PIANO | VOCAL | GUITAR

STORY SONGS

52 NARRATIVE CLASSICS

ISBN 978-1-4950-5034-3

HAL•LEONARD®
CORPORATION
7777 W. BLUEMOUND RD. P.O. BOX 13819 MILWAUKEE, WI 53213

Visit Hal Leonard Online at
www.halleonard.com

ALICE'S RESTAURANT

Words and Music by
ARLO GUTHRIE

You can get ___ an-y-thing ___ you want ___ at Al-ice's ___ res-tau-rant. ___

You can get an-y-thing ___ you want ___ at Al-ice-'s ___ res-tau-rant. ___

Walk right in, it's a-round ___ the back, ___ just a half a mile from the rail-road track. ___

Spoken word: (repeat music from chorus as needed - sing chorus where indicated)
This song is called Alice's Restaurant, and it's about Alice, and the restaurant, but Alice's Restaurant is not the name of the restaurant, that's just the name of the song, and that's why I called the song Alice's Restaurant.

Chorus

Now, it all started two Thanksgivings ago, was on—two years ago on Thanksgiving, when my friend and I went up to visit Alice at the restaurant, but Alice doesn't live in the restaurant, she lives in the church nearby the restaurant, in the bell-tower, with her husband Ray and Fasha the dog. And livin' in the bell tower like that, they got a lot of room downstairs where the pews used to be in. Havin' all that room, seein' as how they took out all the pews, they decided that they didn't have to take out their garbage for a long time.

We got up there, we found all the garbage in there, and we decided it'd be a friendly gesture for us to take the garbage down to the city dump. So we took the half a ton of garbage, put it in the back of a red VW microbus, took shovels and rakes and implements of destruction and headed on toward the city dump.

Well, we got there and there was a big sign and a chain across the dump saying, "Closed on Thanksgiving." And we had never heard of a dump closed on Thanksgiving before, and with tears in our eyes we drove off into the sunset looking for another place to put the garbage.

We didn't find one. Until we came to a side road, and off the side of the side road there was another fifteen-foot cliff and at the bottom of the cliff there was another pile of garbage. And we decided that one big pile is better than two little piles, and rather than bring that one up we decided to throw ours down.

That's what we did, and drove back to the church, had a Thanksgiving dinner that couldn't be beat, went to sleep and didn't get up until the next morning, when we got a phone call from officer Obie. He said, "Kid, we found your name on an envelope at the bottom of a half a ton of garbage, and just wanted to know if you had any information about it." And I said, "Yes, sir, Officer Obie, I cannot tell a lie, I put that envelope under that garbage."

After speaking to Obie for about forty-five minutes on the telephone we finally arrived at the truth of the matter and said that we had to go down and pick up the garbage, and also had to go down and speak to him at the police officer's station. So we got in the red VW microbus with the shovels and rakes and implements of destruction and headed on toward the police officer's station.

Now friends, there was only one or two things that Obie coulda done at the police station, and the first was he could have given us a medal for being so brave and honest on the telephone, which wasn't very likely, and we didn't expect it, and the other thing was he could have bawled us out and told us never to be seen driving garbage around the vicinity again, which is what we expected, but when we got to the police officer's station there was a third possibility that we hadn't even counted upon, and we was both immediately arrested. Handcuffed. And I said "Obie, I don't think I can pick up the garbage with these handcuffs on." He said, "Shut up, kid. Get in the back of the patrol car."

And that's what we did, sat in the back of the patrol car and drove to the quote "Scene of the Crime" unquote. I want tell you about the town of Stockbridge, Massachusetts, where this happened here, they got three stop signs, two police officers, and one police car, but when we got to the Scene of the Crime there was five police officers and three police cars, being the biggest crime of the last fifty years, and everybody wanted to get in the newspaper story about it. And they was using up all kinds of cop equipment that they had hanging around the police officer's station. They was taking plaster tire tracks, footprints, dog smelling prints, and they took twenty-seven eight-by-ten color glossy photographs with circles and arrows and a paragraph on the back of each one explaining what each one was to be used as evidence against us. Took pictures of the approach, the getaway, the northwest corner the southwest corner and that's not to mention the aerial photography.

After the ordeal, we went back to the jail. Obie said he was going to put us in the cell. Said, "Kid, I'm going to put you in the cell, I want your wallet and your belt." And I said, "Obie, I can understand you wanting my wallet so I don't have any money to spend in the cell, but what do you want my belt for?" And he said, "Kid, we don't want any hangings." I said, "Obie, did you think I was going to hang myself for littering?" Obie said he was just making sure, and friends, Obie was, cause he took out the toilet seat so I couldn't hit myself over the head and drown, and he took out the toilet paper so I couldn't bend the bars, roll out the—roll the toilet paper out the window, slide down the roll and have an escape. Obie was making sure, and it was about four or five hours later that Alice (remember Alice? It's a song about Alice), Alice came by and with a few nasty words to Obie on the side, bailed us out of jail, and we went back to the church, had another Thanksgiving dinner that couldn't be beat, and didn't get up until the next morning, when we all had to go to court.

We walked in, sat down, Obie came in with the twenty-seven eight-by-ten color glossy pictures with circles and arrows and a paragraph on the back of each one, sat down. Man came in said, "All rise." We all stood up, and Obie stood up with the twenty-seven eight-by-ten color glossy pictures, and the judge walked in, sat down with a seeing eye dog, and he sat down, we sat down. Obie looked at the seeing eye dog, and then at the twenty-seven eight-by-ten color glossy pictures with circles and arrows and a paragraph on the back of each one, and looked at the seeing eye dog. And then at twenty-seven eight-by-ten color glossy pictures with circles and arrows and a paragraph on the back of each one and began to cry, 'cause Obie came to the realization that it was a typical case of American blind justice, and there wasn't nothing he could do about it, and the judge wasn't going to look at the twenty-seven eight-by-ten color glossy pictures with the circles and arrows and a paragraph on the back of each one explaining what each one was to be used as evidence against us. And we was fined $50 and had to pick up the garbage in the snow, but that's not what I came to tell you about.

Came to talk about the draft.

They got a building down New York City, it's called Whitehall Street, where you walk in, you get injected, inspected, detected, infected, neglected and selected. I went down to get my physical examination one day, and I walked in, I sat down, got good and drunk the night before, so I looked and felt my best when I went in that morning. 'Cause I wanted to look like the all-American kid from New York City, man I wanted, I wanted to feel like the all-, I wanted to be the all-American kid from New York, and I walked in, sat down, I was hung down, brung down, hung up, and all kinds o' mean nasty ugly things. And I walked in and sat down and they gave me a piece of paper, said, "Kid, see the psychiatrist, room 604." And I went up there, I said, "Shrink, I want to kill. I mean, I wanna, I wanna kill. Kill. I wanna, I wanna see, I wanna see blood and gore and guts and veins in my teeth. Eat dead burnt bodies. I mean kill, Kill, KILL, KILL." And I started jumpin' up and down yelling, "KILL, KILL," and he started jumpin' up and down with me and we was both jumpin' up and down yelling, "KILL, KILL." And the Sergeant came over, pinned a medal on me, sent me down the hall, said, "You're our boy."

Didn't feel too good about it.

Proceeded on down the hall gettin' more injections, inspections, detections, neglections and all kinds of stuff that they was doin' to me at the thing there, and I was there for two hours, three hours, four hours, I was there for a long time going through all kinds of mean nasty ugly things and I was just having a tough time there, and they was inspecting, injecting every single part of me, and they was leaving no part untouched. Proceeded through, and when I finally came to see the last man, I walked in, walked in, sat down after a whole big thing there, and I walked up and said, "What do you want?" He said, "Kid, we only got one question. Have you ever been arrested?"

And I proceeded to tell him the story of the Alice's Restaurant Massacre, with full orchestration and five-part harmony and stuff like that and all the phenome... and he stopped me right there and said, "Kid, did you ever go to court?"

And I proceeded to tell him the story of the twenty-seven eight-by-ten color glossy pictures with the circles and arrows and the paragraph on the back of each one, and he stopped me right there and said, "Kid, I want you to go and sit down on that bench that says Group W .... NOW kid!!"

And I, I walked over to the, to the bench there, and there is, Group W's where they put you if you may not be moral enough to join the army after committing your special crime, and there was all kinds of mean nasty ugly-looking people on the bench there. Mother rapers. Father stabbers. Father rapers! Father rapers sitting right there on the bench next to me! And they was mean and nasty and ugly and horrible crime-type guys sitting on the bench next to me. And the meanest, ugliest, nastiest one, the meanest father raper of them all, was coming over to me and he was mean 'n' ugly 'n' nasty 'n' horrible and all kind of things and he sat down next to me and said, "Kid, whad'ya get?" I said, "I didn't get nothing, I had to pay $50 and pick up the garbage." He said, "What were you arrested for, kid?" And I said, "Littering." And they all moved away from me on the bench there, and the hairy eyeball and all kinds of mean nasty things, till I said, "And creating a nuisance." And they all came back, shook my hand, and we had a great time on the bench, talkin' about crime, mother stabbing, father raping, all kinds of groovy things that we was talking about on the bench. And everything was fine, we was smoking cigarettes and all kinds of things, until the Sergeant came over, had some paper in his hand, held it up and said,

"Kids, this-piece-of-paper's-got-47-words-37-sentences-58-words- we-wanna-know-details-of-the-crime-time-of-the-crime-and-any-other-kind-of-thing-you-gotta-say-pertaining-to-and-about-the- crime-I-want-to-know-arresting-officer's-name-and-any-other-kind-of-thing-you-gotta-say," and talked for forty-five minutes and nobody understood a word that he said, but we had fun filling out the forms and playing with the pencils on the bench there, and I filled out the massacre with the four-part harmony, and wrote it down there, just like it was, and everything was fine and I put down the pencil, and I turned over the piece of paper, and there, there on the other side, in the middle of the other side, away from everything else on the other side, in parentheses, capital letters, quoted, read the following words:
"Kid, have you rehabilitated yourself?"

I went over to the Sergeant, said, "Sergeant, you got a lotta damn gall to ask me if I've rehabilitated myself, I mean, I mean, I mean that just, I'm sittin' here on the bench, I mean I'm sittin here on the Group W bench 'cause you want to know if I'm moral enough join the army, burn women, kids, houses and villages after bein' a litterbug." He looked at me and said, "Kid, we don't like your kind, and we're gonna send your fingerprints off to Washington." And friends, somewhere in Washington enshrined in some little folder, is a study in black and white of my fingerprints. And the only reason I'm singing you this song now is 'cause you may know somebody in a similar situation, or you may be in a similar situation, and if you're in a situation like that there's only one thing you can do and that's walk into the shrink wherever you are, just walk in say "Shrink, you can get anything you want at Alice's restaurant." And walk out. You know, if one person, just one person does it they may think he's really sick and they won't take him. And if two people, two people do it, in harmony, they may think they're both faggots and they won't take either of them. And three people do it, three, can you imagine, three people walking in singin' a bar of Alice's Restaurant and walking out. They may think it's an organization. And can you, can you imagine fifty people a day, I said fifty people a day walking in singin' a bar of Alice's Restaurant and walking out? And friends, they may think it's a movement.

And that's what it is, the Alice's Restaurant Anti-Massacre Movement, and all you got to do to join is sing it the next time it come's around on the guitar. With feeling. So we'll wait for it to come around on the guitar here and sing it when it does. Here it comes.

Chorus

That was horrible. If you want to end war and stuff you got to sing loud. I've been singing this song now for twenty-five minutes. I could sing it for another twenty-five minutes. I'm not proud... or tired. So we'll wait till it comes around again, and this time with four-part harmony and feeling. We're just waitin' for it to come around is what we're doing. All right now.

Chorus, take final ending

ALONG CAME JONES

Words and Music by JERRY LEIBER
and MIKE STOLLER

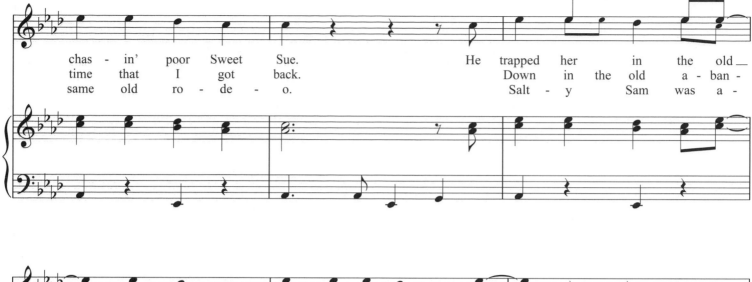

chas - in' poor Sweet Sue. He trapped her in the old __
time that I got back. Down in the old a - ban -
same old ro - de - o. Salt - y Sam was a -

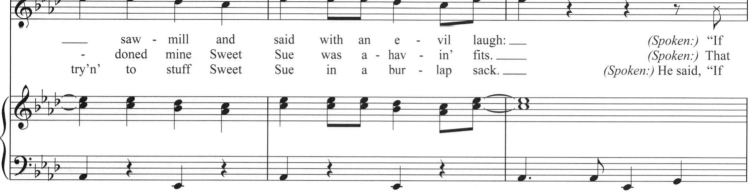

__ saw - mill and said with an e - vil laugh: __ *(Spoken:)* "If
- doned mine Sweet Sue was a - hav - in' fits. __ *(Spoken:)* That
try'n' to stuff Sweet Sue in a bur - lap sack. __ *(Spoken:)* He said, "If

you don't gim - me the deed __ to your ranch, I'll saw you all in
vil - lain said, "Gim - me the deed __ to your ranch, or I'll blow you all to
you don't gim - me the deed __ to your ranch, I'm gon - na throw you on the rail - road

Freely Ddim7

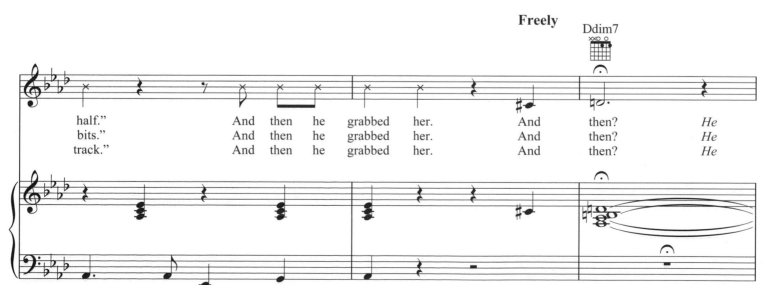

half." And then he grabbed her. And then? *He*
bits." And then he grabbed her. And then? *He*
track." And then he grabbed her. And then? *He*

10

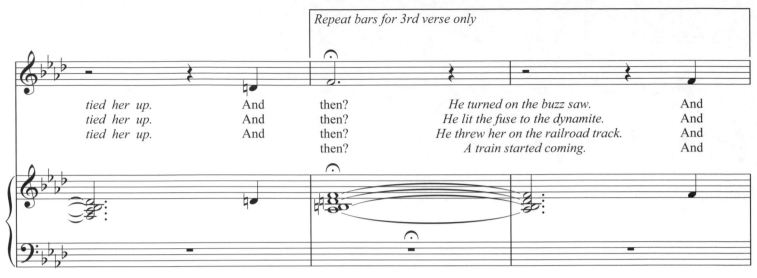

Repeat bars for 3rd verse only

tied her up.   And   then?   He turned on the buzz saw.   And
tied her up.   And   then?   He lit the fuse to the dynamite.   And
tied her up.   And   then?   He threw her on the railroad track.   And
              then?   A train started coming.   And

A tempo

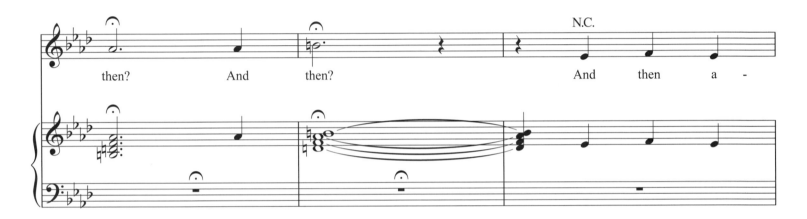

then?   And   then?   And   then   a-

long   came   Jones,

tall   thin   Jones;

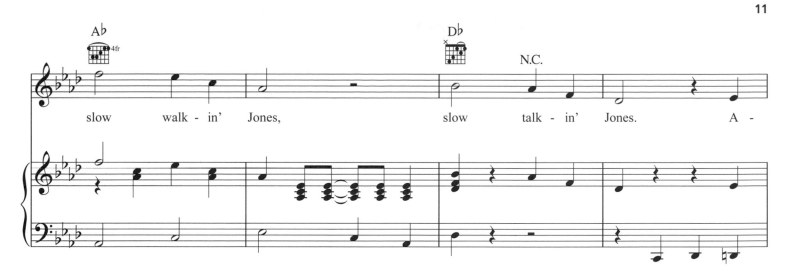

slow walk - in' Jones, slow talk - in' Jones. A -

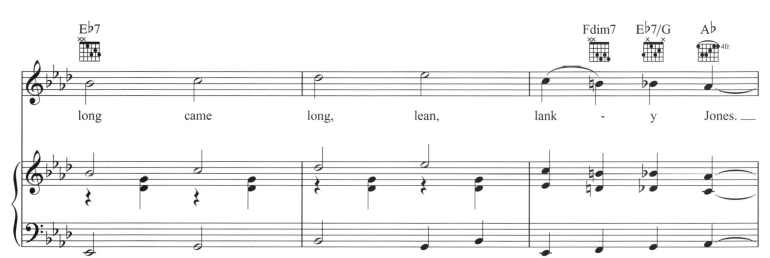

long came long, lean, lank - y Jones. ___

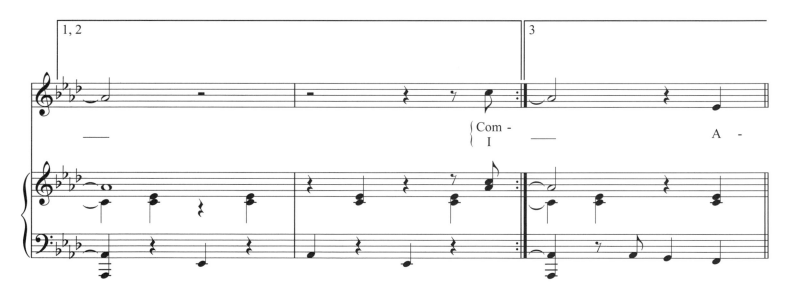

___ { Com -
{ I ___ A -

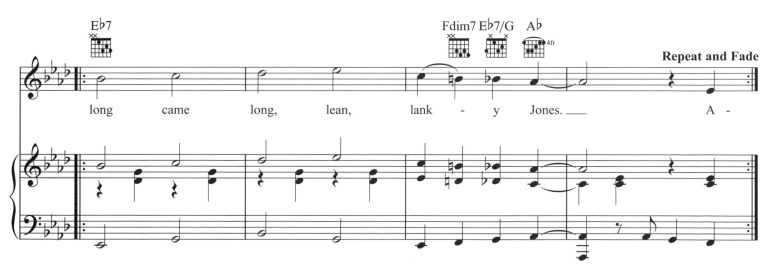

long came long, lean, lank - y Jones. ___ A -

AMERICAN PIE

Words and Music by
DON McLEAN

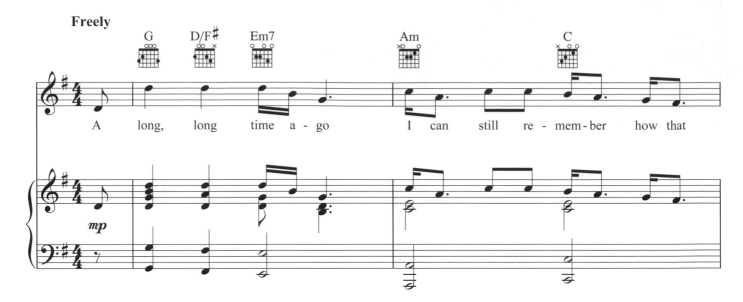

Freely

A long, long time a-go I can still re-mem-ber how that

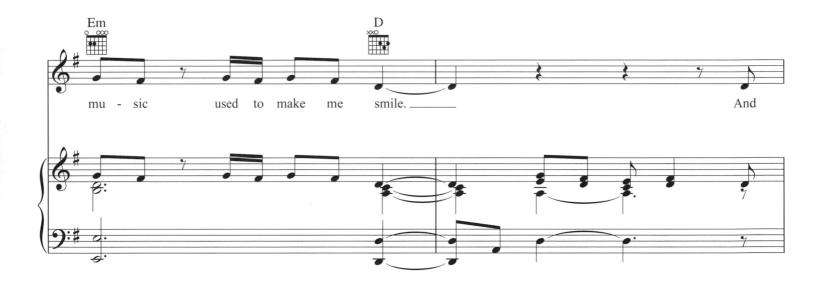

mu - sic used to make me smile. _____ And

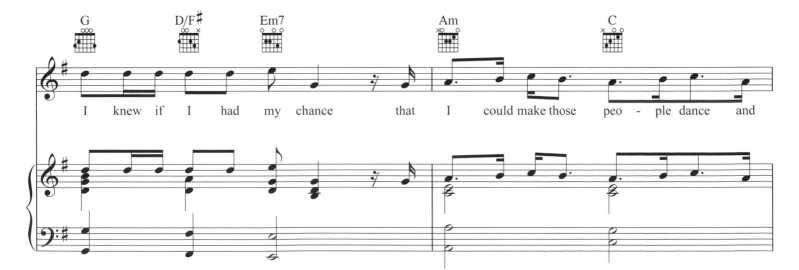

I knew if I had my chance that I could make those peo - ple dance and

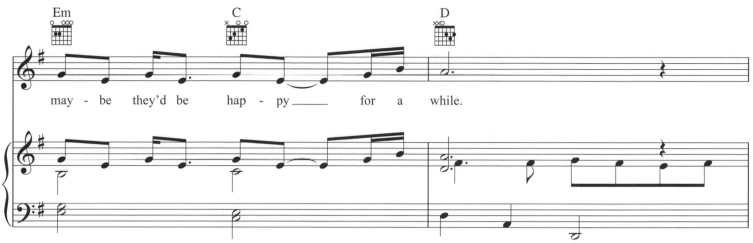

may - be they'd be hap - py _____ for a while.

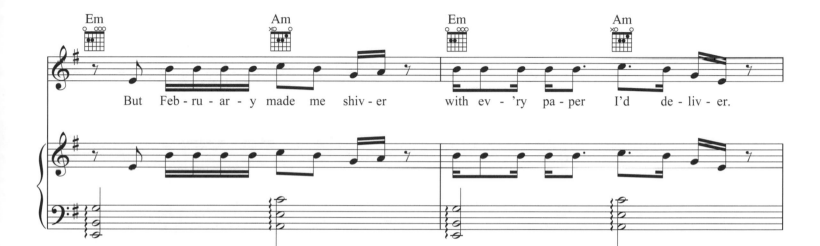

But Feb - ru - ar - y made me shiv - er with ev - 'ry pa - per I'd de - liv - er.

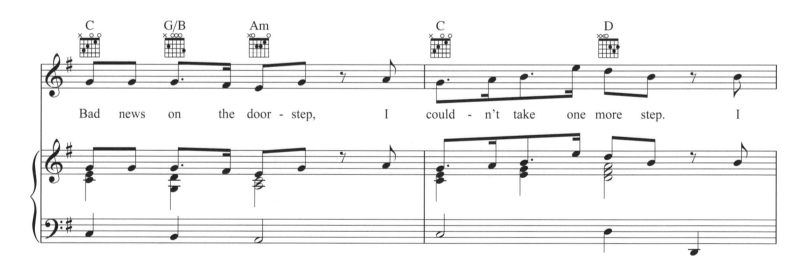

Bad news on the door - step, I could - n't take one more step. I

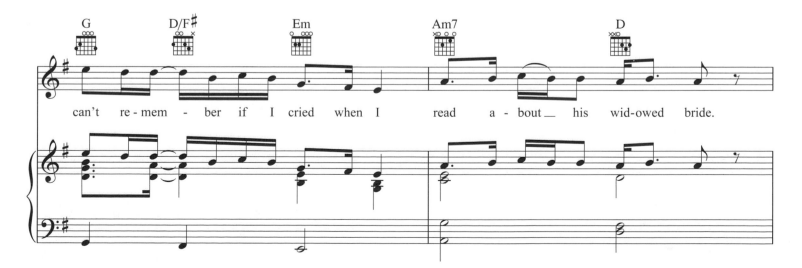

can't re - mem - ber if I cried when I read a - bout ___ his wid - owed bride.

This -'ll be the day __ that I ____ die. ____

1. Did you __ write the book of love __ and do you ____ have faith in
2.–4. *(See additional lyrics)*

God a - bove? _ If the Bi - ble tells ____ you so. ____

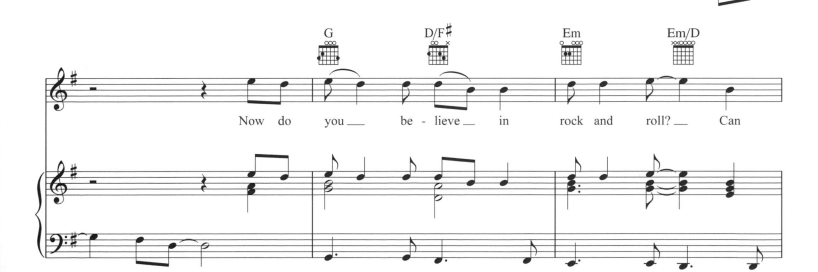

Now do you __ be - lieve __ in rock and roll? __ Can

mu-sic save your mor-tal soul ___ and can you teach me

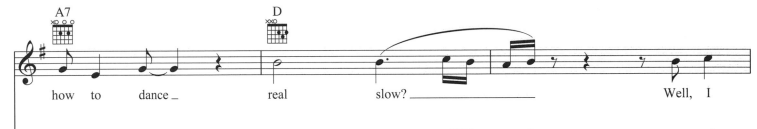

how to dance ___ real slow? _____ Well, I

know that you're ___ in love with him ___ 'cause I _____ saw you danc-in'

in the gym. ___ You both kicked off ___ your shoes. _____ Man, I

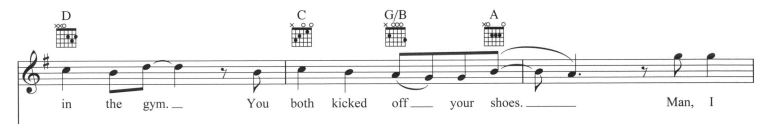

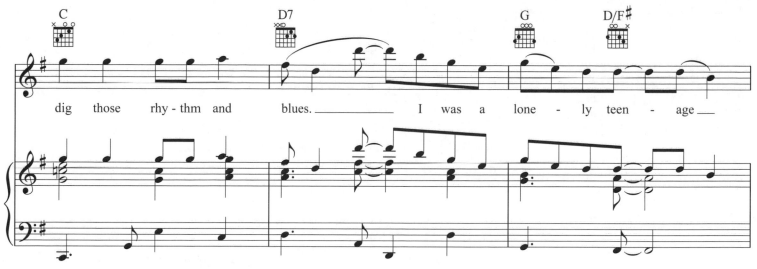

dig those rhy-thm and blues. _____ I was a lone - ly teen - age _____

bronc - in' buck ___ with a pink car - na - tion and a pick - up truck. ___ But

I knew I ___ was out _____ of luck ___ the day _____ the mu -

- sic died. ___   I start - ed sing - ing

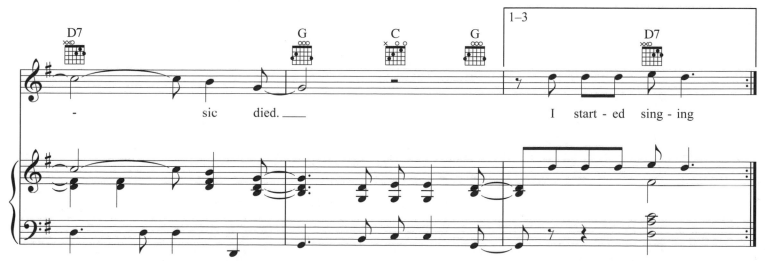

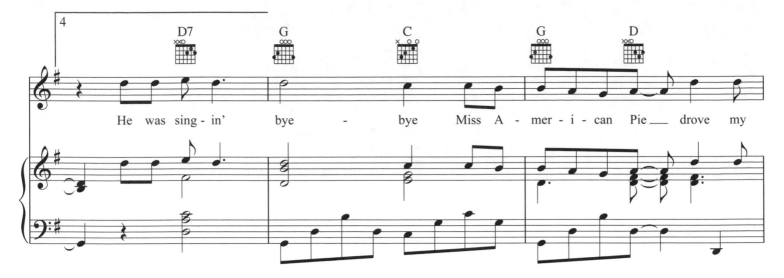

He was sing - in' bye - bye Miss A - mer - i - can Pie___ drove my

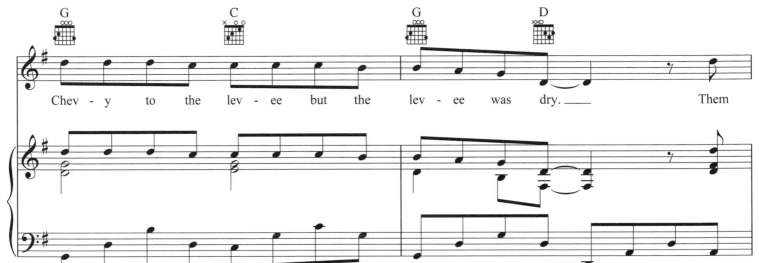

Chev - y to the lev - ee but the lev - ee was dry.___ Them

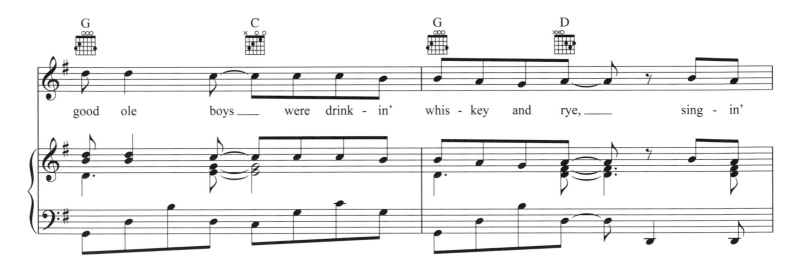

good ole boys___ were drink - in' whis - key and rye,___ sing - in'

this - 'll be the day___ that I___ die.

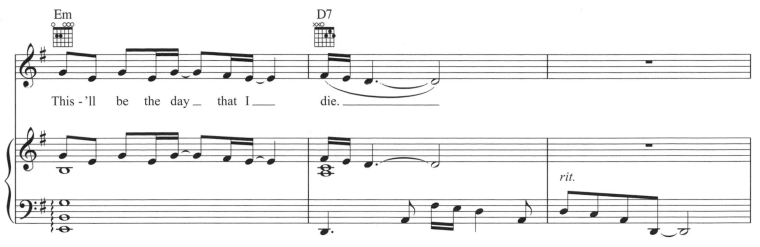

This-'ll be the day _ that I ___ die. ____

Freely

I met a girl who sang _ the blues ____ and I asked her for some hap-py news, ____ but

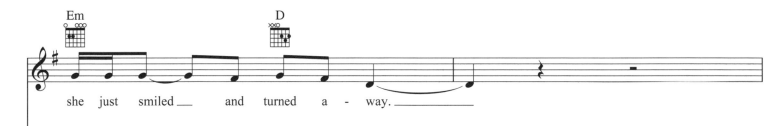

she just smiled ___ and turned a - way. ____

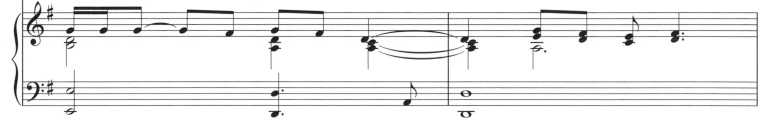

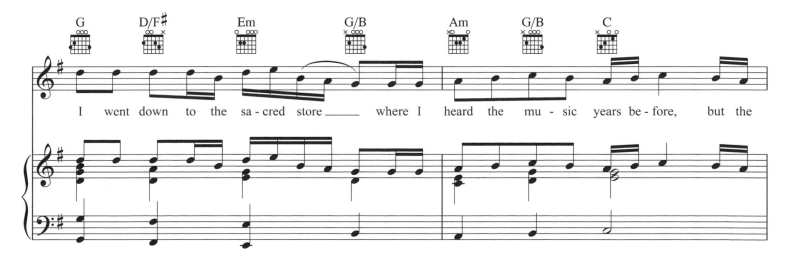

I went down to the sa-cred store ____ where I heard the mu-sic years be-fore, but the

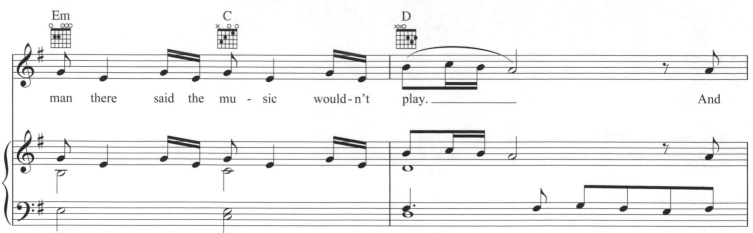

man there said the mu - sic would - n't play. _____ And

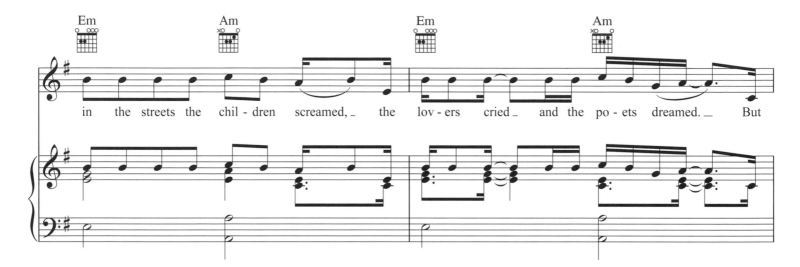

in the streets the chil - dren screamed, _ the lov - ers cried _ and the po - ets dreamed. _ But

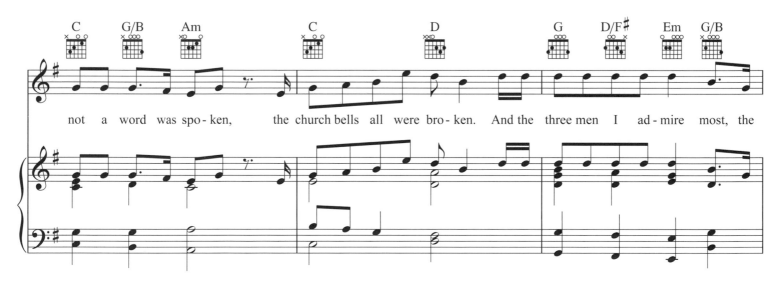

not a word was spo - ken, the church bells all were bro - ken. And the three men I ad - mire most, the

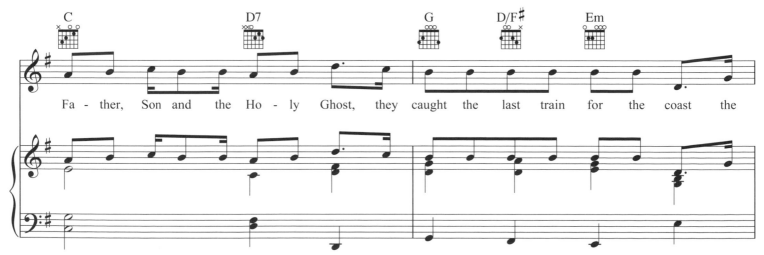

Fa - ther, Son and the Ho - ly Ghost, they caught the last train for the coast the

Additional Lyrics

2. Now for ten years we've been on our own,
And moss grows fat on a rollin' stone
But that's not how it used to be
When the jester sang for the king and queen
In a coat he borrowed from James Dean
And a voice that came from you and me
Oh and while the king was looking down,
The jester stole his thorny crown
The courtroom was adjourned,
No verdict was returned
And while Lenin read a book on Marx
The quartet practiced in the park
And we sang dirges in the dark
The day the music died
We were singin'...bye-bye...etc.

3. Helter-skelter in the summer swelter
The birds flew off with a fallout shelter
Eight miles high and fallin' fast,
It landed foul on the grass
The players tried for a forward pass,
With the jester on the sidelines in a cast
Now the half-time air was sweet perfume
While the sergeants played a marching tune
We all got up to dance
But we never got the chance
'Cause the players tried to take the field,
The marching band refused to yield
Do you recall what was revealed
The day the music died
We started singin'... bye-bye...etc.

4. And there we were all in one place,
A generation lost in space
With no time left to start again
So come on, Jack be nimble, Jack be quick,
Jack Flash sat on a candlestick
'Cause fire is the devil's only friend
And as I watched him on the stage
My hands were clenched in fits of rage
No angel born in hell
Could break that Satan's spell
And as the flames climbed high into the night
To light the sacrificial rite
I saw Satan laughing with delight
The day the music died
He was singin'...bye-bye...etc.

THE BALLAD OF DAVY CROCKETT

from Walt Disney's DAVY CROCKETT

Words by TOM BLACKBURN
Music by GEORGE BRUNS

1. Born on a moun-tain top in Ten-nes-see, green-est state in the
2. eight-een-thir-teen the Creeks up-rose, add-in' red-skin ar-rows to the
3. Off through the woods he's a march-in' a-long, mak-in' up yarns an' a-
4.–10. (See additional lyrics)

Land of the Free. Raised in the woods so's he knew ev-'ry tree,
coun-try's woes. Now, In-jun fight-in' is some-thin' he knows, so he
sing-in' a song, itch-in' fer fight-in' and right-in' a wrong, he's

kilt him a b'ar when he was on-ly three. Da - vy,
shoul - ders his ri - fle, an' off he ___ goes. Da - vy,
rin - gy as a b'ar, an' twict as ___ strong. Da - vy,

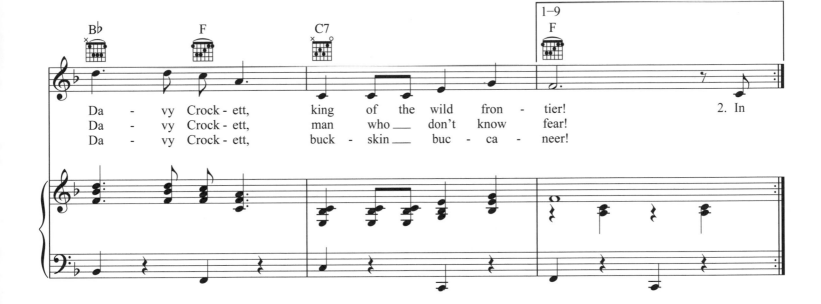

Da - vy Crock - ett, king of the wild fron - tier!
Da - vy Crock - ett, man who ___ don't know fear!
Da - vy Crock - ett, buck - skin ___ buc - ca - neer!

2. In

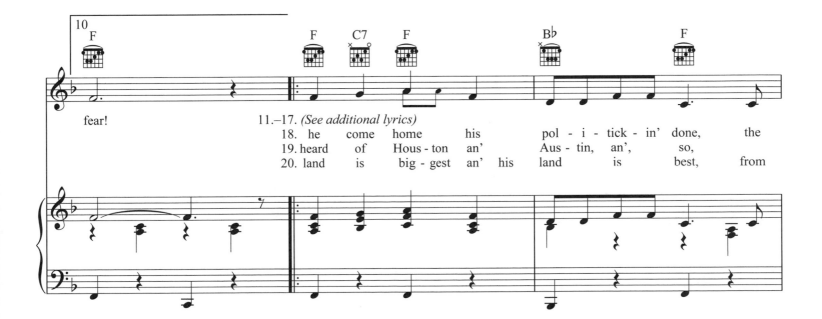

fear!

11.–17. *(See additional lyrics)*

18. he come home his pol - i - tick - in' done, the
19. heard of Hous - ton an' Aus - tin, an', so, the
20. land is big - gest an' his land is best, from

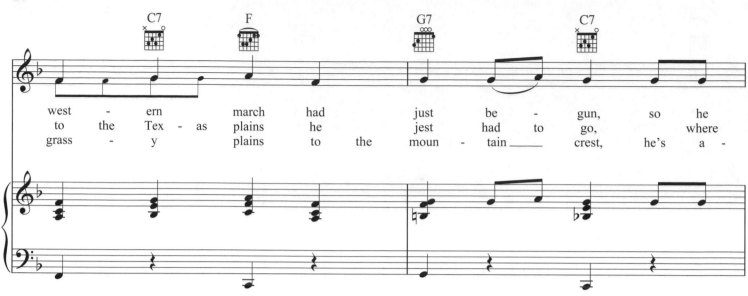

west - ern march had just be - gun, so he
to the Tex - as plains he jest had to go, where
grass - y plains to the moun - tain _____ crest, he's a -

packed his gear an' his trust - y gun, an' lit out grin - nin' to
Free - dom was fight - in' an - oth - er foe, an' they need - ed him at the
head of us all meet - in' the test, fol - low - in' his leg - end

fol - low the sun. Da - vy, Da - vy Crock - ett,
Al - a - mo. Da - vy, Da - vy Crock - ett,
in - to the West. Da - vy, Da - vy Crock - ett, the

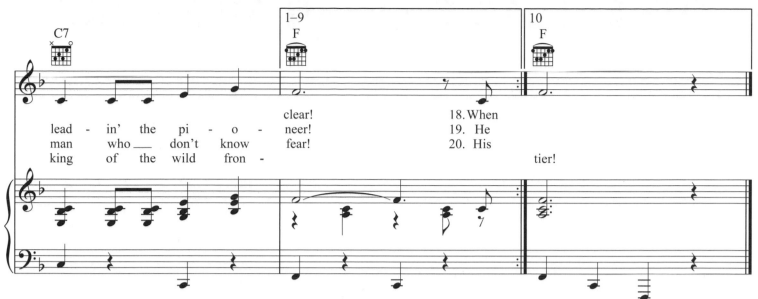

lead - in' the pi - o - neer!   18. When
man who___ don't know fear!   19. He
king of the wild fron - tier!   20. His

Additional Lyrics

4. Andy Jackson is our gen'ral's name,
His reg'lar soldiers we'll put to shame,
Them redskin varmints us Volunteers'll tame,
'Cause we got the guns with the sure-fire aim.
Davy – Davy Crockett,
The champion of us all!

5. Headed back to war from the ol' home place,
But Red Stick was leadin' a merry chase,
Fightin' an' burnin' at a devil's pace
South to the swamps on the Florida Trace.
Davy – Davy Crockett,
Trackin' the redskins down!

6. Fought single-handed through the Injun War
Till the Creeks was whipped an' peace was in store,
An' while he was handlin' this risky chore,
Made hisself a legend forevermore.
Davy – Davy Crockett,
King of the wild frontier!

7. He give his word an' he give his hand
That his Injun friends could keep their land,
An' the rest of his life he took the stand
That justice was due every redskin band.
Davy – Davy Crockett,
Holdin' his promise dear!

8. Home fer the winter with his family,
Happy as squirrels in the ol' gum tree,
Bein' the father he wanted to be,
Close to his boys as the pod an' the pea.
Davy – Davy Crockett,
Holdin' his young 'uns dear!

9. But the ice went out an' the warm winds came
An' the meltin' snow showed tracks of game,
An' the flowers of Spring filled the woods with flame,
An' all of a sudden life got too tame.
Davy – Davy Crockett,
Headin' on West again!

10. Off through the woods we're ridin' along,
Makin' up yarns an' singin' a song.
He's ringy as a b'ar and twice as strong,
An' knows he's right 'cause he ain't often wrong.
Davy – Davy Crockett,
The man who don't know fear!

11. Lookin' fer a place where the air smells clean,
Where the tree is tall an' the grass is green,
Where the fish is fat in an untouched stream,
An' the teemin' woods is a hunter's dream.
Davy – Davy Crockett,
Lookin' fer Paradise!

12. Now he'd lost his love an' his grief was gall.
In his heart he wanted to leave it all,
An' lose himself in the forests tall,
But he answered instead his country's call.
Davy – Davy Crockett,
Beginnin' his campaign!

13. Needin' his help they didn't vote blind,
They put in Davy 'cause he was their kind,
Sent up to Nashville the best they could find,
A fightin' spirit an' a thinkin' mind.
Davy – Davy Crockett,
Choice of the whole frontier!

14. The votes were counted an' he won hands down,
So they sent him off to Washin'ton town
With his best dress suit still his buckskins brown,
A livin' legend of growin' renown.
Davy – Davy Crockett,
The Canebrake Congressman!

15. He went off to Congress an' served a spell,
Fixin' up the Gover'ment an' laws as well,
Took over Washin'ton so we heered tell
An' patched up the crack in the Liberty Bell.
Davy – Davy Crockett,
Seein' his duty clear!

16. Him an' his jokes travelled all through the land,
An' his speeches made him friends to beat the band,
His politickin' was their favorite brand
An' everyone wanted to shake his hand.
Davy – Davy Crockett,
Helpin' his legend grow!

17. He knew when he spoke he sounded the knell
Of his hopes for White House an' fame as well,
But he spoke out strong so hist'ry books tell
An' patched up the crack in the Liberty Bell.
Davy – Davy Crockett,
Seein' his duty clear!

THE BALLAD OF JOHN AND YOKO

Words and Music by JOHN LENNON
and PAUL McCARTNEY

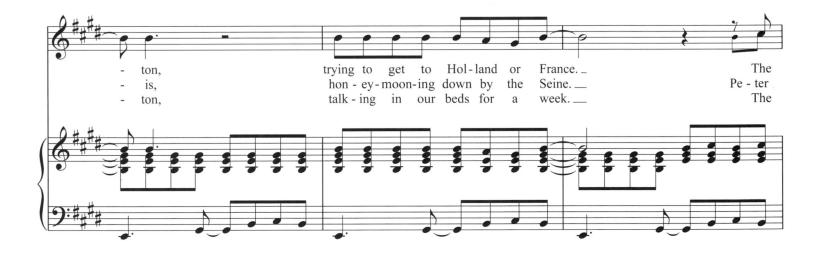

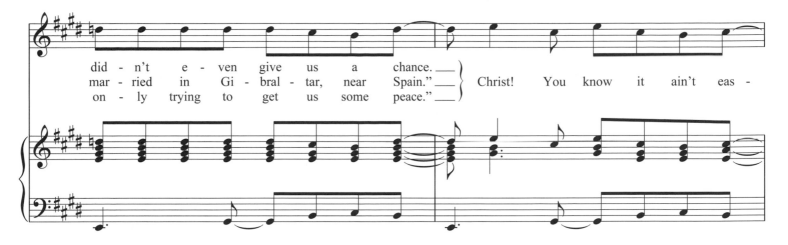

did - n't e - ven give us a chance. ___
mar - ried in Gi - bral - tar, near Spain." ___ } Christ! You know it ain't eas -
on - ly trying to get us some peace." ___

A
- y, ___   you know how hard it can be. ___

E

B7
The way things are go - ing, ___   they're gon - na cru - ci - fy ___

E
me.   1   2   Drove from

eat - ing choc'late cake in a bag. ____ The news - pa - pers said, ____ "She's
fif - ty a - corns tied in a sack. ____ The men from the press ___ said, ___ "We

gone to his head; _____ they look just like two gu - rus in drag." _
wish you suc - cess; _____ it's good to have the both of you back." _

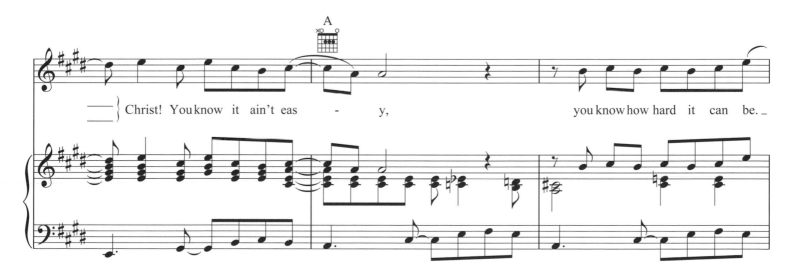

— { Christ! You know it ain't eas - y,   you know how hard it can be. _

The way things are go - ing, ___

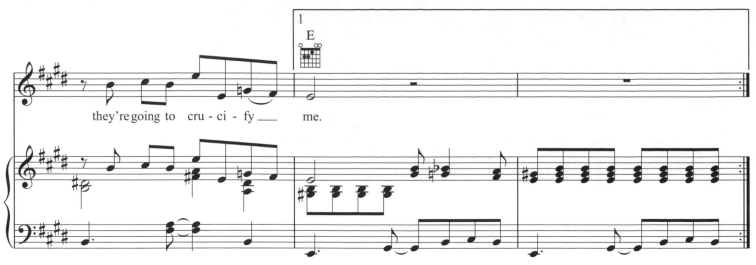

they're going to cru - ci - fy ___ me.

me.   The way things are go - ing, ___

they're going to cru - ci - fy ___ me.

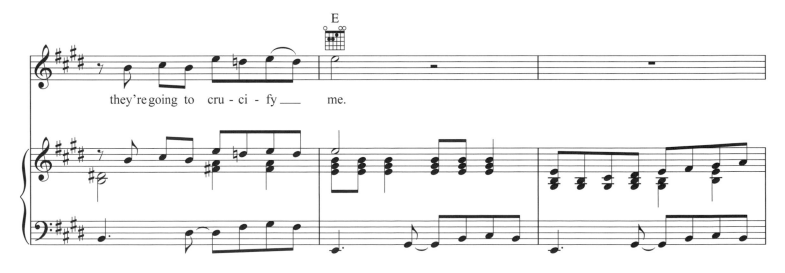

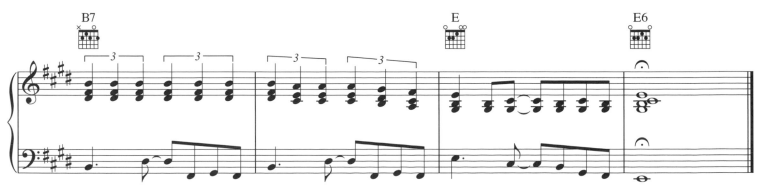

A BOY NAMED SUE

Words and Music by
SHEL SILVERSTEIN

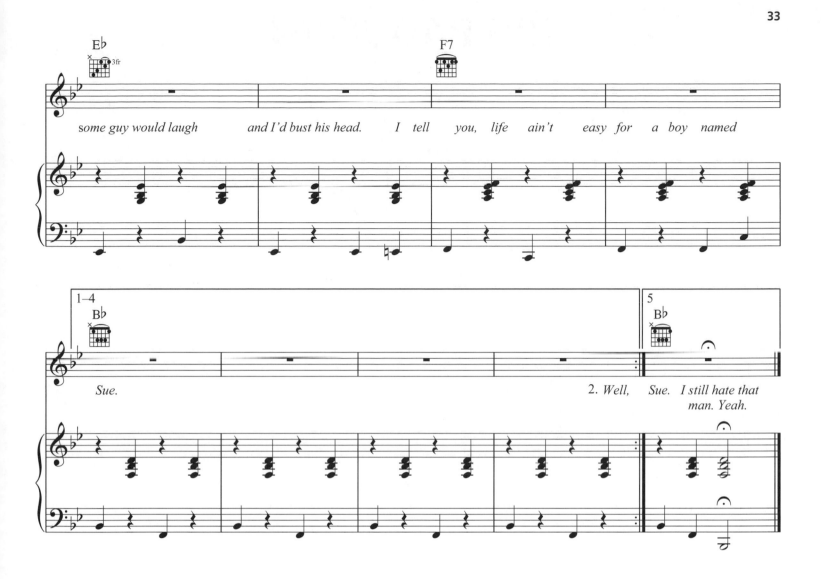

some guy would laugh and I'd bust his head. I tell you, life ain't easy for a boy named

Sue.

2. Well, Sue. I still hate that man. Yeah.

Additional Lyrics

2. Well, I grew up quick and I grew up mean;
My fists got hard and my wits got keen.
Roamed from town to town to hide my shame,
But I made me a vow to the moon and stars,
I'd search the honky-tonks and bars,
And kill that man that give me that awful name.

Well, it was Gatlinburg in mid July,
And I had just hit town and my throat was dry.
I'd thought I'd stop and have myself a brew.
At an old saloon on a street of mud,
There at a table dealin' stud,
Sat the dirty, mangy dog that named me Sue.

3. Well, I knew that snake was my own sweet dad
From a worn-out picture that my mother had.
And I knew that scar on his cheek and his evil eye.
He was big and bent and gray and old,
And I looked at him and my blood ran cold,
And I said, "My name is Sue. How do you do?
Now you gonna die." Yeah, that's what I told him.

Well, I hit him hard right between the eyes,
And he went down, but to my surprise
He come up with a knife and cut off a piece of my ear.
But I busted a chair right across his teeth.
And we crashed through the wall and into the street,
Kickin' and a-gougin' in the mud and the blood and the beer.

4. I tell you, I've fought tougher men,
But I really can't remember when.
He kicked like a mule and he bit like a crocodile.
I heard him laugh and then I heard him cussin';
He went for his gun and I pulled mine first.
He stood there lookin' at me and I saw him smile.

And he said, "Son, this world is rough,
And if a man's gonna make it, he's gotta be tough.
And I know I wouldn't be there to help you along.
So I give you that name and I said, 'Goodbye.'
I knew you'd have to get tough or die.
And it's that name that helped to make you strong."

5. Yeah, he said, "Now you just fought one helluva fight,
And I know you hate me and you've got the right
To kill me now and I wouldn't blame you if you do.
But you ought to thank me before I die
For the gravel in your guts and the spit in your eye,
'Cause I'm the _____ that named you Sue."
Yeah, what could I do? What could I do?

I got all choked up and I threw down my gun,
Called him my pa and he called me his son.
And I come away with a different point of view.
And I think about him now and then,
Ev'ry time I try and ev'ry time I win.
And if I ever have a son, I think I'm gonna name him...
Bill or George. Anything but Sue.
I still hate that man. Yeah.

BIG BAD JOHN

Words and Music by
JIMMY DEAN

Medium Country, in 2

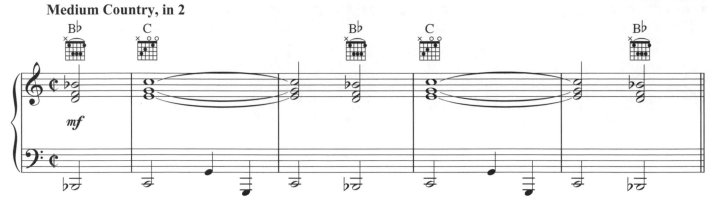

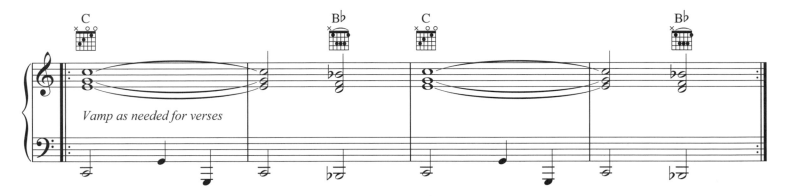

Vamp as needed for verses

Refrain

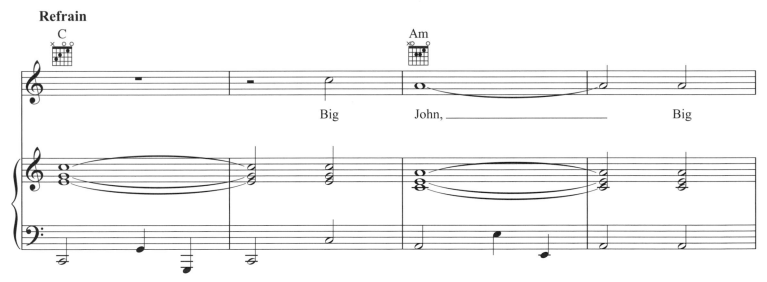

Big   John, _____   Big

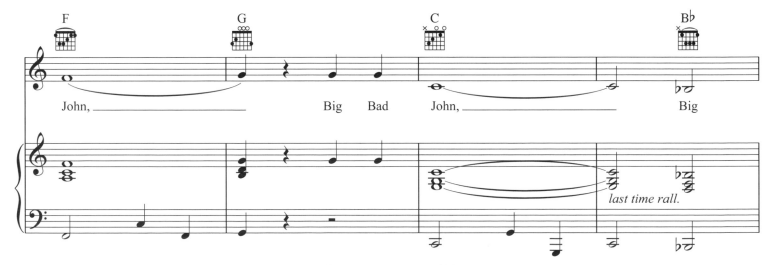

John, _____   Big Bad   John, _____   Big

last time rall.

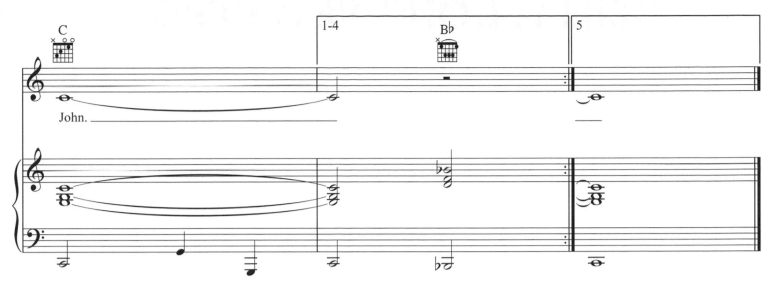

Verses

1. Every morning at the mine you could see him arrive,
   He stood six-foot-six and weighed two-forty-five.
   Kind of broad at the shoulder and narrow at the hip,
   And everybody knew you didn't give no lip to Big John!
   Refrain

2. Nobody seemed to know where John called home,
   He just drifted into town and stayed all alone.
   He didn't say much, a-kinda quiet and shy,
   And if you spoke at all, you just said, "Hi" to Big John!
   Somebody said he came from New Orleans,
   Where he got in a fight over a Cajun queen.
   And a crashing blow from a huge right hand
   Sent a Louisiana fellow to the promised land. Big John!
   Refrain

3. Then came the day at the bottom of the mine
   When a timber cracked and the men started crying.
   Miners were praying and hearts beat fast,
   And everybody thought that they'd breathed their last 'cept John.
   Through the dust and the smoke of this man-made hell
   Walked a giant of a man that the miners knew well.
   Grabbed a sagging timber and gave out with a groan,
   And, like a giant oak tree, just stood there alone. Big John!
   Refrain

4. And with all of his strength, he gave a mighty shove;
   Then a miner yelled out, "There's a light up above!"
   And twenty men scrambled from a would-be grave,
   And now there's only one left down there to save; Big John!
   With jacks and timbers they started back down
   Then came that rumble way down in the ground,
   And smoke and gas belched out of that mine,
   Everybody knew it was the end of the line for Big John!
   Refrain

5. Now they never re-opened that worthless pit,
   They just placed a marble stand in front of it;
   These few words are written on that stand:
   "At the bottom of this mine lies a big, big man; Big John!"
   Refrain

BILLY, DON'T BE A HERO

Words and Music by PETER CALLENDER
and MITCH MURRAY

And with her head up- on his shoul - der, his young and love - ly
I need a vol - un - teer to ride__ up and bring us back some

fi - an - cée, from where I stood__ I saw she was cry - ing,
ex - tra men." And Bil - ly's hand__ was up in a mo - ment,

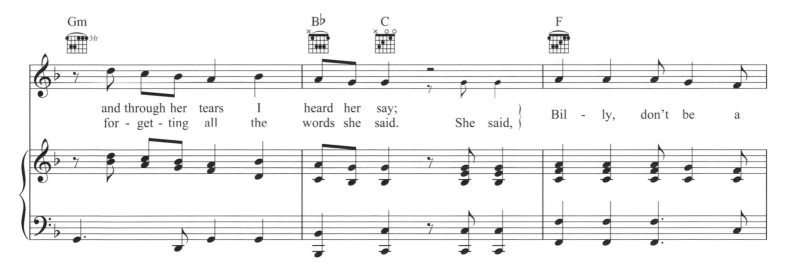

and through her tears I heard her say;
for - get - ting all the words she said. She said, } Bil - ly, don't be a

he - ro, don't be a fool with your life. _____

Bil - ly, don't be a he - ro, come back and make me your wife."

And as they start - ed to go she said,

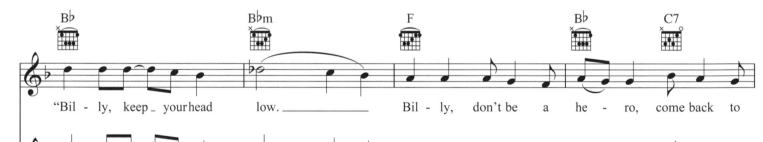

"Bil - ly, keep your head low. Bil - ly, don't be a he - ro, come back to

me."

D.S. al Coda

I heard she threw that let - ter _____ a - way. _____

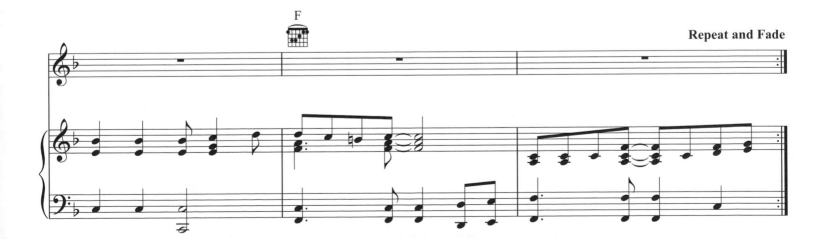

Repeat and Fade

CAT'S IN THE CRADLE

Words and Music by HARRY CHAPIN
and SANDY CHAPIN

Moderate Folk style, in 2

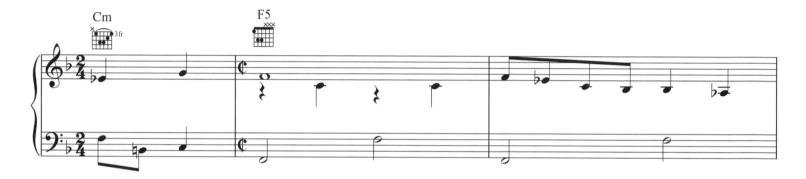

My child ar- rived ____ just the oth- er day.
He came to the world in the u- su- al way, ___ but there were

son turned ten ____ just the oth- er day.
He said, "Thanks for the ball, Dad. Come on, let's play. ____ Can you

came from col- lege just the oth- er day,
so much like a man. I just had to say, ____ "Son, I'm

sil - ver spoon, _ lit - tle boy blue and the man ___ in the moon. _

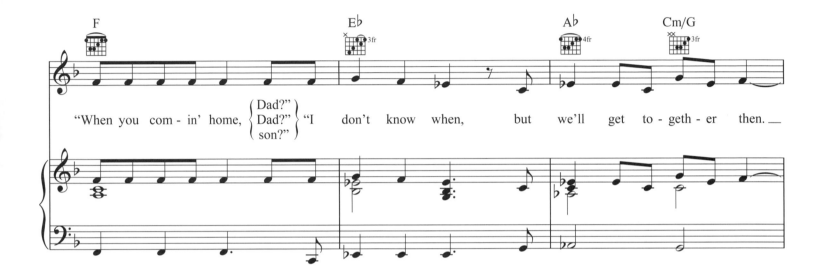

"When you com - in' home, {Dad?" / Dad?" / son?"} "I don't know when, but we'll get to - geth - er then. __

__ You know we'll have a good time then."

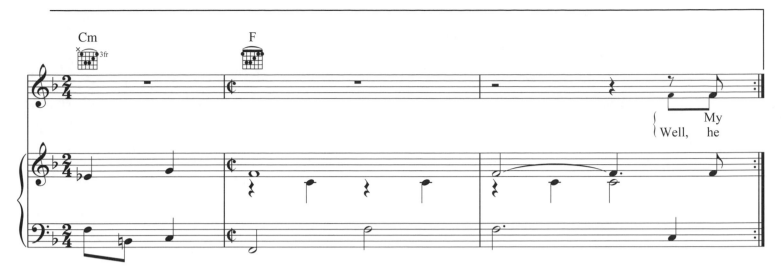

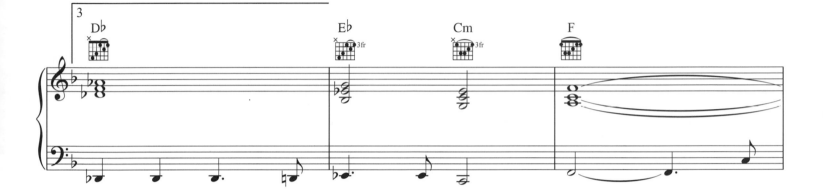

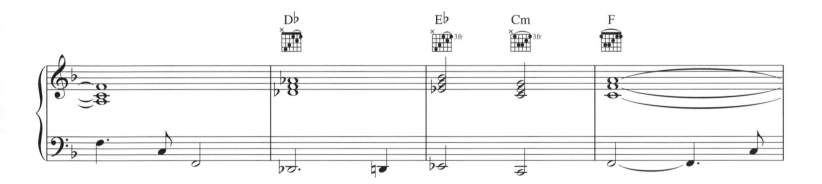

I called him up just the oth-er day. I said, "I'd

like to see ___ you if you don't mind." ___ He said, "I'd love to, Dad, ___ if I can

find the time. ___ You see, my new job's a has-sle and the

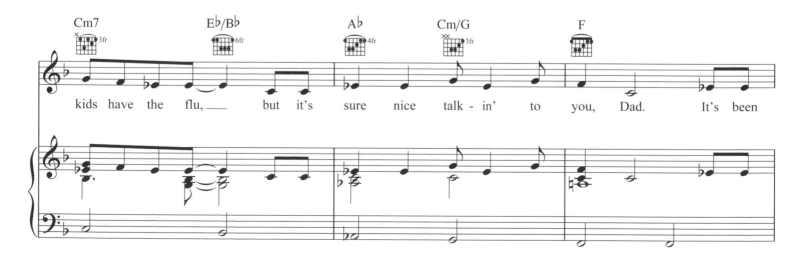

kids have the flu, ___ but it's sure nice talk-in' to you, Dad. It's been

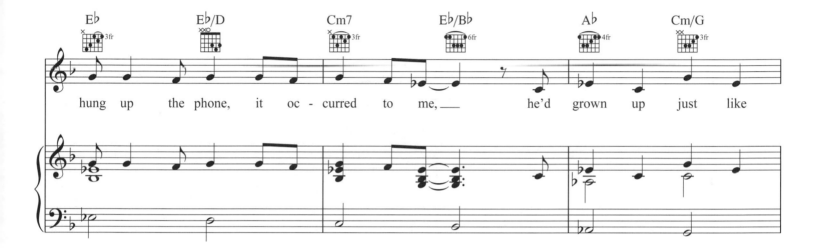

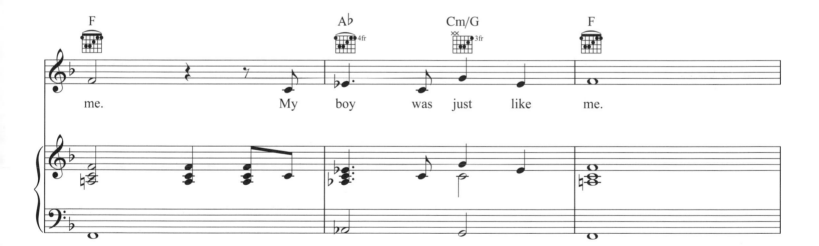

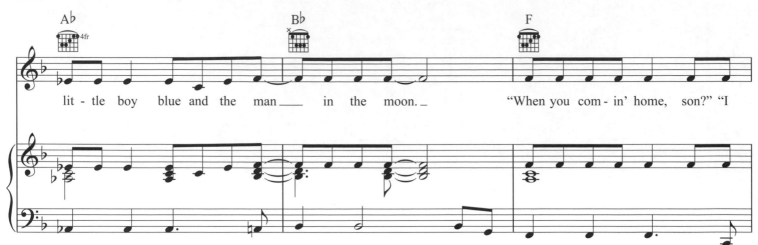

lit - tle boy blue and the man___ in the moon.___ "When you com - in' home, son?" "I

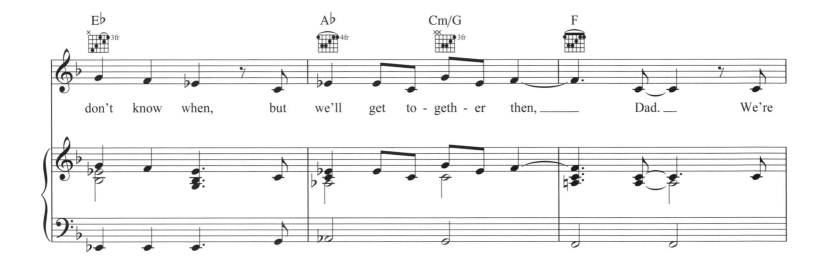

don't know when, but we'll get to - geth - er then,_____ Dad.___ We're

A little slower

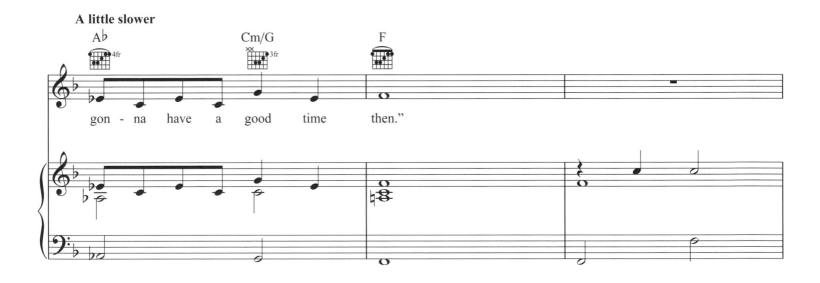

gon - na have a good time then."

THE DEVIL WENT DOWN TO GEORGIA

Words and Music by CHARLIE DANIELS,
JOHN THOMAS CRAIN, JR., WILLIAM JOEL DiGREGORIO,
FRED LAROY EDWARDS, CHARLES FRED HAYWARD
and JAMES WAINWRIGHT MARSHALL

Fast Hoedown

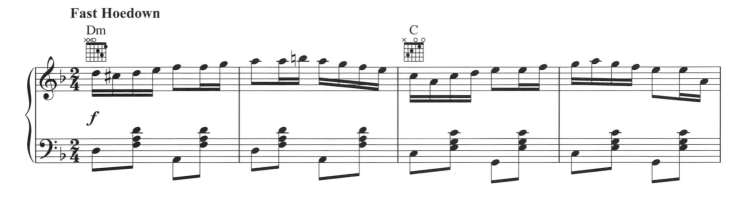

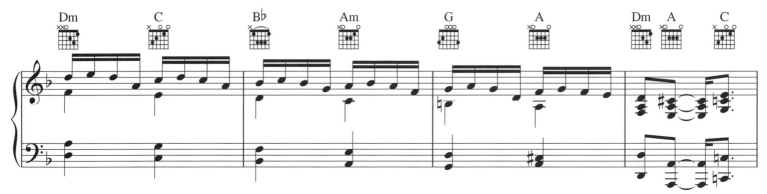

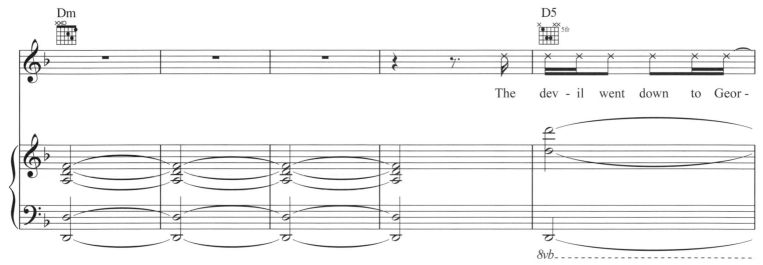

The dev-il went down to Geor-gia. He was look-in' for a soul to steal. He was in a bind 'cause he was

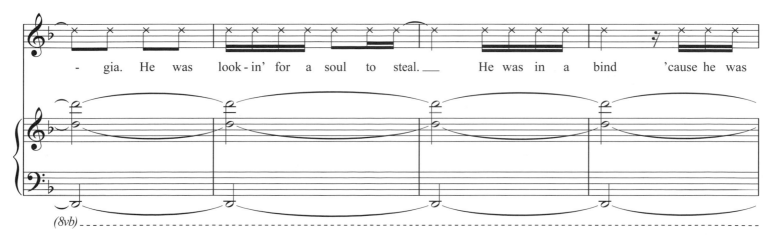

48

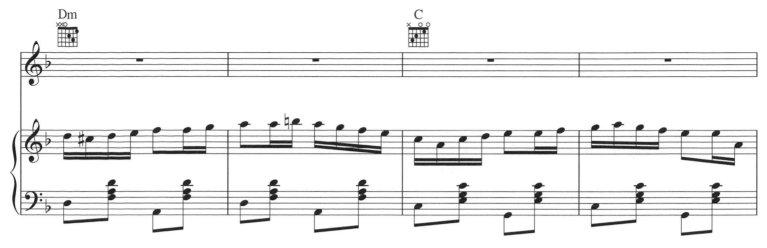

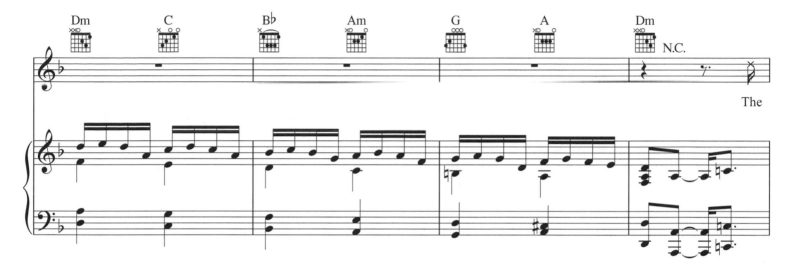

The

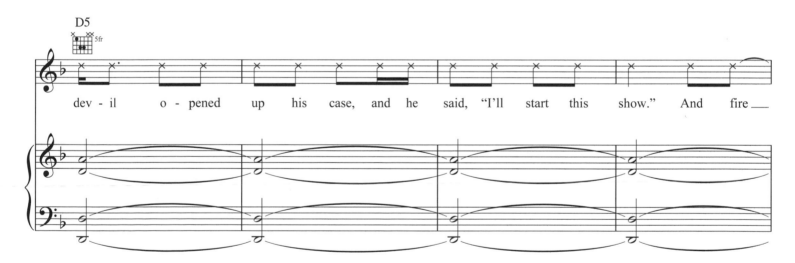

dev - il o - pened up his case, and he said, "I'll start this show." And fire ___

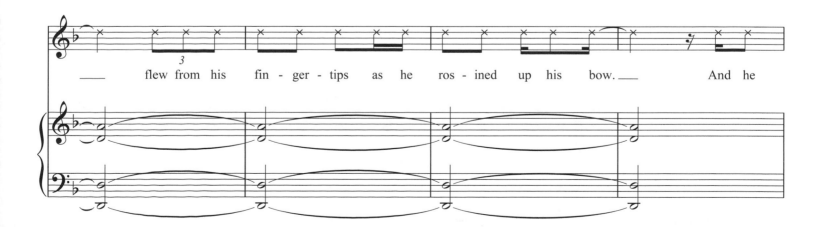

___ flew from his fin - ger - tips as he ros - ined up his bow. ___ And he

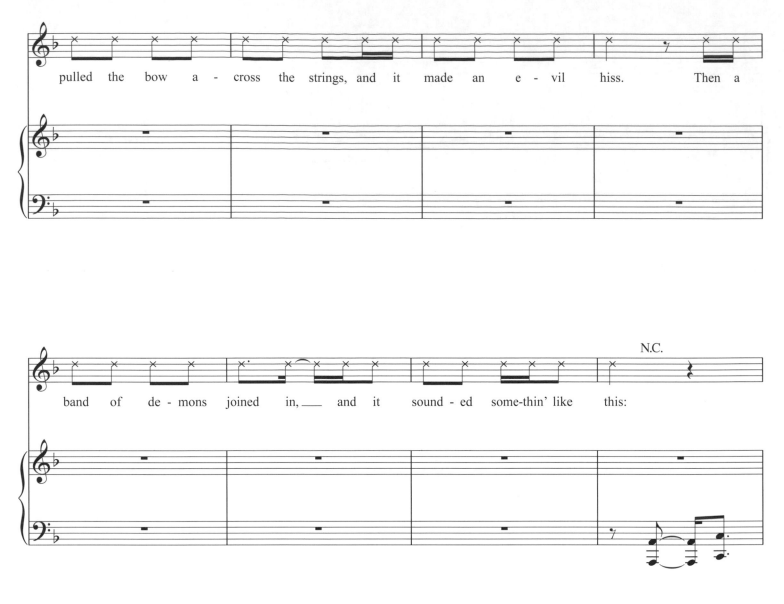

pulled the bow a - cross the strings, and it made an e - vil hiss. Then a

band of de - mons joined in, ___ and it sound - ed some - thin' like this:

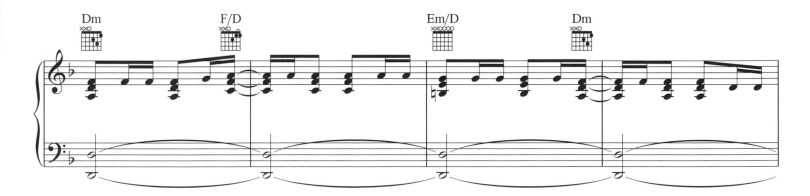

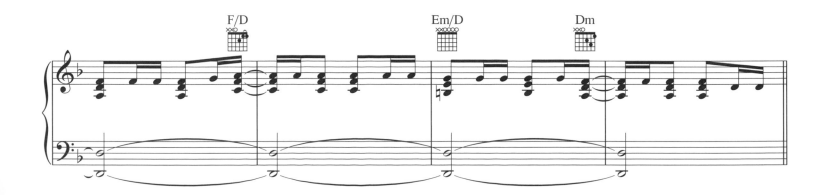

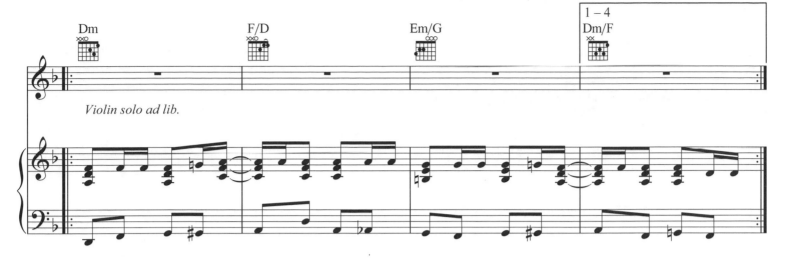

Violin solo ad lib.

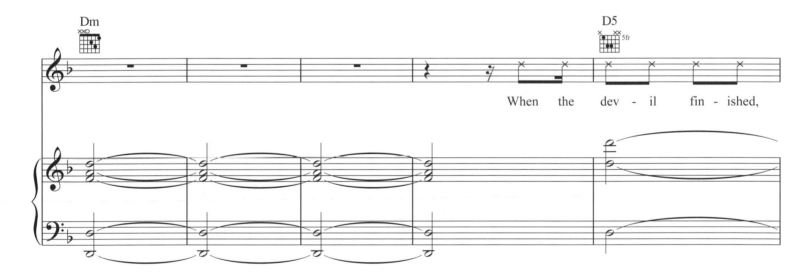

When the dev - il fin - ished,

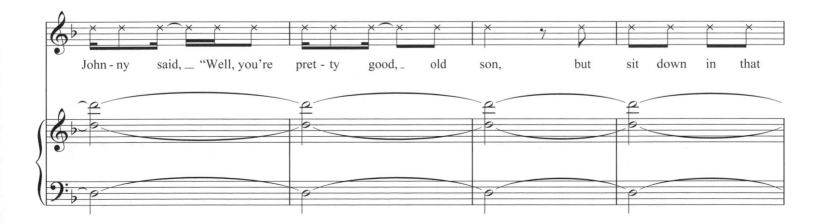

John - ny said, _ "Well, you're pret - ty good, _ old son, but sit down in that

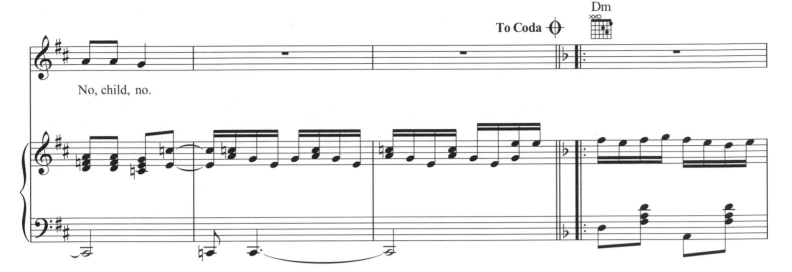

No, child, no.

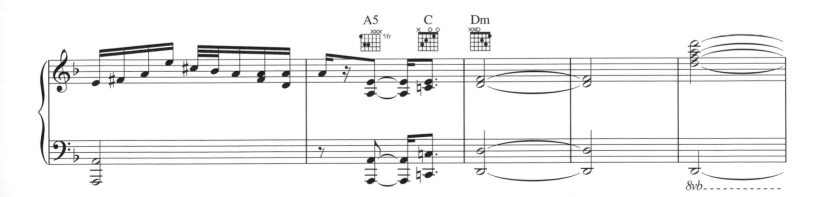

The dev-il bowed his head be-cause he knew that he'd_ been beat. And he

laid that gold-en fid-dle on the ground_ at John-ny's feet.

John-ny said, "Dev-il, just come on back_ if you ev-er want to try a-gain. _ 'Cause I

D.S. al Coda

told you once, you son-of-a-gun, _ I'm the best that's ev-er been." _ He played,

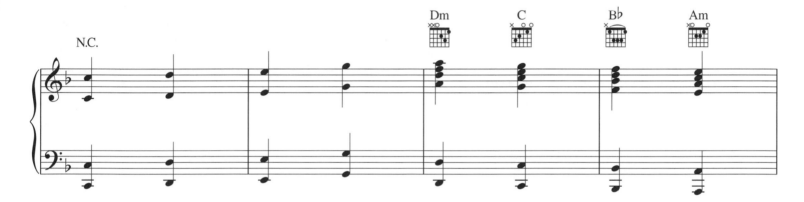

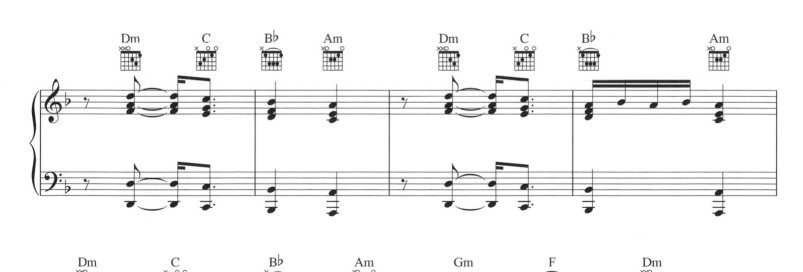

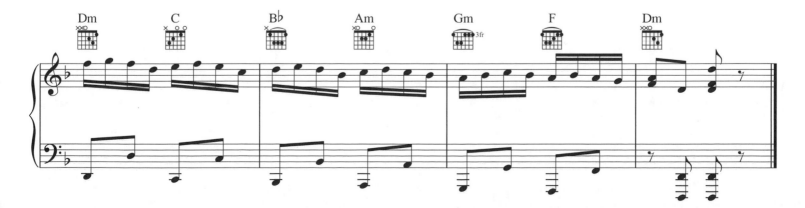

THE CIRCLE GAME

Words and Music by
JONI MITCHELL

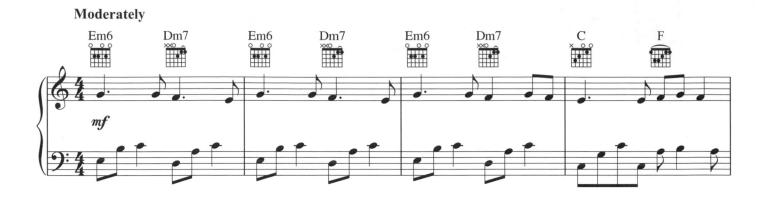

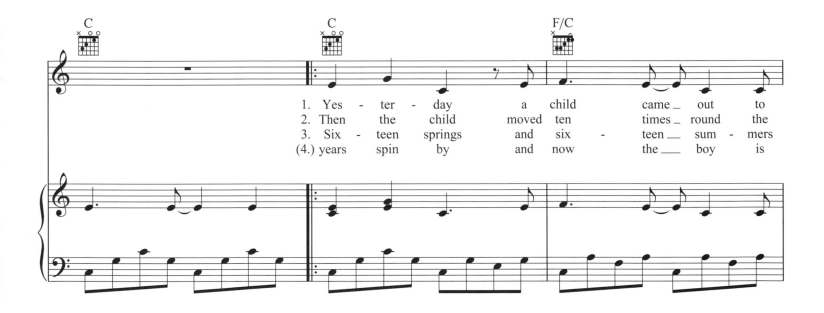

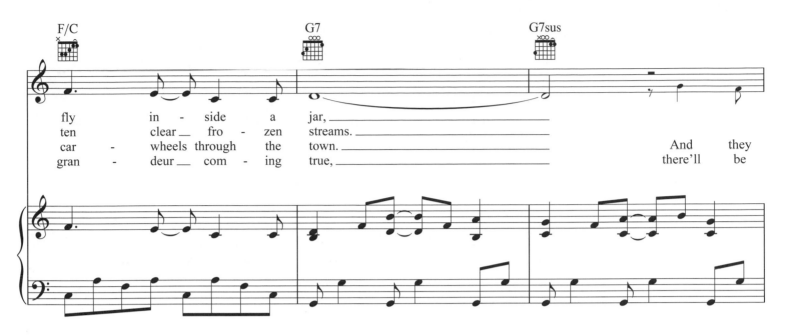

fly in - side a jar, _____
ten clear fro - zen streams. _____
car - wheels through the town. _____
gran - deur com - ing true, _____ And they there'll be

fear - ful when the sky was full ____ of thun - der _____
Words like "when you're old - er" must ____ ap - pease him, _____
tell him, "Take your time, it won't ____ be long now _____
new dreams, may - be bet - ter dreams, ___ and plen - ty _____

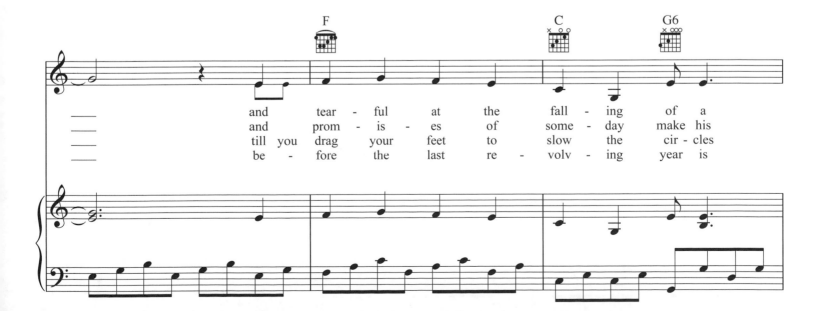

____ and tear - ful at the fall - ing of a
____ and prom - is - es of some - day make his
____ till you drag your feet to slow the cir - cles
____ be - fore the last re - volv - ing year is

star. _____
dreams. _____
down." _____
through. _____

And the sea - sons, they go

round and round, and the paint - ed po - nies go up and down.

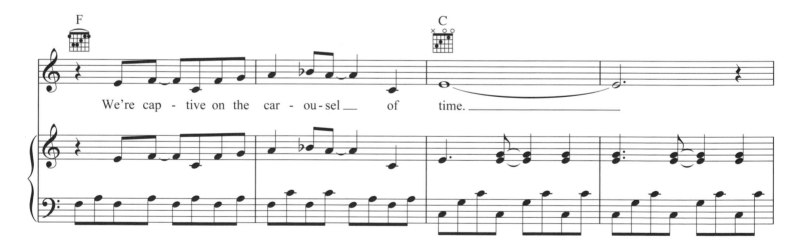

We're cap - tive on the car - ou - sel ___ of time. _____

We can't re - turn, we can on - ly look ___ be - hind from where we

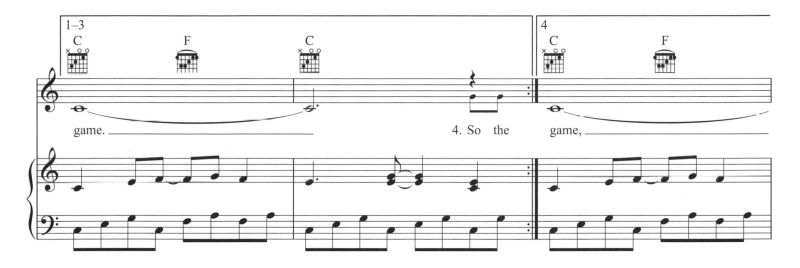

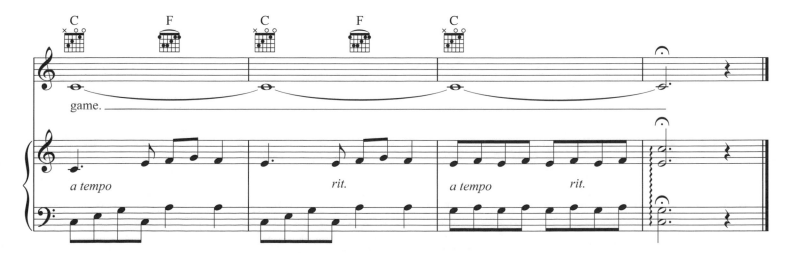

COAT OF MANY COLORS

Words and Music by
DOLLY PARTON

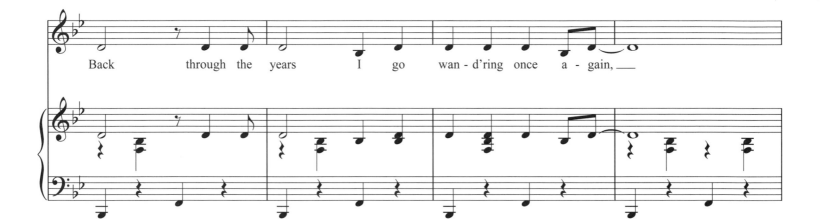

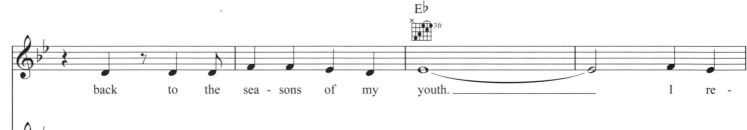

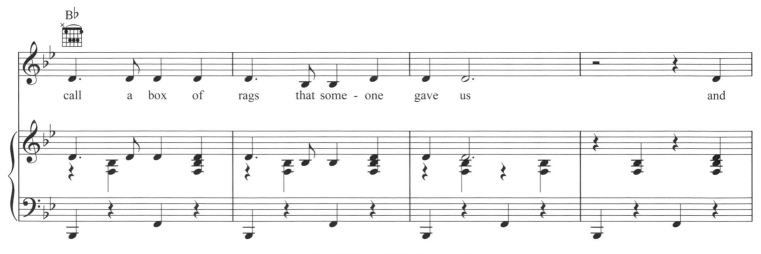

Back through the years I go wan-d'ring once a-gain, back to the sea-sons of my youth. I re-call a box of rags that some-one gave us and

63

coat of man - y col - ors that I was so proud of. _____
could - n't wait to wear it, and Ma - ma blessed it with a kiss. _____
coat of man - y col - ors my ma - ma made for me. _____
coat of man - y col - ors was worth more than all their clothes. _____

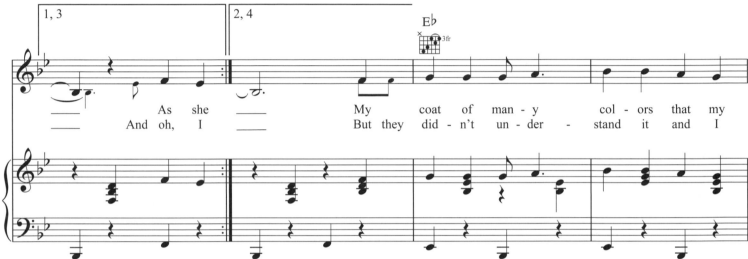

_____ As she _____ My coat of man - y col - ors that my
_____ And oh, I _____ But they did - n't un - der - stand it and I

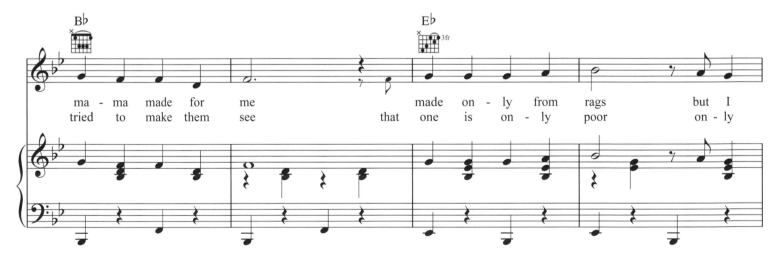

ma - ma made for me made on - ly from rags but I
tried to make them see that one is on - ly poor on - ly

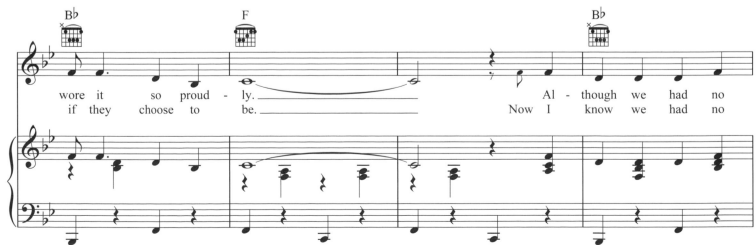

wore it so proud - ly. _____ Al - though we had no
if they choose to be. _____ Now I know we had no

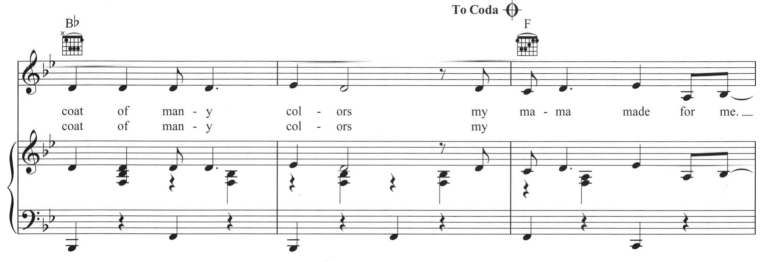

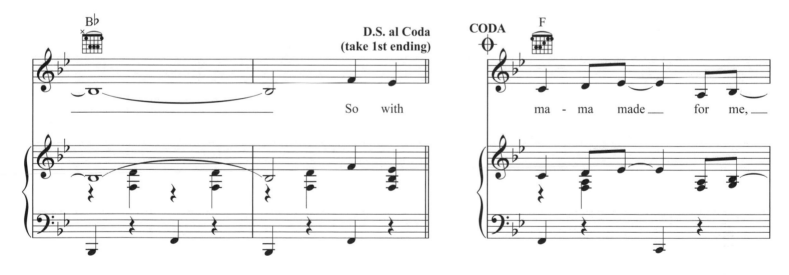

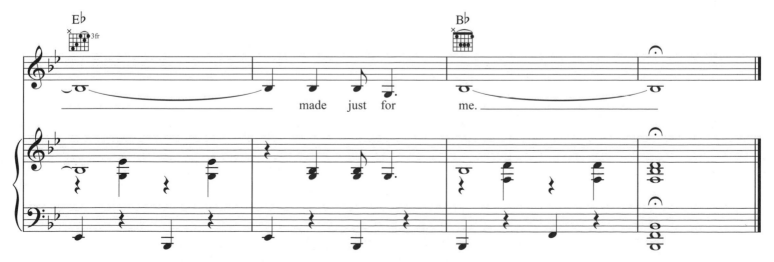

CONVOY

Words and Music by WILLIAM D. FRIES
and CHIP DAVIS

Moderately

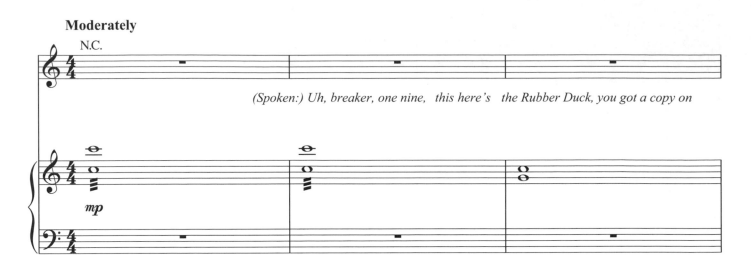

(Spoken:) Uh, breaker, one nine, this here's the Rubber Duck, you got a copy on

me, Pig-Pen, c'mon?   Uh, yeah, ten-four, Pig-Pen, fer   sure, fer sure, by golly.

It's clean clear to flag town, c'mon?   Yeah, that's a big ten-four, there,   Pig-Pen, yeah, we

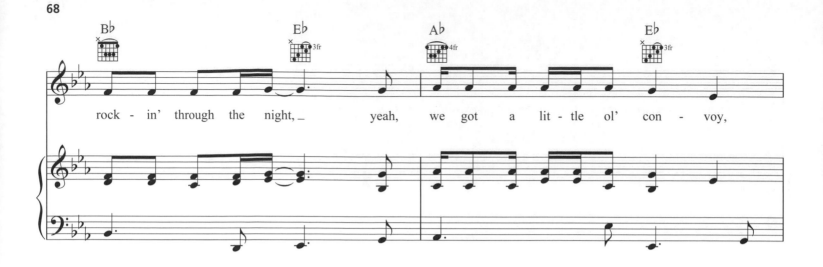

rock - in' through the night, _ yeah, we got a lit - tle ol' con - voy,

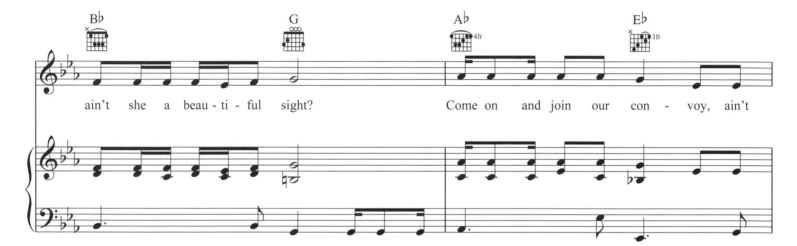

ain't she a beau - ti - ful sight? Come on and join our con - voy, ain't

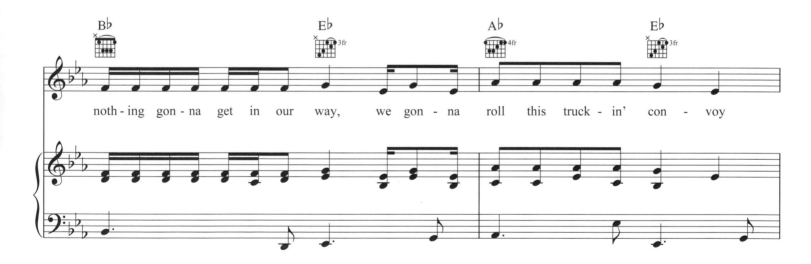

noth - ing gon - na get in our way, we gon - na roll this truck - in' con - voy

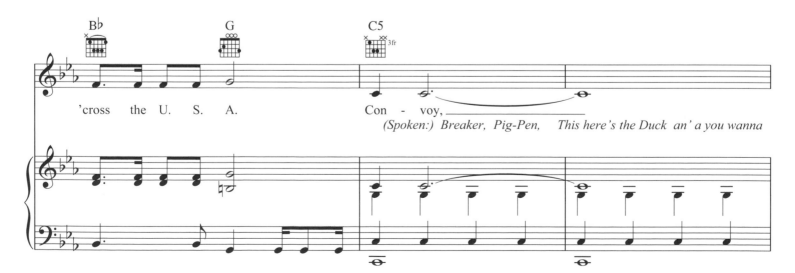

'cross the U. S. A. Con - voy, _____

(Spoken:) Breaker, Pig-Pen, This here's the Duck an' a you wanna

we got a {great big / might-y} con-voy, ain't she a beau-ti-ful sight?

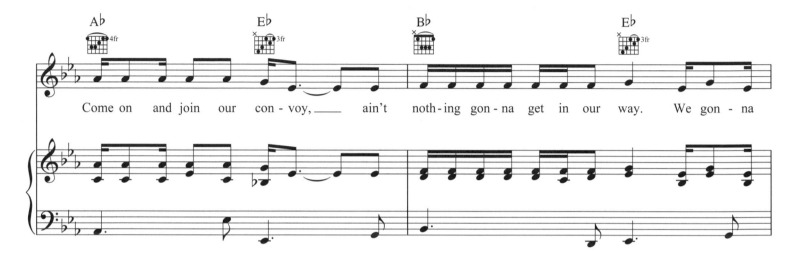

Come on and join our con-voy,___ ain't noth-ing gon-na get in our way. We gon-na

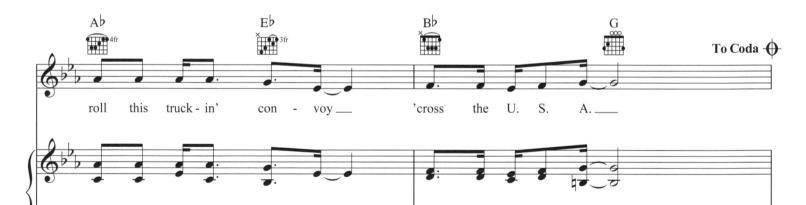

To Coda ⊕

roll this truck-in' con - voy___ 'cross the U. S. A.___

Con - voy,_____
(Spoken:) Uh, you wanna give me a ten-nine on that, Pig-Pen?

con - voy.___
Uh, negatory, Pig-Pen, you're

Uh, Rubber Duck to Sod Buster, come on there, yeah, ten-four Sod Buster. Listen, you wanna put that micro-bus in behind that

suicide jockey? Yeah, he's haulin' dynamite an' he needs all the help he can get. Well, we

laid a strip for the Jersey shore and prepared to cross the line. I could
Pig-Pen, this here's the Rubber Duck, we just ain't gonna pay no toll, so we

see the bridge was lined with Bears, but I didn't have a doggoned dime. I sez,
crashed the gate doin' ninety-eight, I sez,

"Let them truckers roll." 'Cause

D.S. al Coda

COPACABANA
(At the Copa)

Music by BARRY MANILOW
Lyric by BRUCE SUSSMAN and JACK FELDMAN

Moderately, with a Latin feel

Her name was Lo - la; ___ she was a
Ri - co; ___ he wore a
Lo - la; ___ she was a

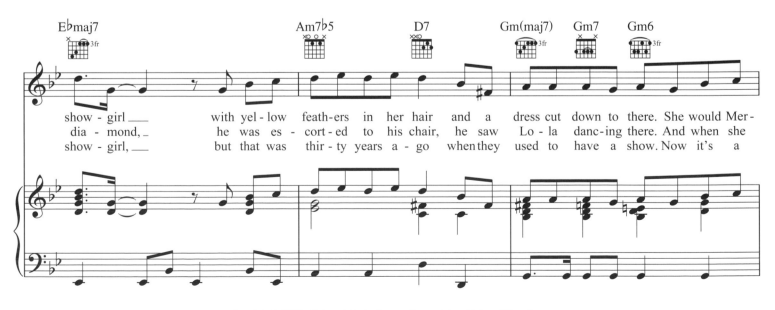

show - girl ___ with yel - low feath-ers in her hair and a dress cut down to there. She would Mer-
dia - mond, ___ he was es - cort-ed to his chair, he saw Lo - la danc-ing there. And when she
show - girl, ___ but that was thir-ty years a - go when they used to have a show. Now it's a

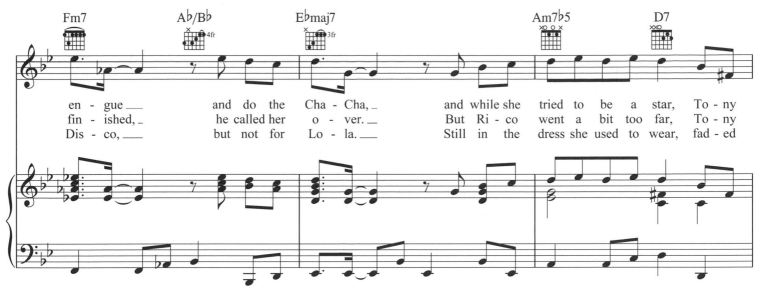

en - gue ___ and do the Cha - Cha, ___ and while she tried to be a star, To - ny
fin - ished, ___ he called her o - ver. ___ But Ri - co went a bit too far, To - ny
Dis - co, ___ but not for Lo - la. ___ Still in the dress she used to wear, fad - ed

al - ways tend - ed bar, a - cross the crowd - ed ___ floor. They worked from
sailed a - cross the bar. And then the punch - es ___ flew and chairs were
feath - ers in her hair, she sits there so re - fined and drinks her -

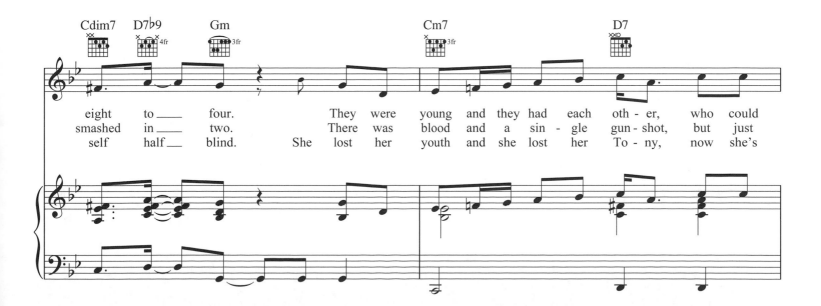

eight to ___ four. They were young and they had each oth - er, who could
smashed in ___ two. There was blood and a sin - gle gun - shot, but just
self half ___ blind. She lost her youth and she lost her To - ny, now she's

ask for more? }
who shot who? } At the Co - pa, Co - pa - ca - ban - a, the
lost her mind. }

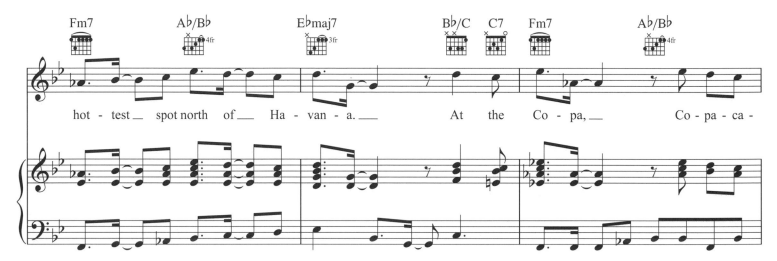

hot - test spot north of Ha - van - a. At the Co - pa, Co - pa - ca -

ban - a, mu - sic and pas - sion were al - ways the fash - ion, at the

To Coda ⊕

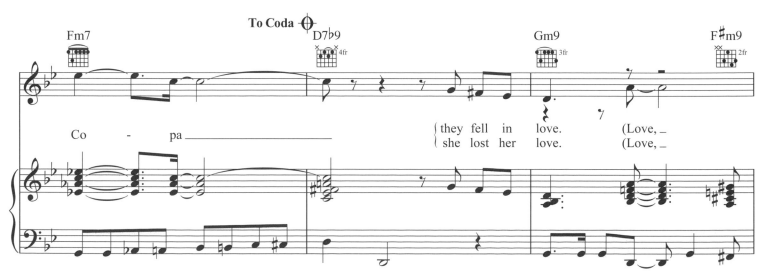

Co - pa
{ they fell in love. (Love, _
{ she lost her love. (Love, _

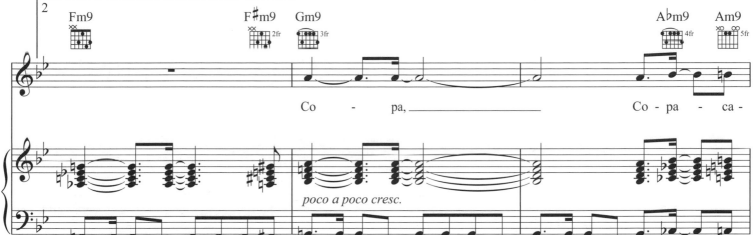

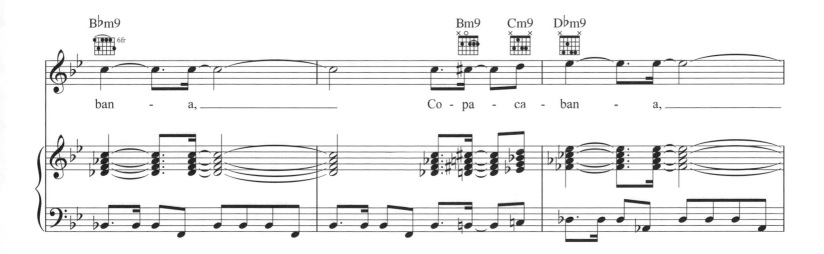

ban - a, _____ like in ___ Ha - van - a, _____

____ have a ___ ba - nan - a, _____ mu - sic __ and

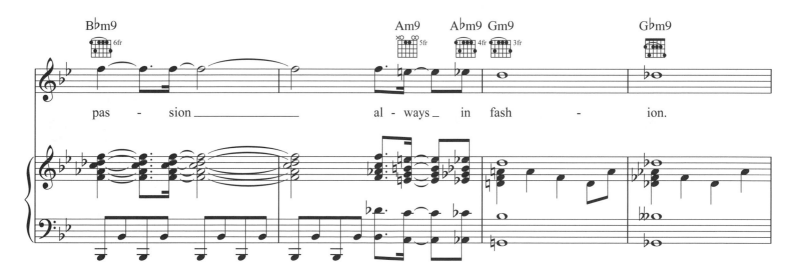

pas - sion _____ al - ways _ in fash - ion.

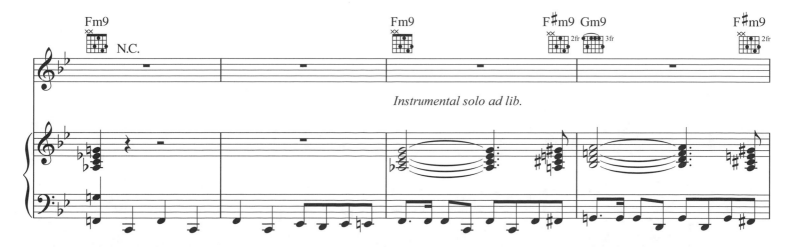

Instrumental solo ad lib.

D.S. al Coda

Solo ends   Her name is

don't fall in love,   Co - pa - ca - don't fall in

CODA

(Co - pa, ___   Co - pa - ca -

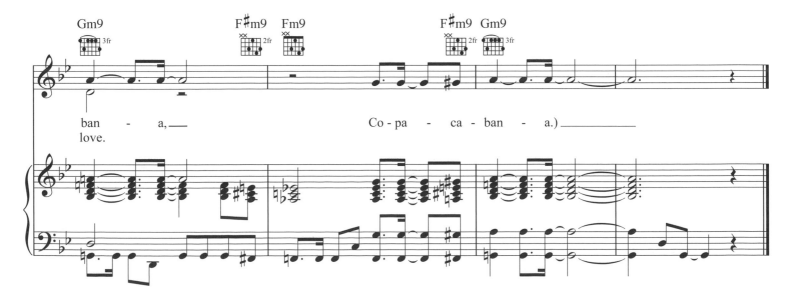

ban - a, ___   Co - pa - ca - ban - a.) ___
love.

DON'T STAND SO CLOSE TO ME

Music and Lyrics by
STING

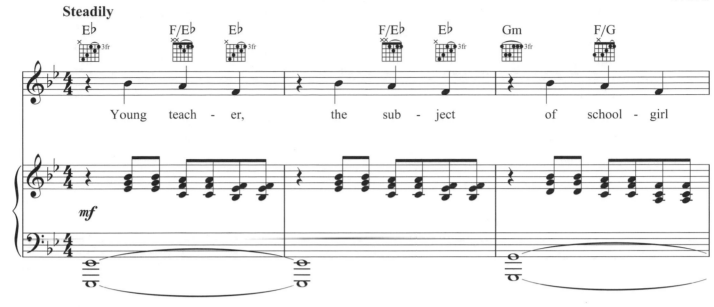

Young teach - er, the sub - ject of school - girl

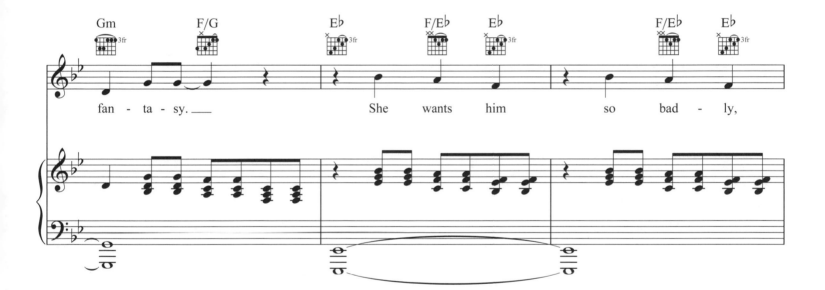

fan - ta - sy.___ She wants him so bad - ly,

knows what she wants to be. ___ In - side her

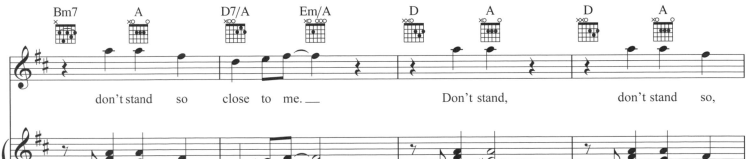

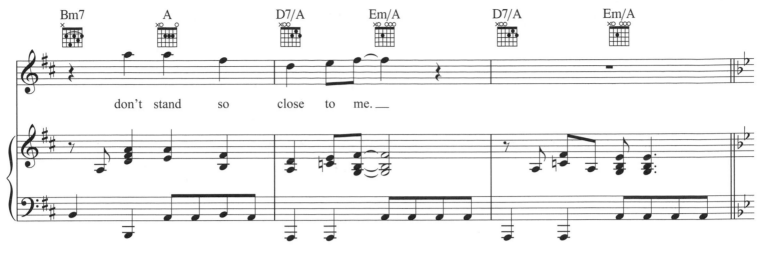

don't stand so close to me. ___

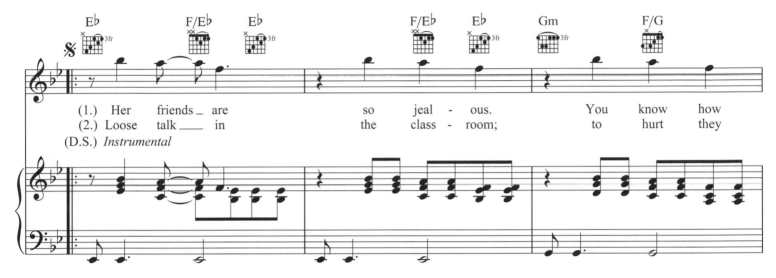

(1.) Her friends ___ are so jeal - ous. You know how
(2.) Loose talk ___ in the class - room; to hurt they
(D.S.) *Instrumental*

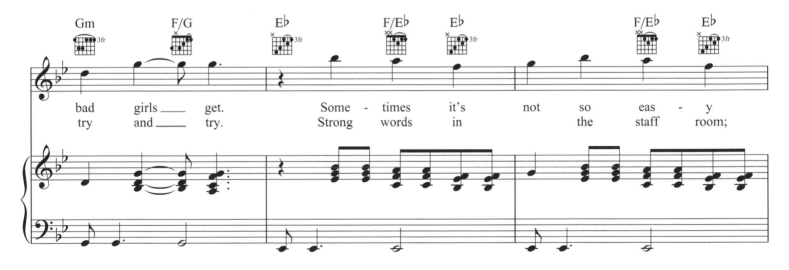

bad girls ___ get. Some - times it's not so eas - y
try and ___ try. Strong words in the staff room;

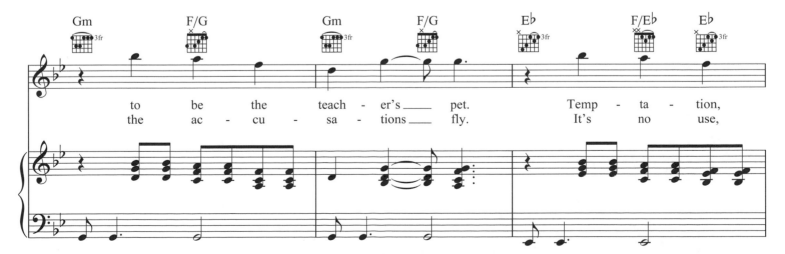

to be the teach - er's ___ pet. Temp - ta - tion,
the ac - cu - sa - tions ___ fly. It's no use,

84

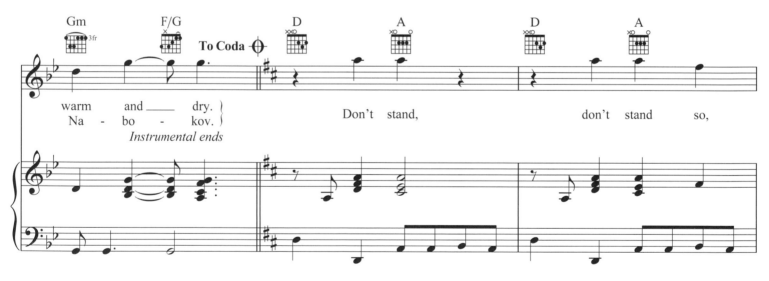

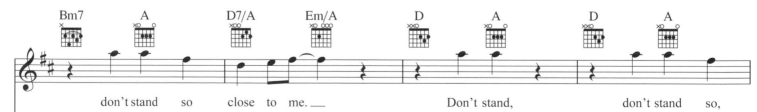

don't stand so close to me. ___

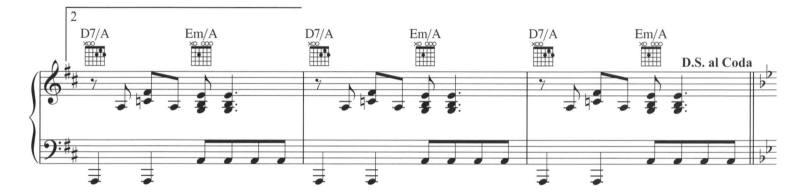

D.S. al Coda

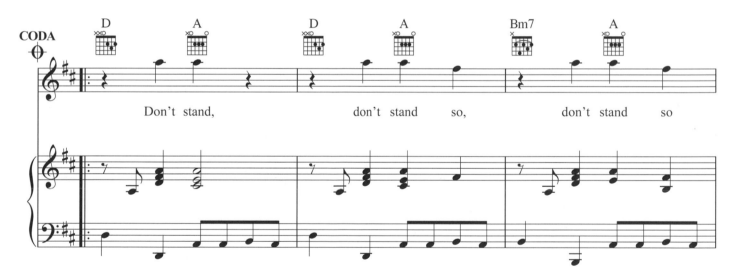

CODA

Don't stand,   don't stand so,   don't stand so

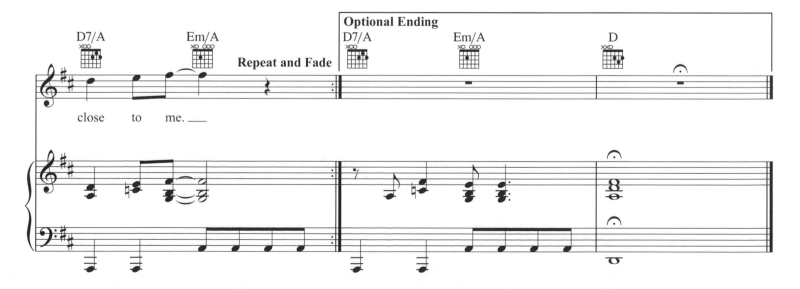

close to me. ___

Optional Ending

Repeat and Fade

COWARD OF THE COUNTY

Words and Music by ROGER BOWLING
and BILLY EDD WHEELER

Moderate Country, in 2

Ev-'ry-one __ con-sid-ered him __ the cow-ard of __ the coun-ty. __

He'd nev-er stood __ one sin-gle time to prove the coun-ty wrong. __

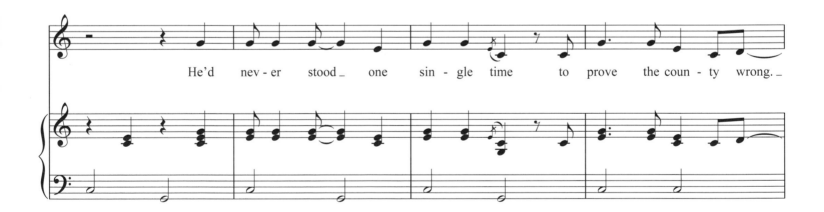

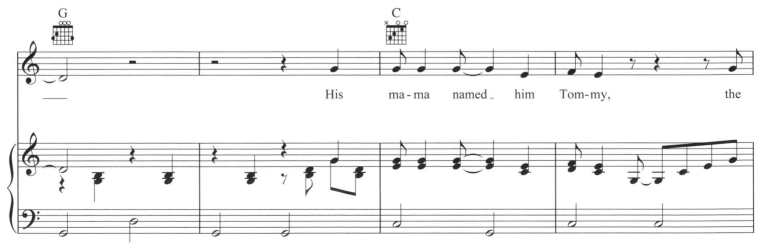

His ma-ma named __ him Tom-my, the

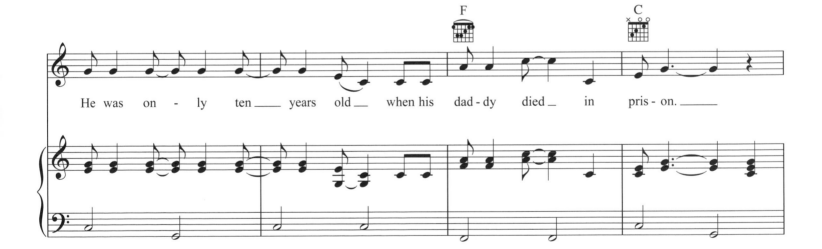

I still re-call the fi-nal words _ my

broth-er said _ to Tom-my, "Son, my life is o-

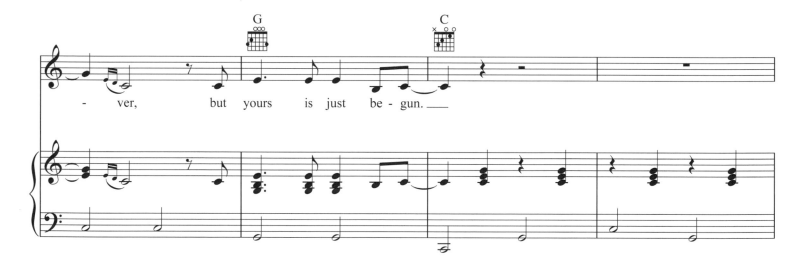

-ver, but yours is just be-gun. _

Prom-ise me, son, _ not to do _ the things _ I've done.

some - one for ev - 'ry - one __ and Tom-my's love __ was Beck-y. _____

In her arms __ he did-n't have __ to prove he was a man. _

One day while he was work - in' _____ the

Gat-lin boys __ came call - in'. They took turns __ at Beck-

down his dad-dy's pic - ture. As his tears fell on his

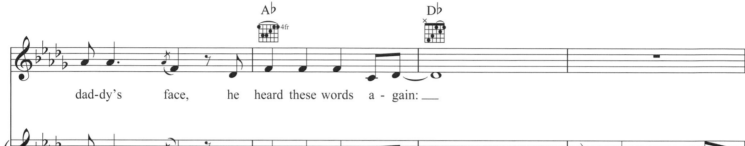

dad-dy's face, he heard these words a - gain: ___

"Prom - ise me, son, ___ not to do ___ the things I've done.

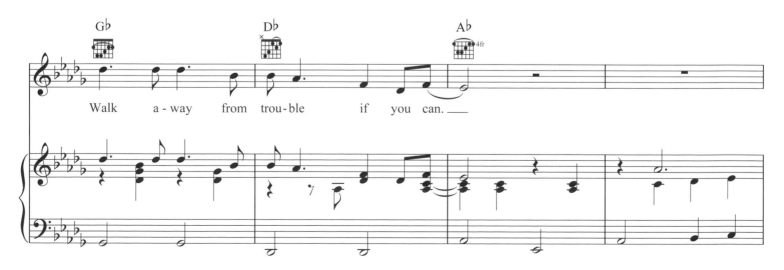

Walk a - way from trou - ble if you can. ___

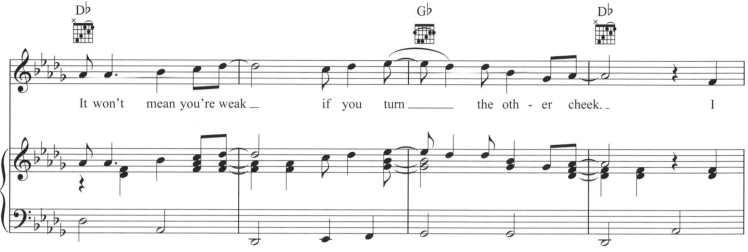

It won't mean you're weak _ if you turn ____ the oth - er cheek. _ I

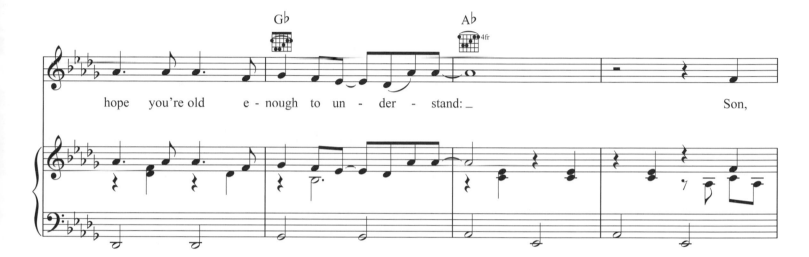

hope you're old e - nough to un - der - stand: _ Son,

you don't have to fight ___ to be a man." _ The

Gat - lin boys _ just laughed _ at him _ when he walked in - to the bar - room.

One of them got up and met him half - way 'cross the floor.

When Tom-my turned a - round they said, "Hey

look! Ol' Yel-low's leav - in'." *(Spoken:) But you coulda heard*

a pin drop when Tommy stopped and blocked the door.

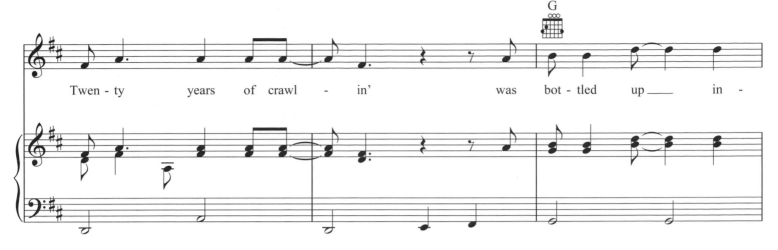

Twen-ty years of crawl-in' was bot-tled up__ in-

side him. He was-n't hold-in' noth-in' back,__ he

let 'em have it all.__ When Tom-my left__ the bar-

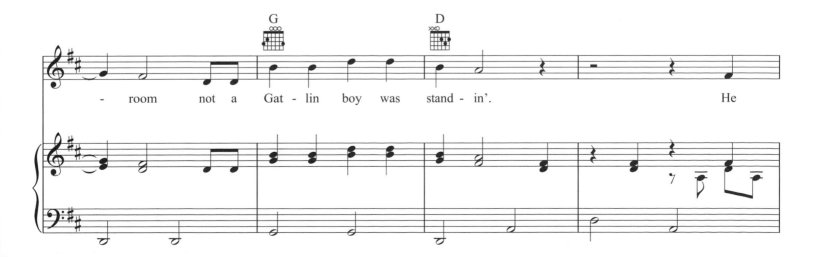

-room not a Gat-lin boy was stand-in'. He

said, "This one's ___ for Beck - y," as he watched the last one

D

fall. *(Spoken:) And I heard him say,* "I prom - ised you, Dad, ___ not to do ___

G **D** **G** **D**

_____ the things you done. I walk a - way from trou - ble when I can. ___

A **D**

___ Now please don't think I'm weak, ___ I did - n't turn ___

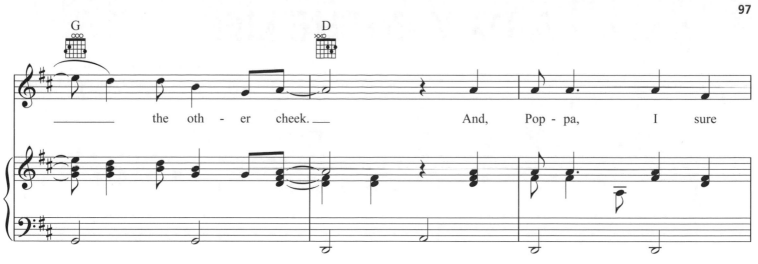

the oth - er cheek. ___ And, Pop - pa, I sure

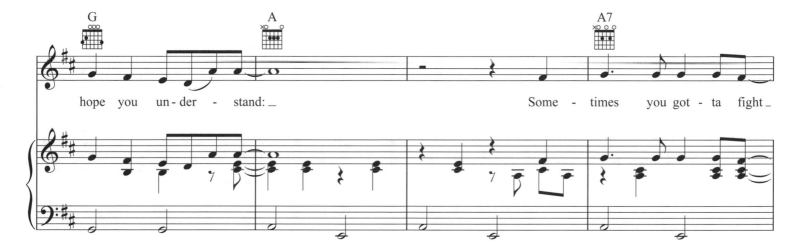

hope you un - der - stand: ___ Some - times you got - ta fight ___

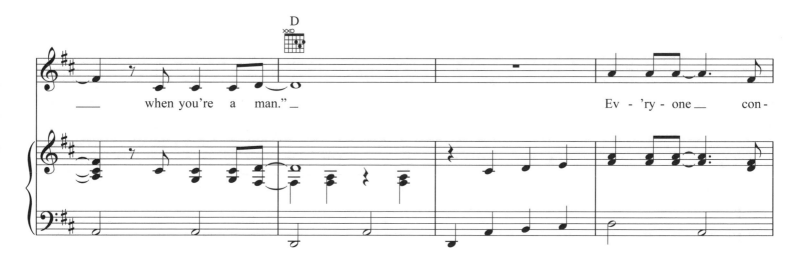

___ when you're a man." ___ Ev - 'ry - one ___ con -

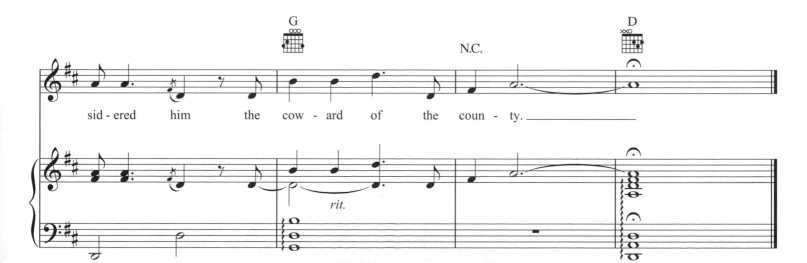

sid - ered him the cow - ard of the coun - ty. ___

A DAY IN THE LIFE

Words and Music by JOHN LENNON
and PAUL McCARTNEY

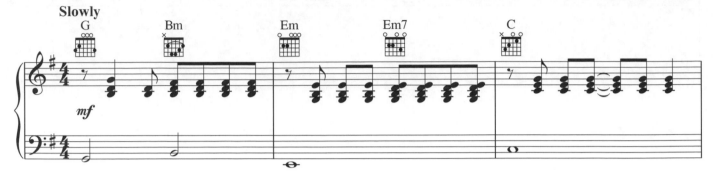

I read the news to-day, _ oh boy,

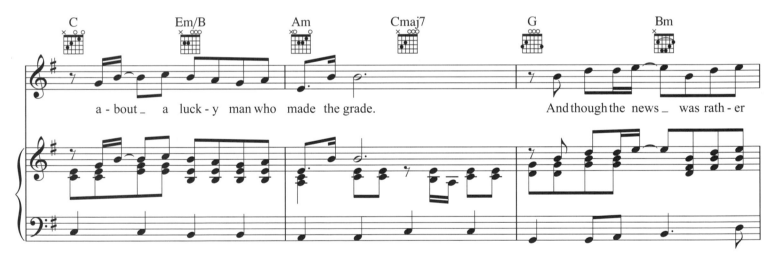

a - bout _ a luck - y man who made the grade.   And though the news _ was rath - er

sad,   well, I just had to laugh, _____

I saw the pho-to-graph. _____
He blew his mind out in ___ a
I saw a film to-day, _ oh

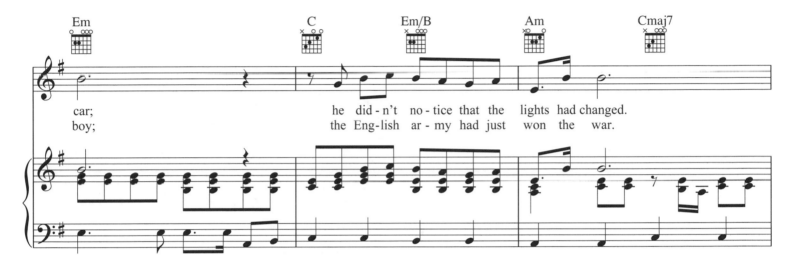

car;
boy;
he did-n't no-tice that the lights had changed.
the Eng-lish ar-my had just won the war.

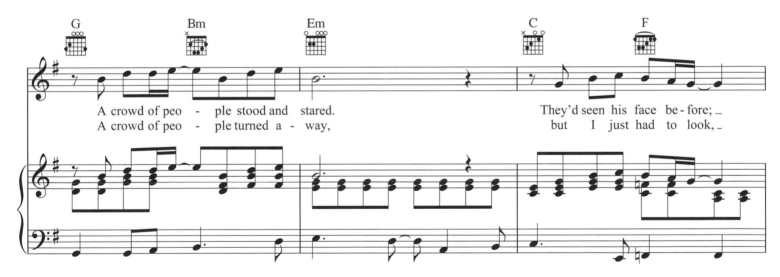

A crowd of peo - ple stood and stared.
A crowd of peo - ple turned a - way,
They'd seen his face be-fore; _
but I just had to look, _

no-bod-y was real-ly sure if he was from the House of Lords. __

hav - ing read the book. I'd

love to turn ____ you ____ on. ____

Woke up,

fell out of bed, dragged a comb a cross my head. ____ Found my

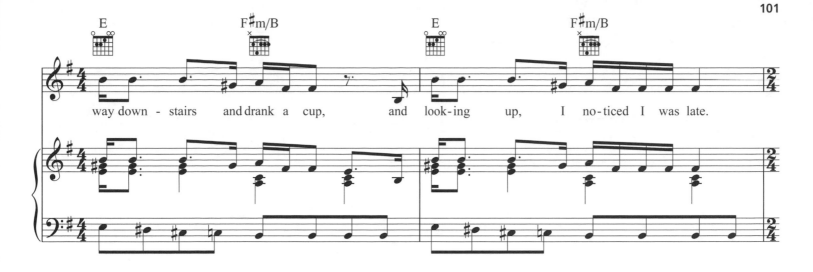

way down - stairs and drank a cup, and look-ing up, I no-ticed I was late.

Found my coat and grabbed my hat ___ made the bus in sec-onds

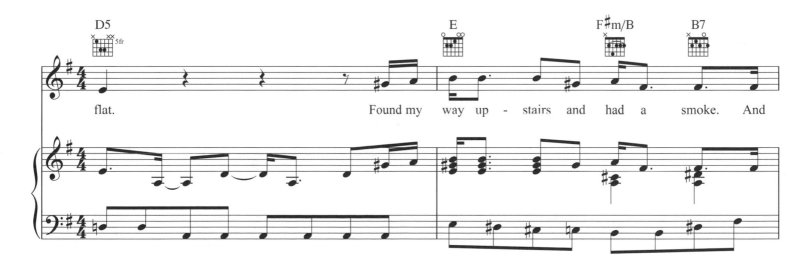

flat. Found my way up - stairs and had a smoke. And

some-bod - y spoke and I went in-to a dream. Ah ___

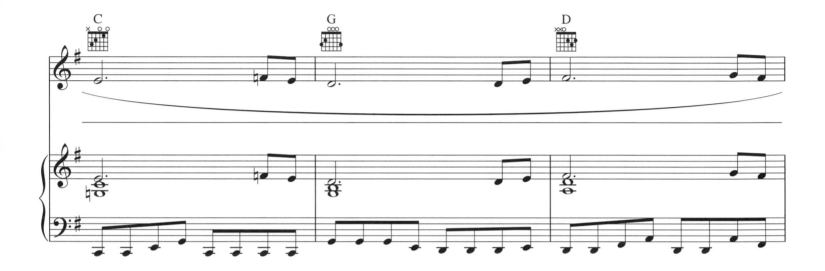

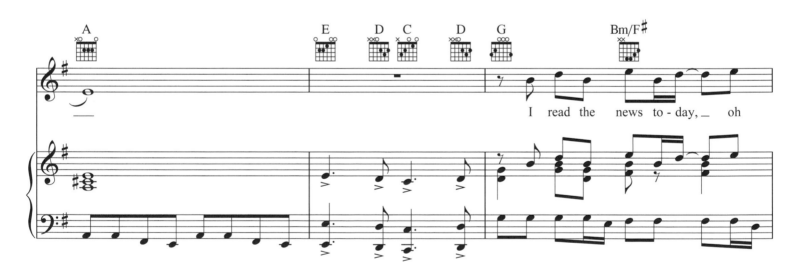

I read the news to-day, __ oh boy,

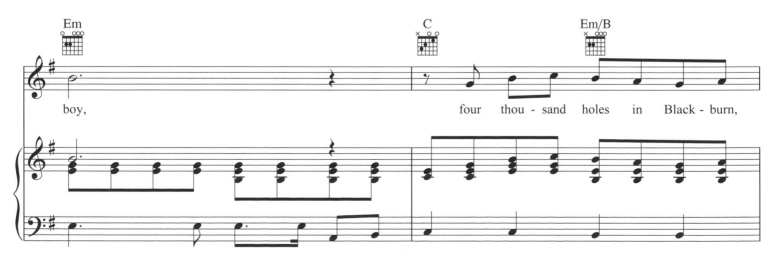

four thou-sand holes in Black-burn,

Lan - ca - shire. And though the holes _ were rath - er

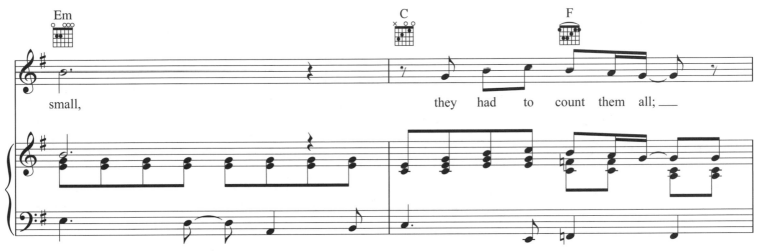

small, they had to count them all; ___

now they know how man - y holes it takes to fill the Al - bert Hall. I'd

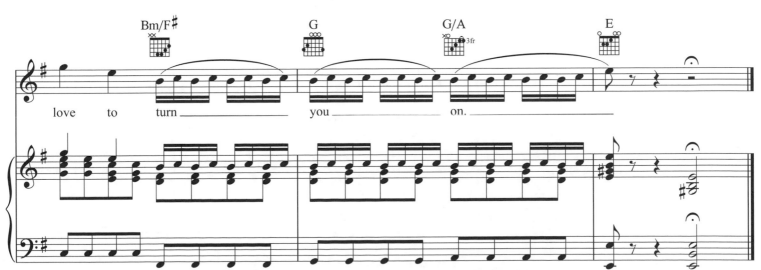

love to turn _____ you _____ on. _____

DON'T TAKE YOUR GUNS TO TOWN

Words and Music by
JOHNNY R. CASH

C

man.   I can shoot as quick and straight as
hips.   He rode in - to a cat - tle town, a
hand,   and tried to tell him - self at last he
draw,   but the stran - ger drew his gun and fired be -

G   C   F

an - y - bod - y can.   But I would - n't shoot with - out
smile up - on his lips.   He stopped and walked in - to
had be - come a man.   A dust - y cow - poke at
- fore he e - ven saw.   As Bil - ly Joe fell to

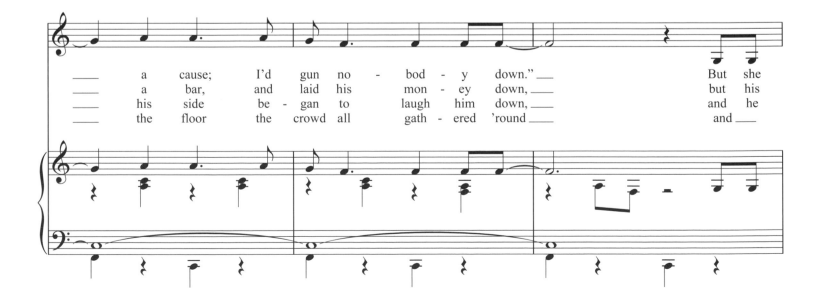

a cause; I'd gun no - bod - y down."   But she
a bar, and laid his mon - ey down,   but his
his side be - gan to laugh him down,   and he
the floor the crowd all gath - ered 'round   and

EL PASO

Words and Music by
MARTY ROBBINS

Out in the West Tex - as town of El
Night - time would find me in Ro - sa's Can -

Pa - so, I fell in love with a Mex - i - can
ti - na. Mu - sic would play and Fe - li - na would

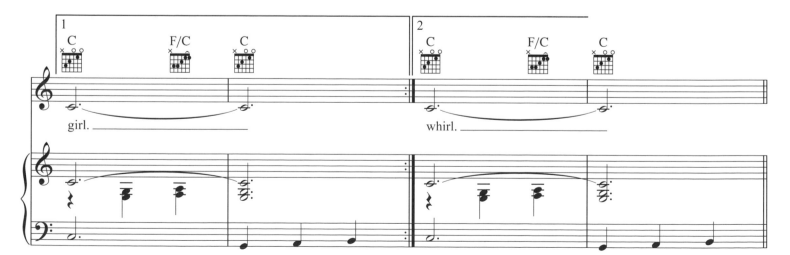

1.
girl. _____

2.
whirl. _____

Black - er than night were the eyes of Fe - li - na,
Just for a mo - ment, I stood there in si - lence,
Back in El Pa - so my life would be worth - less;
Off to my right I see five mount - ed cow - boys.

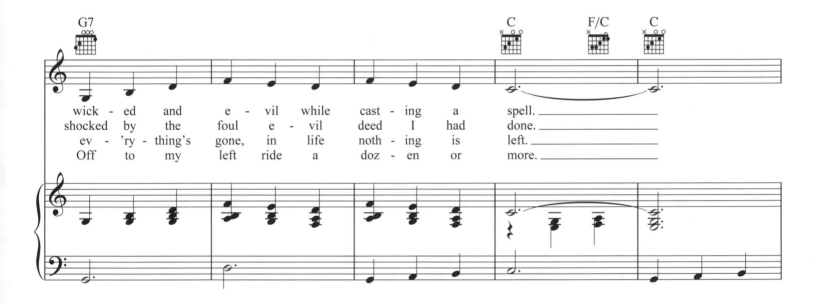

wick - ed and e - vil while cast - ing a spell. _____
shocked by the foul e - vil deed I had done. _____
ev - 'ry - thing's gone, in life noth - ing is left. _____
Off to my left ride a doz - en or more. _____

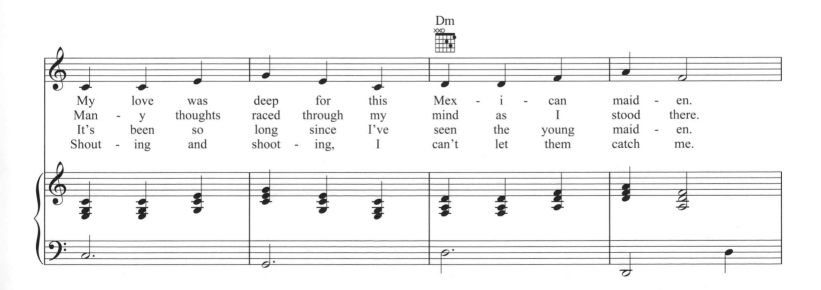

My love was deep for this Mex - i - can maid - en.
Man - y thoughts raced through my mind as I stood there.
It's been so long since I've seen the young maid - en.
Shout - ing and shoot - ing, I can't let them catch me.

I was in love, but in vain, I could tell. _____
I had but one chance, and that was to run. _____
My love is strong-er than my fear of death. _____
I have to make it to Ro-sa's back door. _____

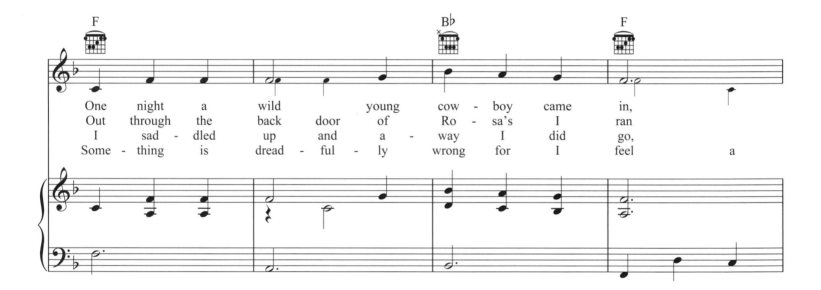

One night a wild young cow-boy came in,
Out through the wild back door of Ro-sa's I ran
I sad-dled up and a-way I did go,
Some-thing is dread-ful-ly wrong for I feel a

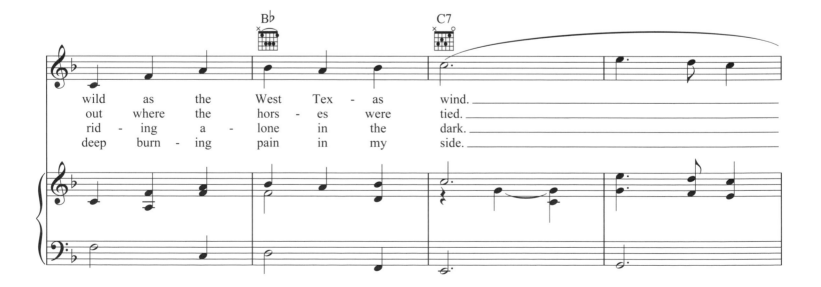

wild as the West Tex-as wind. _____
out where the hors-es were tied. _____
rid-ing a-lone in the dark. _____
deep burn-ing pain in my side. _____

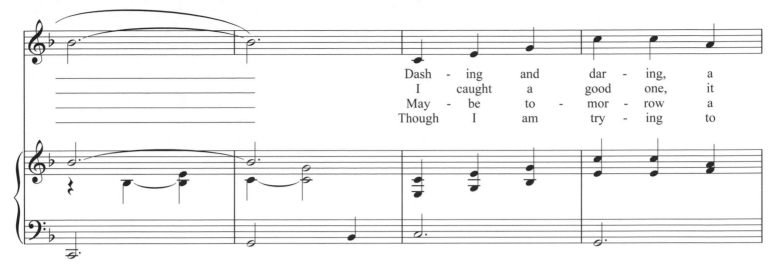

Dash - ing and dar - ing, a
I caught a good one, it
May - be to - mor - row a
Though I am try - ing to

drink he was shar - ing with wick - ed Fe - li - na, the
looked like it could run. Up on its back and a -
bul - let will find me. To - night, noth - ing's worse than this
stay in the sad - dle, I'm get - ting wea - ry, un -

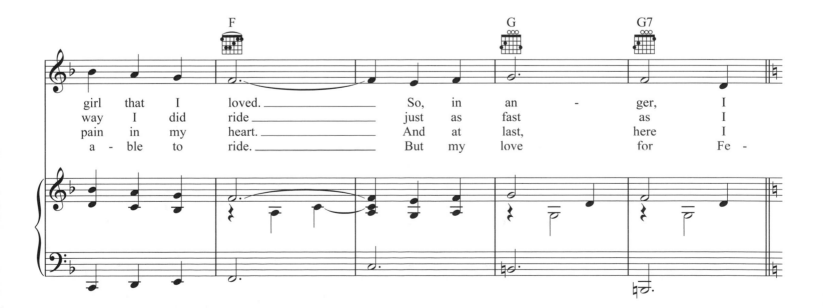

girl that I loved. So, in an - ger, I
way I did ride just as fast as I
pain in my heart. And at last, here I
a - ble to ride. But my love for Fe -

C   Dm

chal - lenged his right for the love of this maid - en.
could from the West Tex - as town of El Pa - so,
li - na is strong and I rise where I've fall - en.

G7   C   F/C

Down went his hand for the gun that he wore. _____
out to the bad - lands of New Mex - i - co. _____
I can see Ro - sa's Can - ti - na be - low. _____
Though I am wea - ry, I can't stop to rest. _____

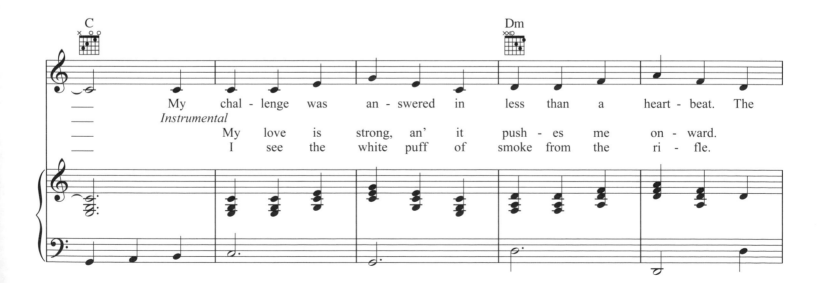

C   Dm

___ My chal - lenge was an - swered in less than a heart - beat. The
___ *Instrumental*
___ My love is strong, an' it push - es me on - ward.
___ I see the white puff of smoke from the ri - fle.

ELEANOR RIGBY

Words and Music by JOHN LENNON
and PAUL McCARTNEY

Moderately, with a steady beat

Ah, _____ look at all _____ the lone - ly peo - ple! _____

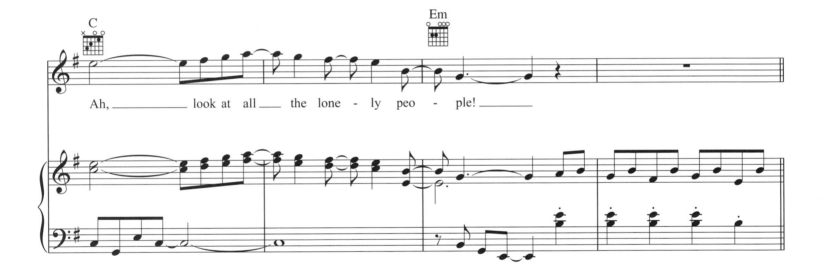

Ah, _____ look at all _____ the lone - ly peo - ple! _____

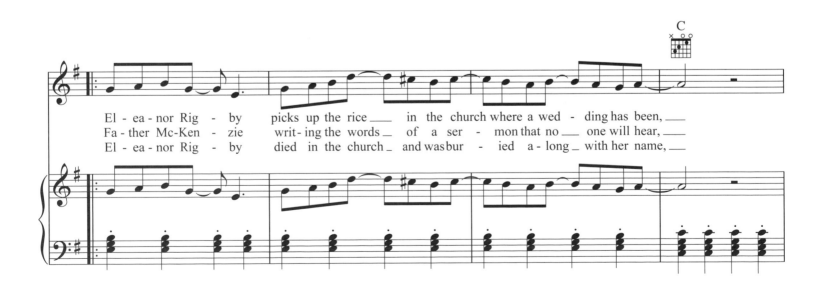

El - ea - nor Rig - by picks up the rice _____ in the church where a wed - ding has been, _____
Fa - ther Mc-Ken - zie writ - ing the words _____ of a ser - mon that no _____ one will hear, _____
El - ea - nor Rig - by died in the church _____ and was bur - ied a - long _____ with her name, _____

115

ESCAPE
(The Piña Colada Song)

Words and Music by
RUPERT HOLMES

Moderate groove

lady,   we'd been to-geth-er too long. ___   Like a worn-out re-cord-
lady,   I know I sound kind of mean. ___   But me and my old la-
hopes   and she walked in - to the place. ___   I knew her smile in an in-

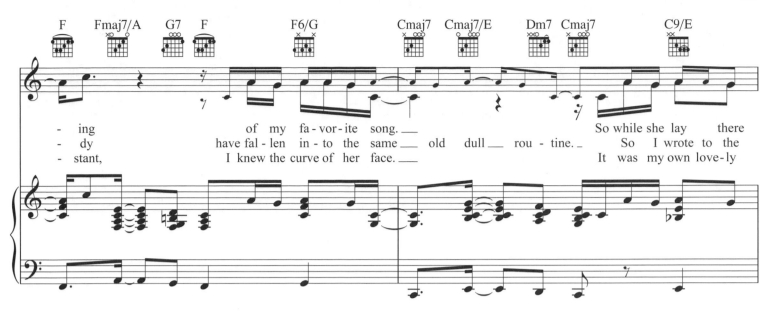

- ing of my fa-vor-ite song. ___ So while she lay there
- dy have fal - len in - to the same ___ old dull ___ rou - tine. ___ So I wrote to the
- stant, I knew the curve of her face. ___ It was my own love-ly

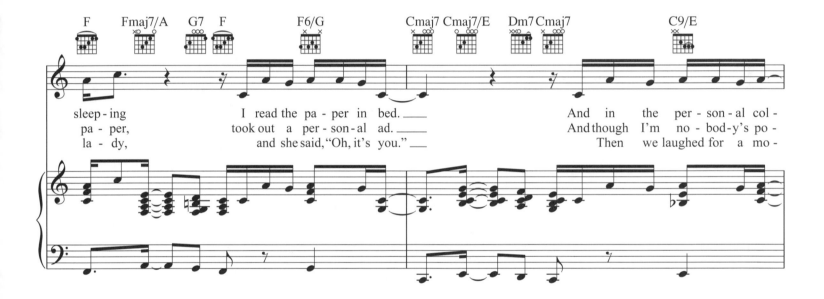

sleep - ing I read the pa - per in bed. ___ And in the per - son - al col -
pa - per, took out a per-son-al ad. ___ And though I'm no-bod-y's po -
la - dy, and she said, "Oh, it's you." ___ Then we laughed for a mo -

- umns, there was this let - ter I read: ___ If you like pi - ña co -
- et, I thought it was-n't half bad. ___ Yes, I like pi - ña co -
- ment, and I said, "I nev - er knew ___ that you liked pi - ña co -

la - das   and get-ting caught in the rain,   if you're not in-to
la - das   and get-ting caught in the rain.   I'm not much in-to
la - das,   get-ting caught in the rain,   and the feel of the

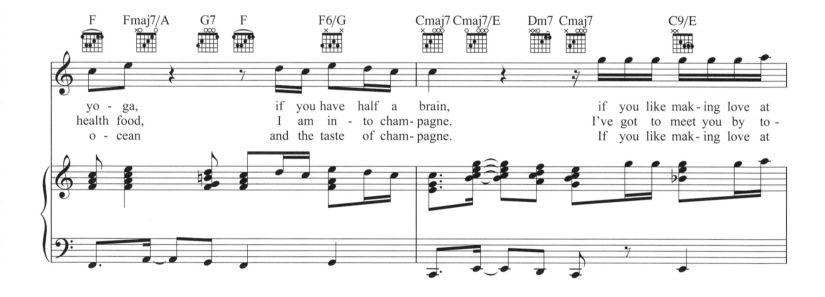

yo - ga,   if you have half a brain,   if you like mak-ing love at
health food,   I am in-to cham-pagne.   I've got to meet you by to-
o - cean   and the taste of cham-pagne.   If you like mak-ing love at

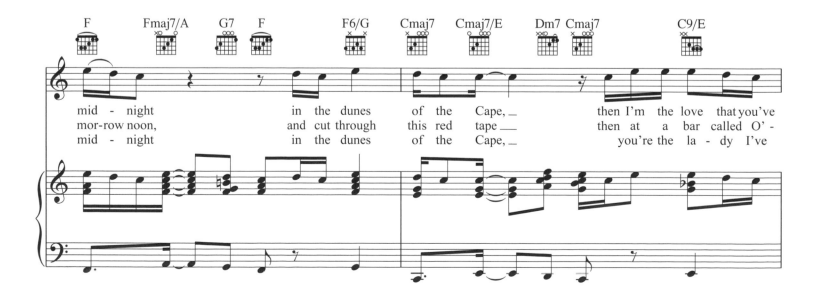

mid - night   in the dunes of the Cape, __   then I'm the love that you've
mor-row noon,   and cut through this red tape __   then at a bar called O'-
mid - night   in the dunes of the Cape, __   you're the la - dy I've

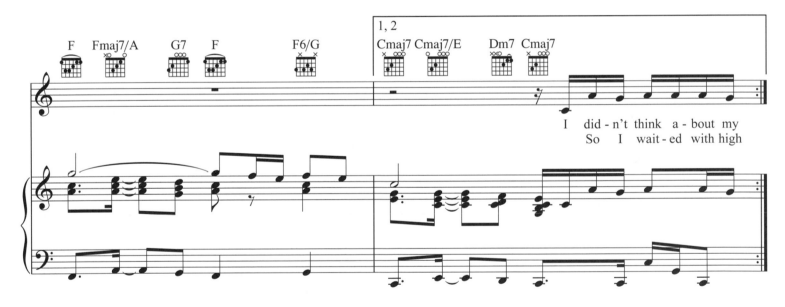

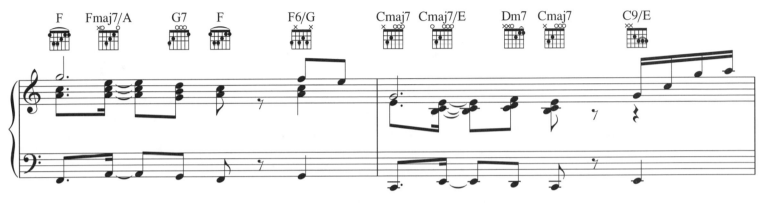

FAST CAR

Words and Music by
TRACY CHAPMAN

May - be we'll make some - thing. But me my - self I've got noth-ing to prove.
You and I can both get jobs and fin - 'lly see what it means to be liv - ing. __

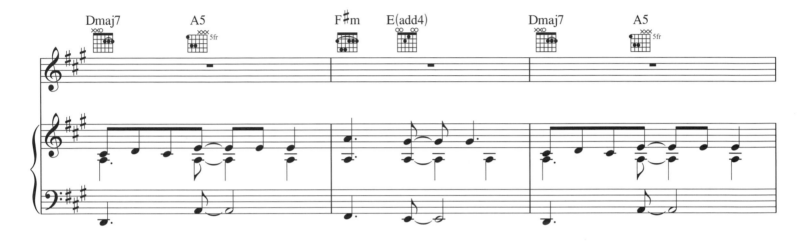

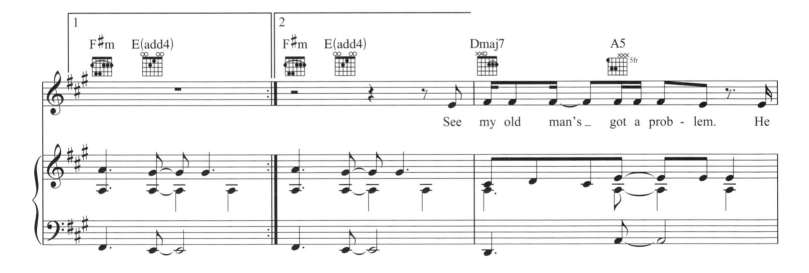

1 **2**

See my old man's __ got a prob - lem. He

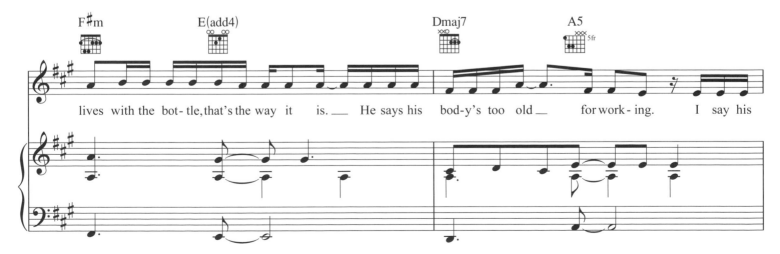

lives with the bot - tle, that's the way it is. __ He says his bod-y's too old __ for work - ing. I say his

bod-y's too young to look like his. My ma-ma went off ___ and left him. She

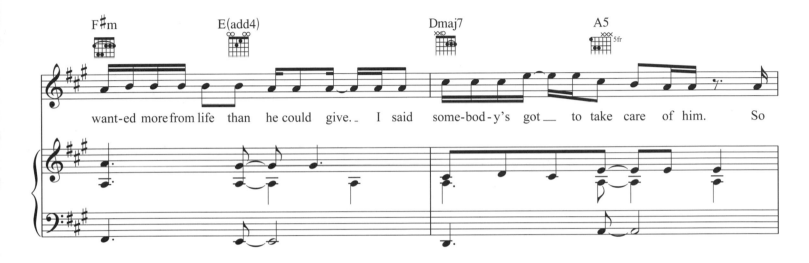

want-ed more from life than he could give. ___ I said some-bod-y's got ___ to take care of him. So

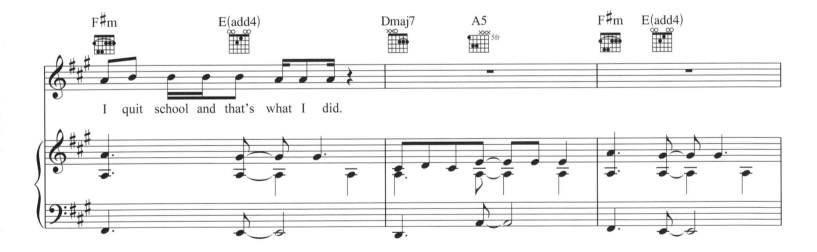

I quit school and that's what I did.

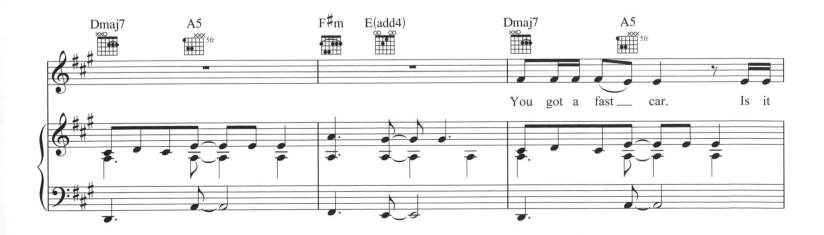

You got a fast ___ car. Is it

fast e - nough _ so we could fly a - way? _ We got - ta make a de - ci - sion, we

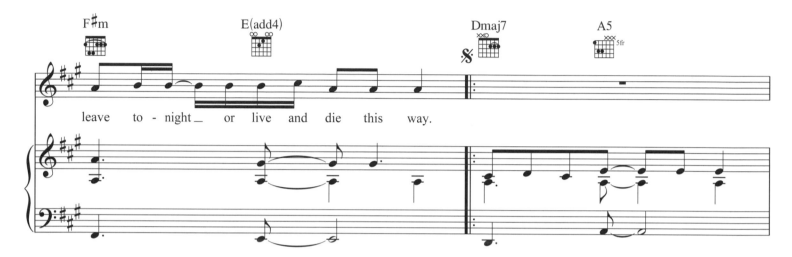

leave to - night _ or live and die this way.

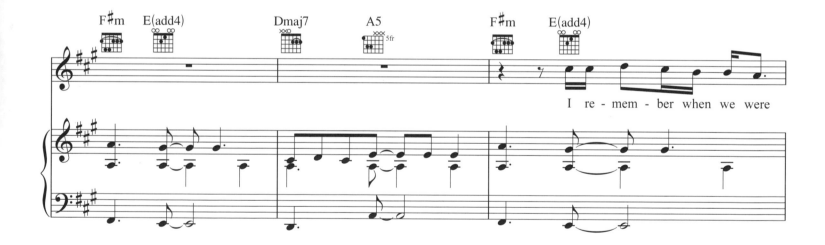

I re - mem - ber when we were

driv - ing, driv - ing in your car, _ speed so fast _ I felt like _ I was drunk,

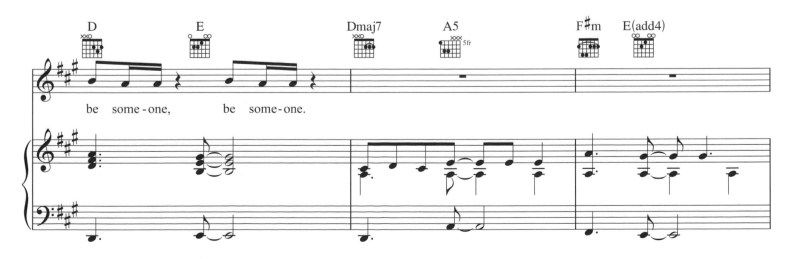

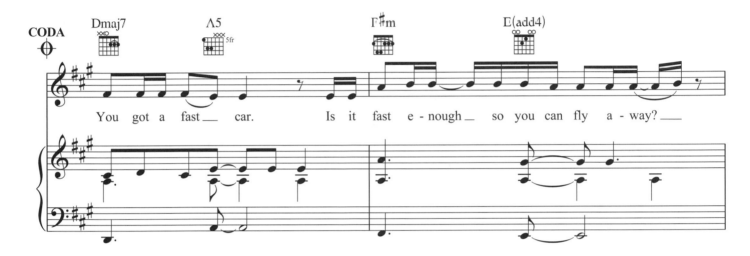

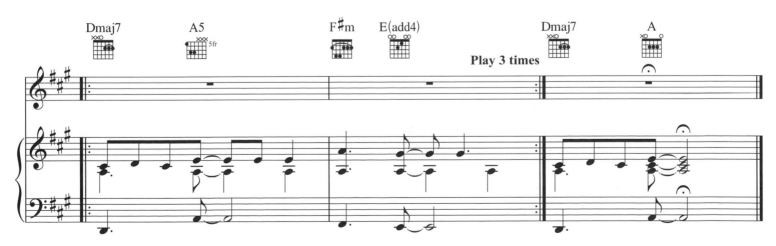

THE GAMBLER

Words and Music by
DON SCHLITZ

Moderate Country, in 2

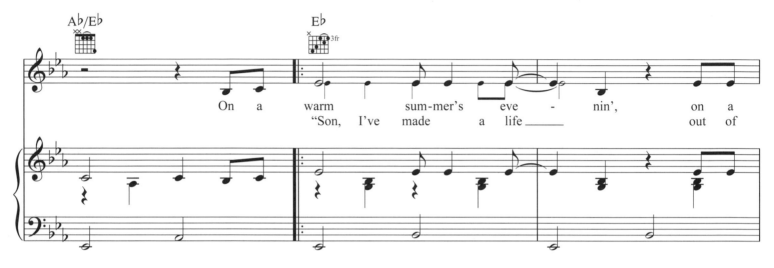

On a warm sum-mer's eve - nin', on a
"Son, I've made a life _____ out of

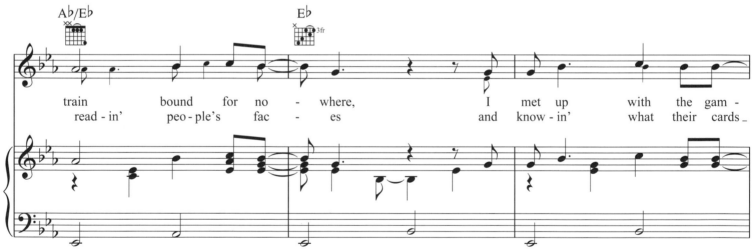

train bound for no - where, I met up with the gam -
read - in' peo - ple's fac - es and know - in' what their cards _

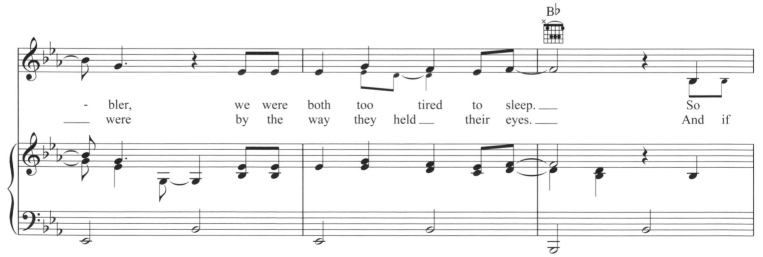

- bler, we were both too tired to sleep. _____ So
_____ were by the way they held _____ their eyes. _____ And if

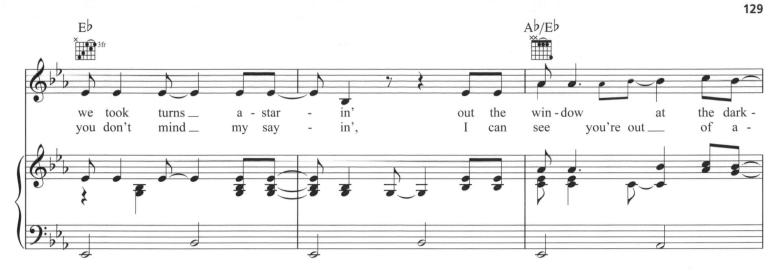

we took turns __ a - star - in', out the win - dow at the dark -
you don't mind __ my say - in', I can see you're out __ of a -

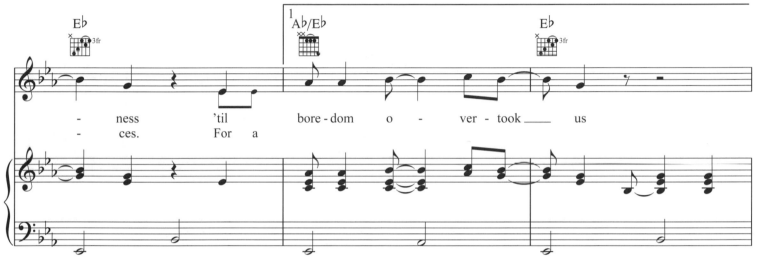

- ness 'til bore - dom o - ver - took __ us
- ces. For a

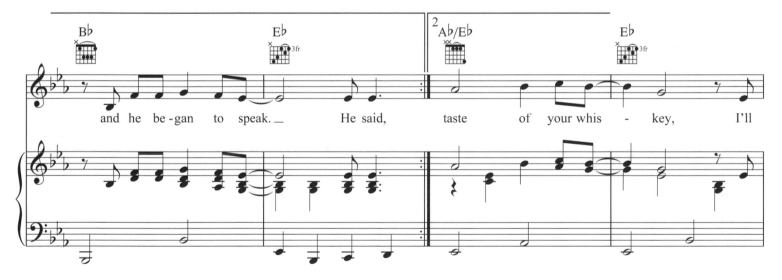

and he be - gan to speak. __ He said, taste of your whis - key, I'll

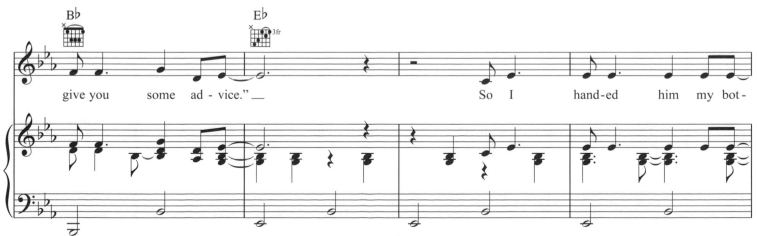

give you some ad - vice." __ So I hand - ed him my bot -

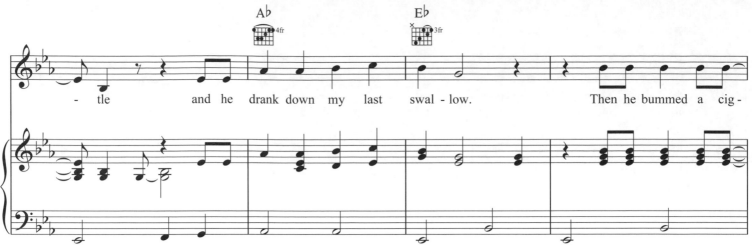

-tle ___ and he drank down my last swal-low. ___ Then he bummed a cig-

-a-rette ___ and asked me for a light. ___ And the night got death-ly qui-

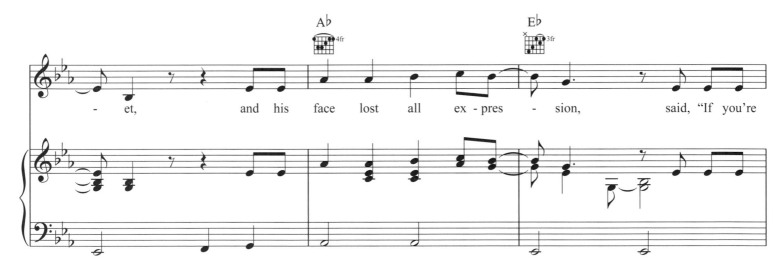

-et, ___ and his face lost all ex-pres-sion, ___ said, "If you're

gon-na play ___ the game, ___ boy, ___ ya got-ta learn to play ___ it right. ___ You got to

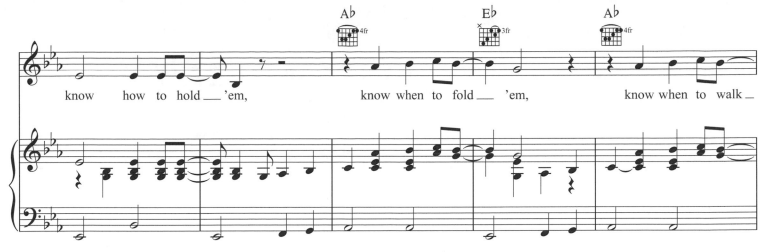

know how to hold __ 'em, know when to fold __ 'em, know when to walk __

__ a-way __ and know when to run. __ You nev-er count your mon-ey when you're

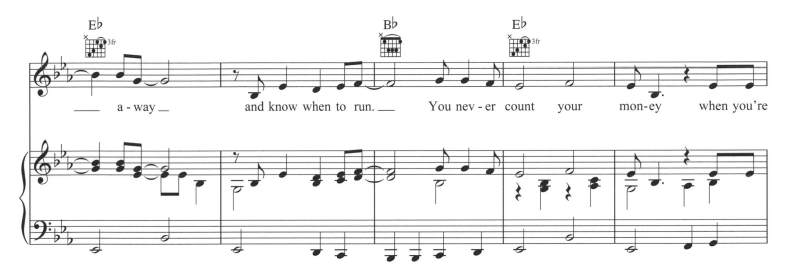

sit-tin' at the ta - ble. There'll be time e-nough __ for count - in'

when the deal-in's done.

know when to hold ___ 'em,   know when to fold ___ 'em,   know when to walk ___

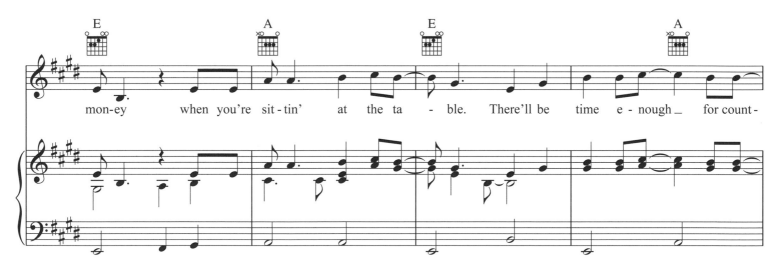

___ a - way ___   and know when to run. ___   You nev - er count   your

mon-ey   when you're sit-tin'   at the ta - ble. There'll be   time e - nough ___ for count-

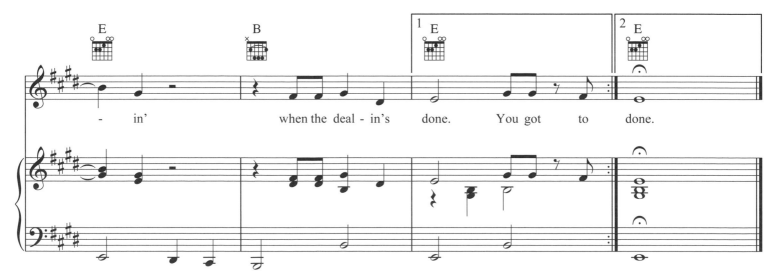

- in'   when the deal - in's   done. You got   to   done.

HOTEL CALIFORNIA

Words and Music by DON HENLEY,
GLENN FREY and DON FELDER

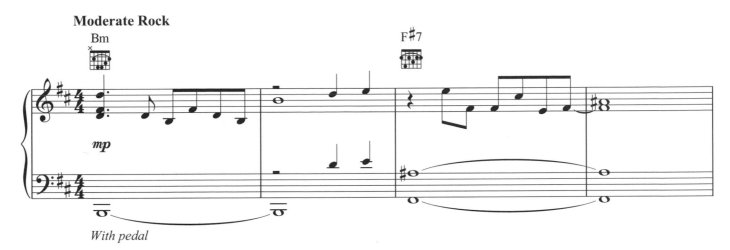

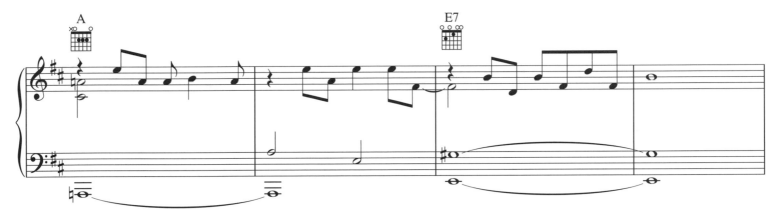

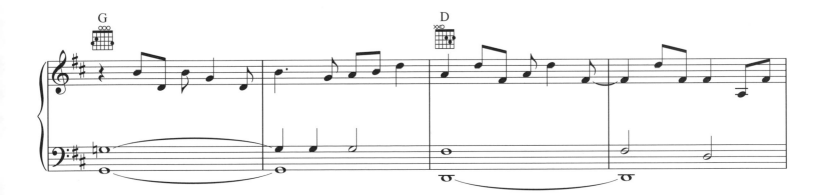

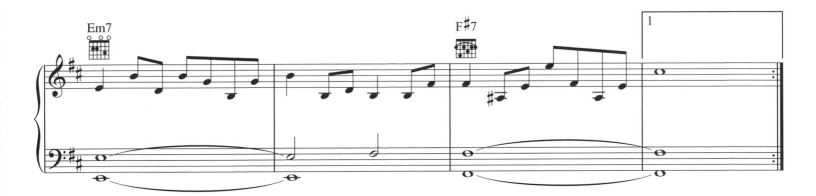

138

Such a love - ly place, (such a
Such a love - ly place, (such a

love - ly place) ___ such a love - ly face. ___
love - ly place) ___ such a love - ly face. ___

Plen - ty of room ___ at the Ho - tel Cal - i - for-
They liv - in' it up ___ at the Ho - tel Cal - i - for-

- nia.   An - y time ___ of year, ___ (an - y
- nia.   What a nice ___ sur - prise; ___ (what a

HARPER VALLEY P.T.A.

Words and Music by
TOM T. HALL

HAZARD

Words and Music by
RICHARD MARX

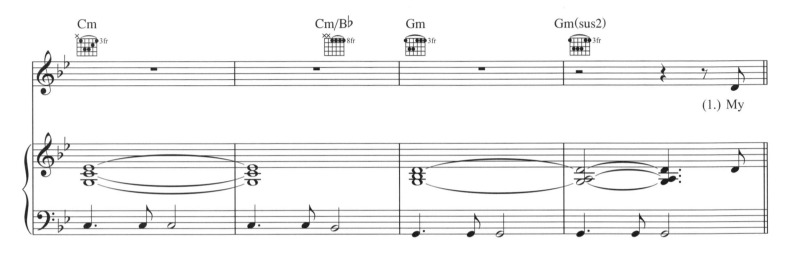

(1.) My

moth-er came to Haz-ard when I _____ was just sev-en.
(2.) No one un-der-stood ___ what I felt ___ for Mar-y.
_____ (3.) *Instrumental*

E- ven then ___ the folks ___
No one cared ___ un-til ___

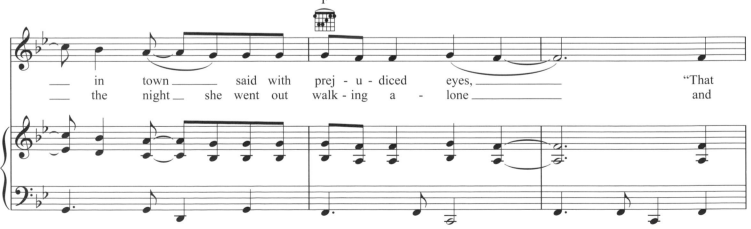

___ in town _____ said with prej-u-diced eyes, _____
___ the night ___ she went out walk-ing a- lone _____

"That
and

C   Gm

boy's not right."   Three years a - go___ when I
nev - er came home. ___ Man with a badge_ came

came to know Mar - y,   first time_ that some - one looked_ be - yond the
knock-ing next morn - ing. Here I was_ sur-round - ed by a thou - sand

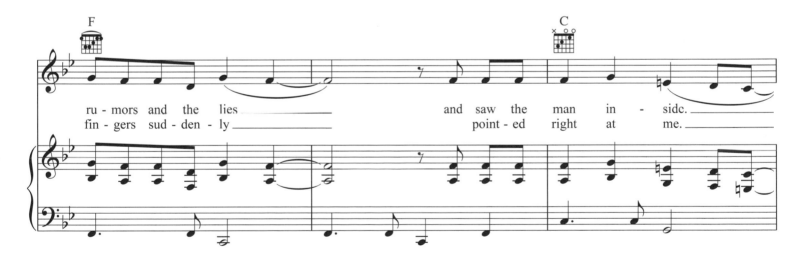

F   C

ru - mors and the lies ___ and saw the man in - side. ___
fin - gers sud - den - ly ___ point - ed right at me. ___

Eb

Instrumental ends

(1.) We used   to walk___ down by ___ the
(2.,3.) I swear   I left ___ her by ___ the

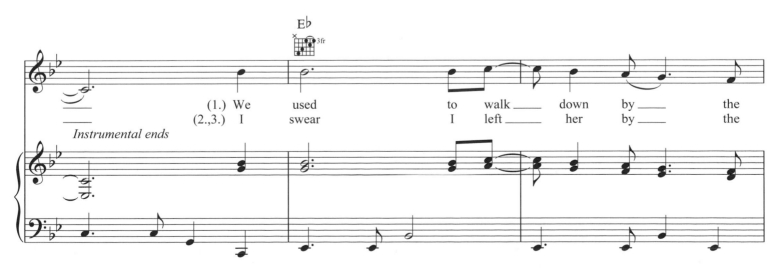

riv - er. ___ She loved to watch ___ the sun go down. ___
riv - er. ___ I swear I left ___ her safe ___ and sound. ___

___ We loved to walk ___ a - long ___ the
___ I need to make ___ it to ___ the

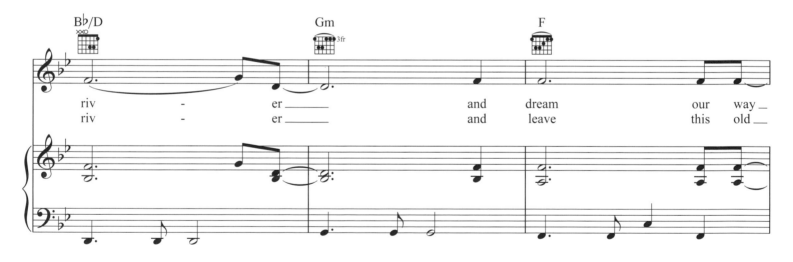

riv - er _____ and dream our way ___
riv - er _____ and leave this old ___

To Coda

(D.C. on repeat)

___ out of ___ this town. _____
___ Ne - bras - ka town. _____

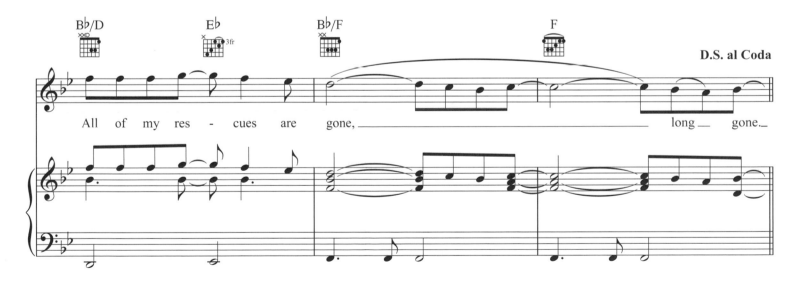

A HORSE WITH NO NAME

Words and Music by
DEWEY BUNNELL

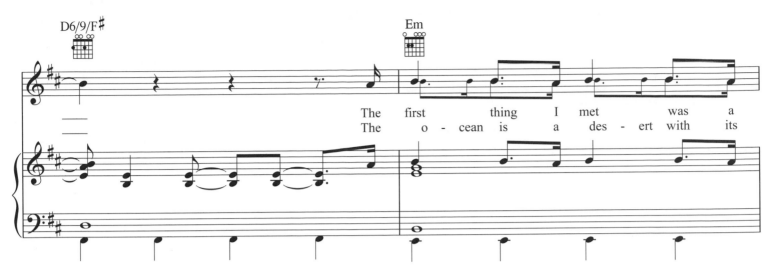

The first thing I met was a
The o- cean is a des - ert with its

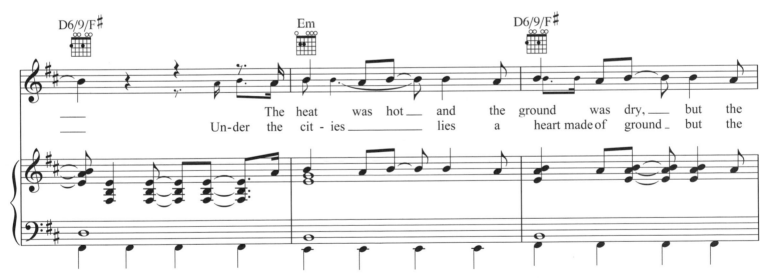

fly with a buzz ___ and the sky with no ___ clouds.
life un - der - ground ___ and the per - fect dis - guise ___ a - bove. ___

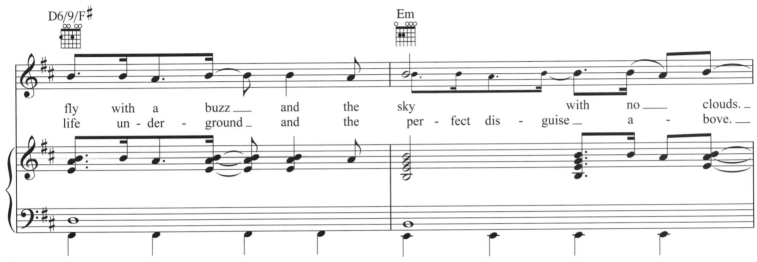

The heat was hot ___ and the ground was dry, ___ but the
Un - der the cit - ies ___ lies a heart made of ground ___ but the

air was full ___ of ___ sound. ___ You see, I've
hu - mans will give ___ no ___ love. ___ You see, I've

been through the des - ert on a horse with no name. ___ It felt

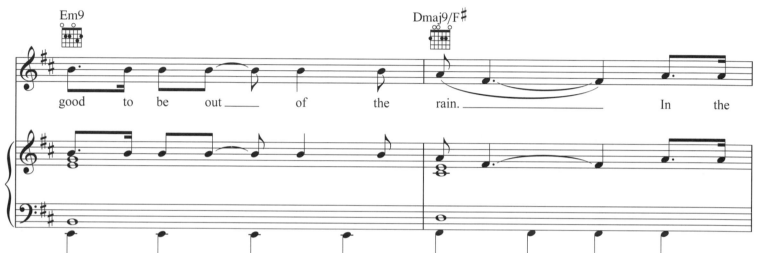

good to be out ___ of the rain. _____ In the

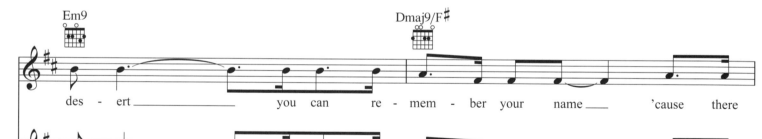

des - ert _____ you can re - mem - ber your name ___ 'cause there

To Coda ⊕

ain't no one for to give you no pain. ___ La la la

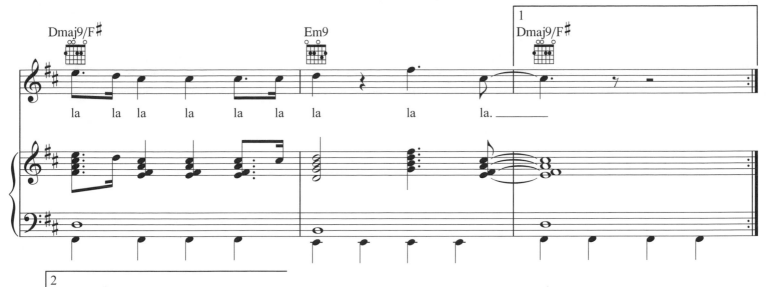

la la la la la la la la la.____

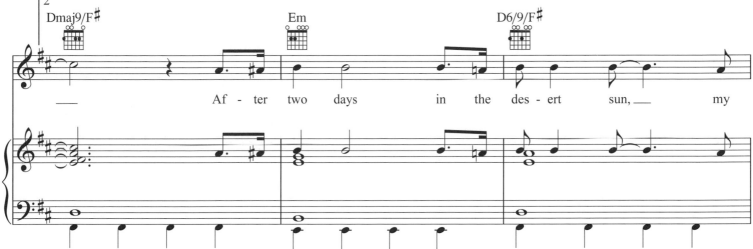

____ Af - ter two days in the des - ert sun,____ my

skin be - gan ___ to turn red. Af - ter three days in the

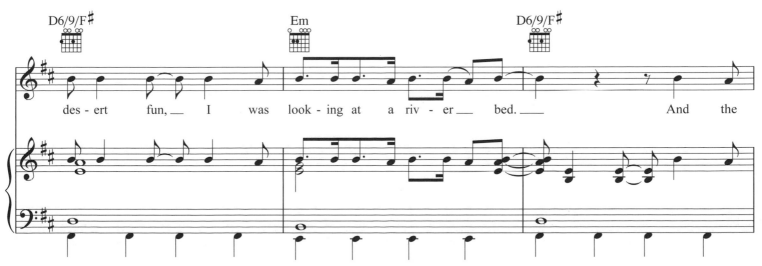

des - ert fun, ___ I was look - ing at a riv - er ___ bed. ___ And the

sto - ry is told _ of a riv - er that flowed; _ made me sad to think _ it was

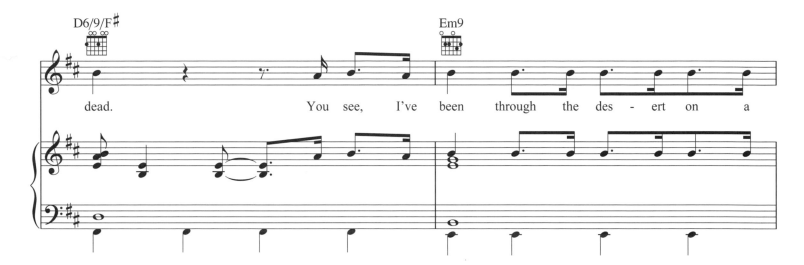

dead. You see, I've been through the des - ert on a

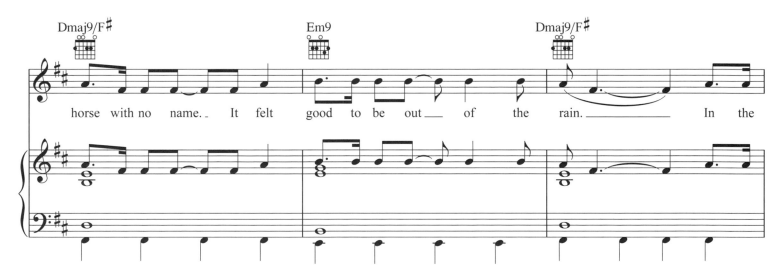

horse with no name. _ It felt good to be out _ of the rain. _____ In the

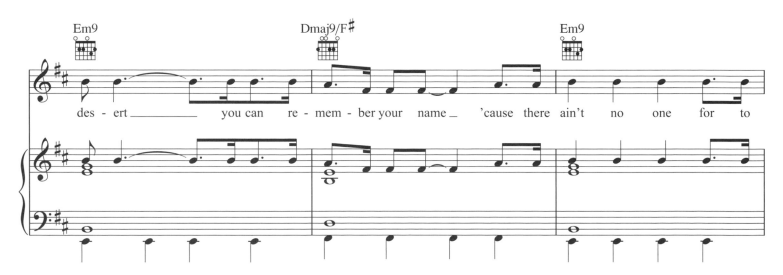

des - ert _____ you can re - mem - ber your name _ 'cause there ain't no one for to

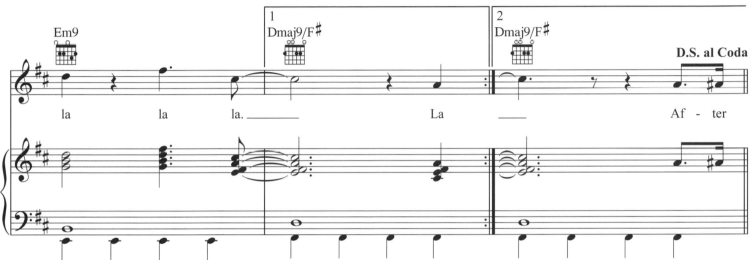

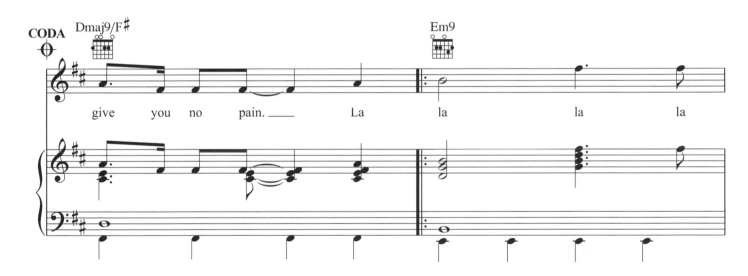

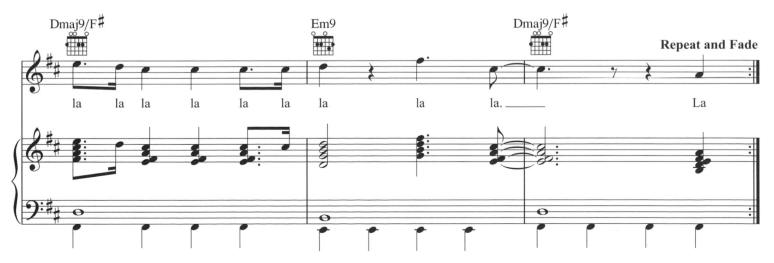

INTO THE GREAT WIDE OPEN

Words and Music by TOM PETTY
and JEFF LYNNE

o - pen, _____ un - der the skies _ of blue.

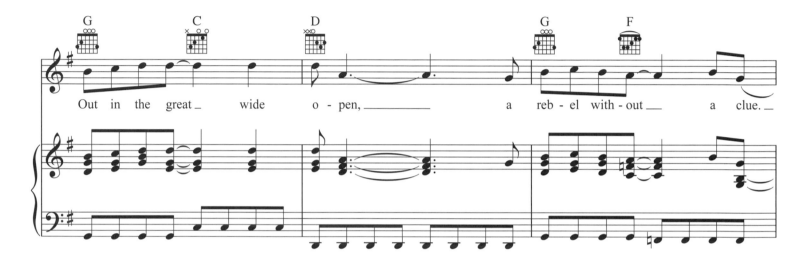

Out in the great _ wide o - pen, _____ a reb - el with - out _ a clue. _

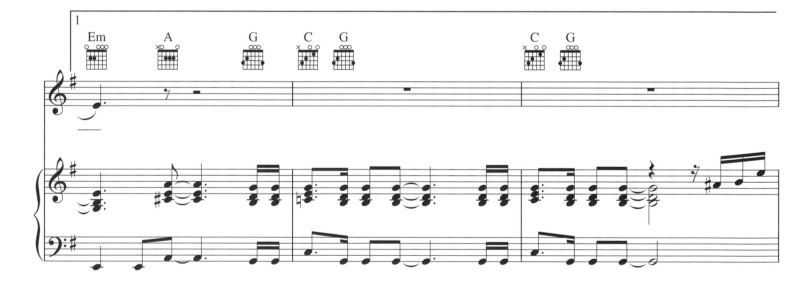

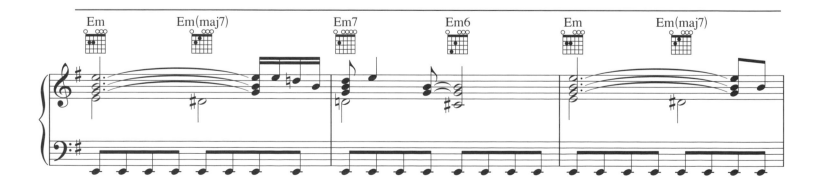

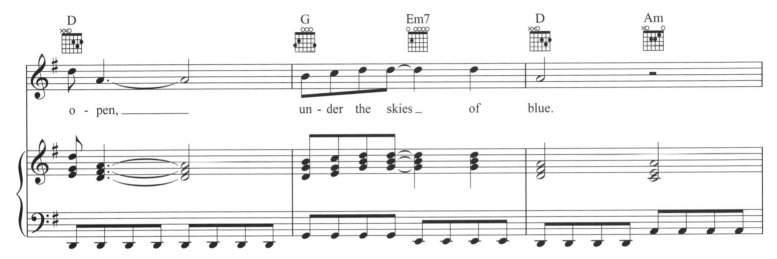

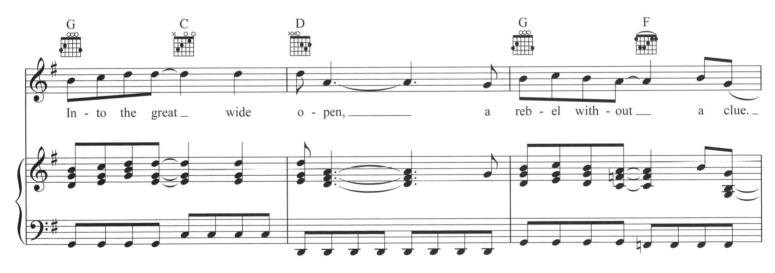

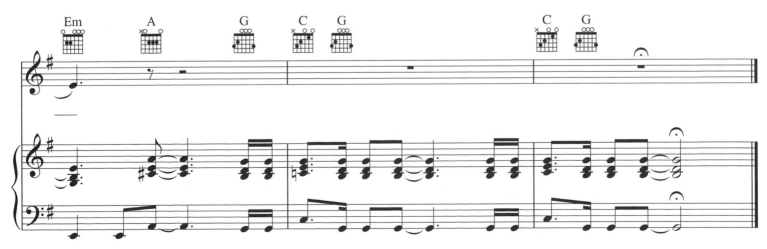

JACK AND DIANE

Words and Music by
JOHN MELLENCAMP

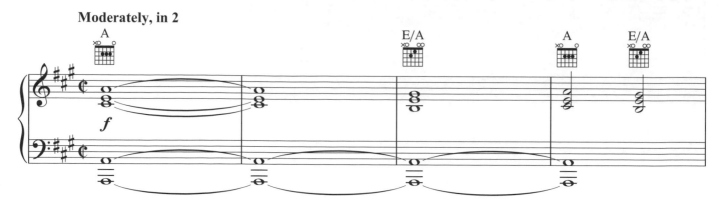

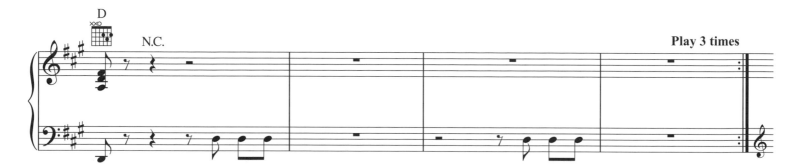

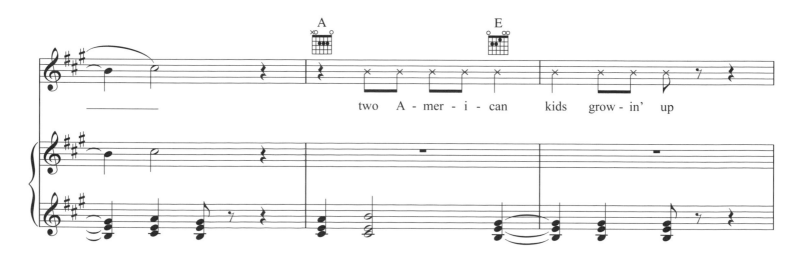

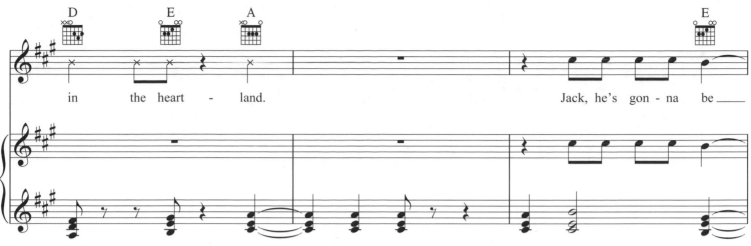

in the heart - land.   Jack, he's gon - na be ___

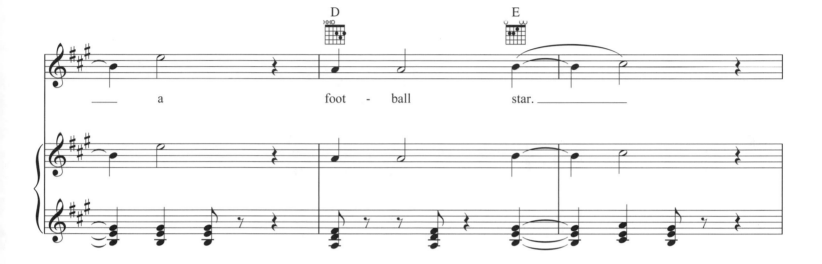

___ a   foot - ball   star. ___

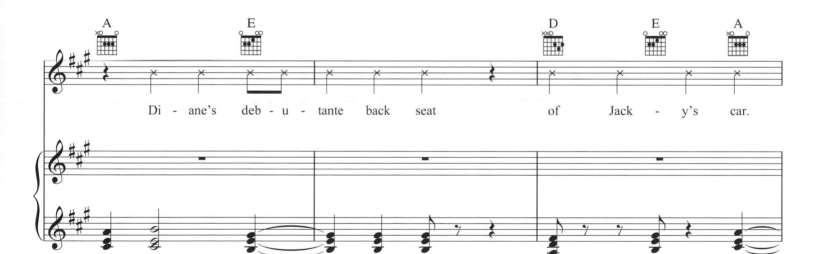

Di - ane's deb - u - tante back seat   of   Jack - y's   car.

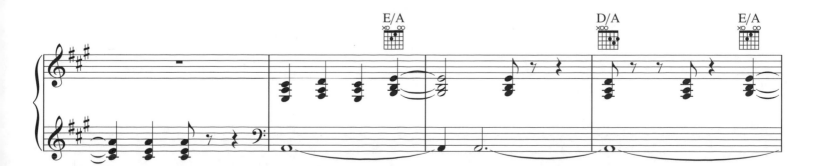

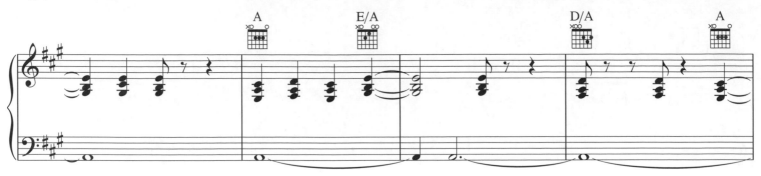

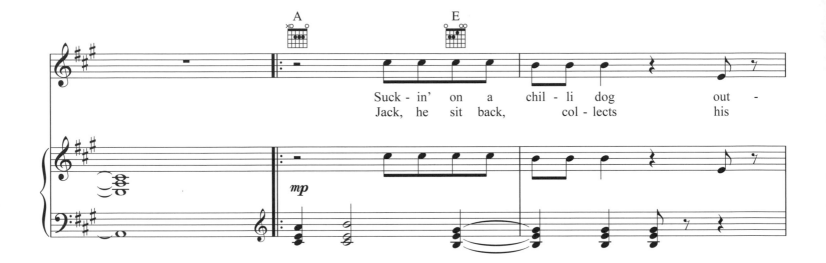

Suck - in' on a chil - li dog out -
Jack, he sit back, col - lects his

side the Tas - tee Freez; _____ Di - ane sit - tin' on
thoughts for a ____ mo - ment; scratch - es his

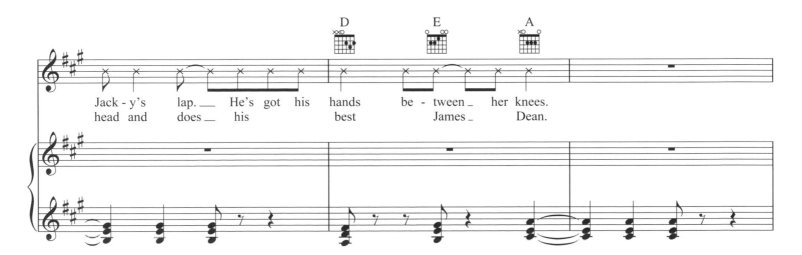

Jack - y's lap. __ He's got his hands be - tween __ her knees.
head and does __ his best James __ Dean.

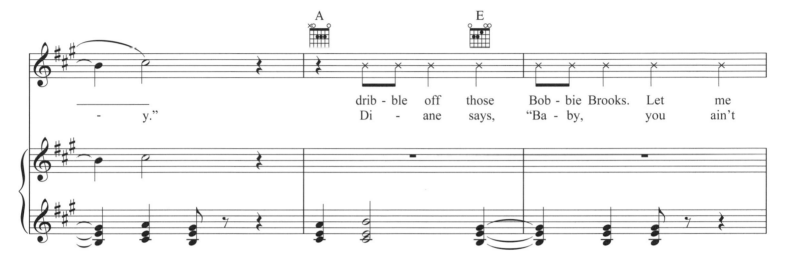

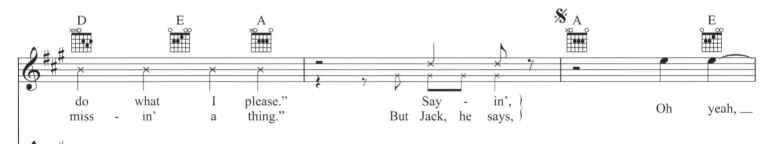

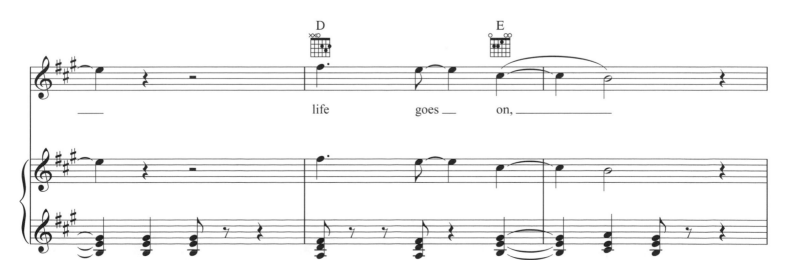

long af - ter the thrill of liv - ing is ___ gone. ___

___ Say - in', oh yeah, ___

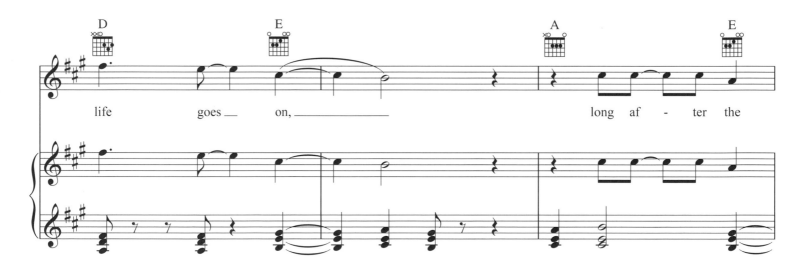

life goes ___ on, ___ long af - ter the

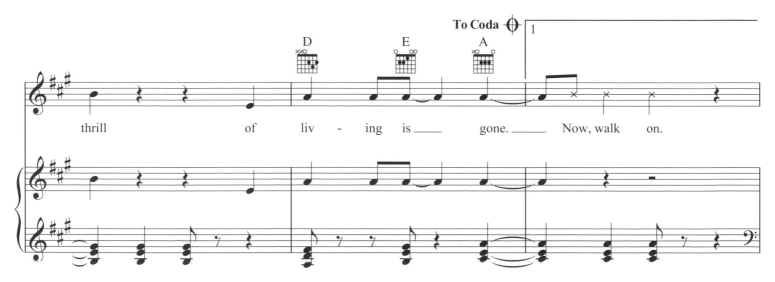

thrill of liv - ing is ___ gone. ___ Now, walk on.

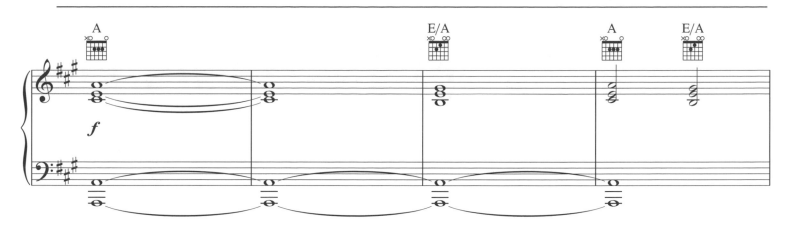

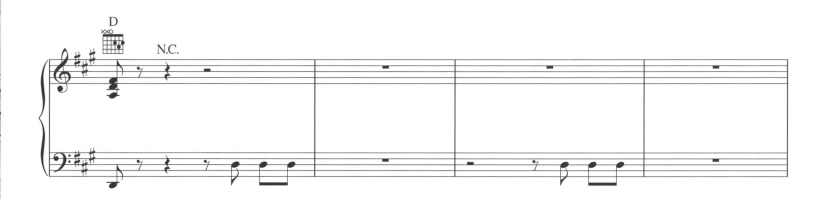

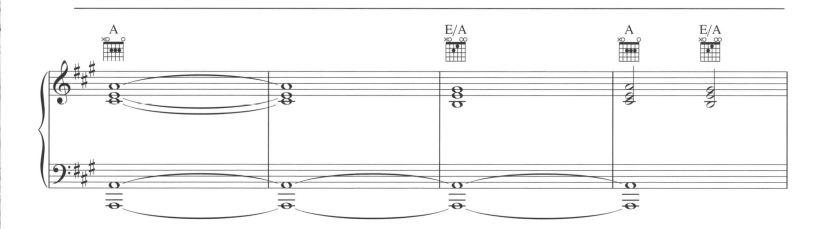

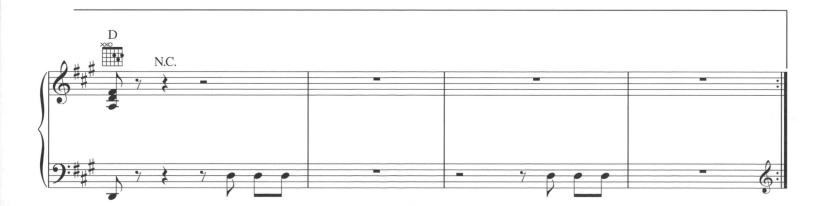

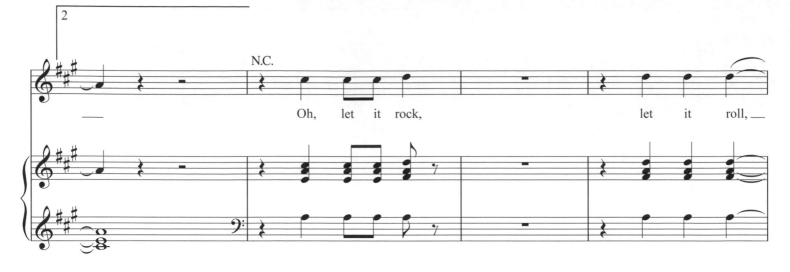

Oh, let it rock, let it roll, __

__ let the Bi - ble Belt come and

save my soul. _____ Hold - in' on to

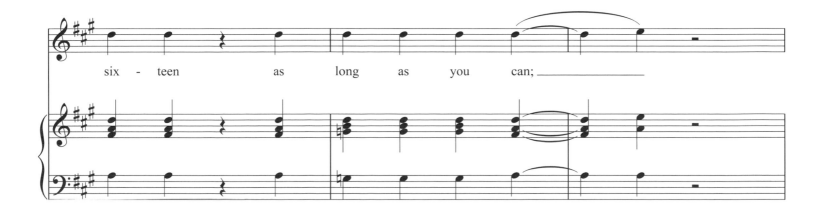

six - teen as long as you can; _____

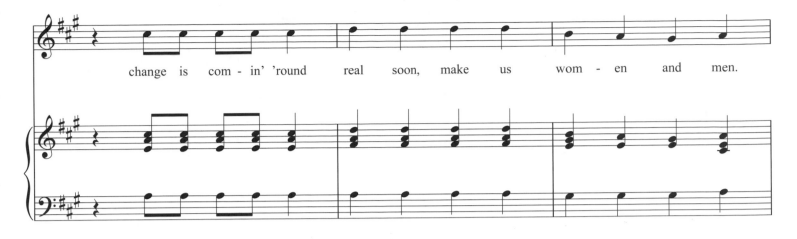

change is com - in' 'round   real   soon,   make   us   wom - en   and   men.

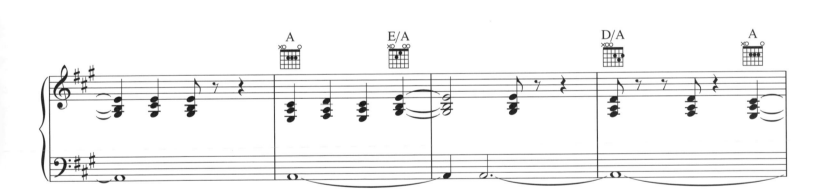

A lit - tle

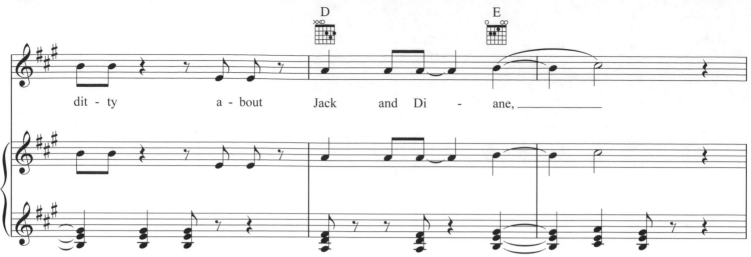

dit - ty   a - bout   Jack   and   Di -   ane, _____

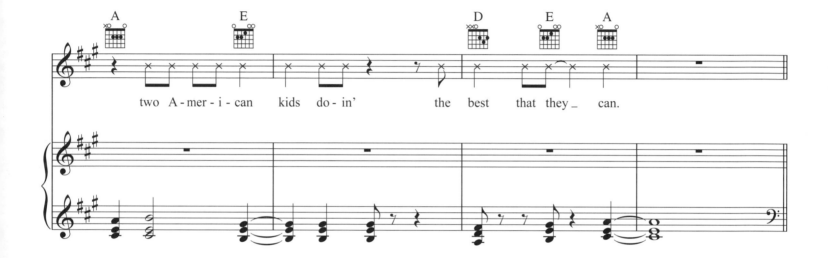

two A - mer - i - can   kids   do - in'   the   best   that they _ can.

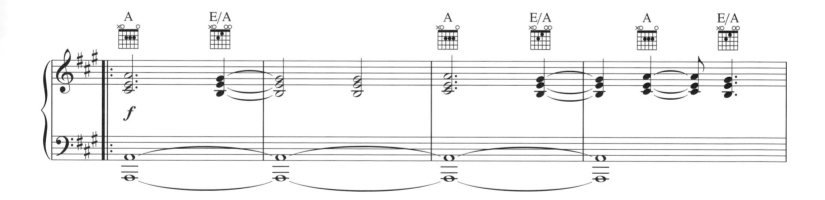

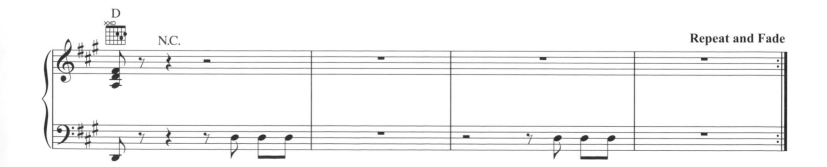

Repeat and Fade

N.C.

IN THE GHETTO
(The Vicious Circle)

Words and Music by
MAC DAVIS

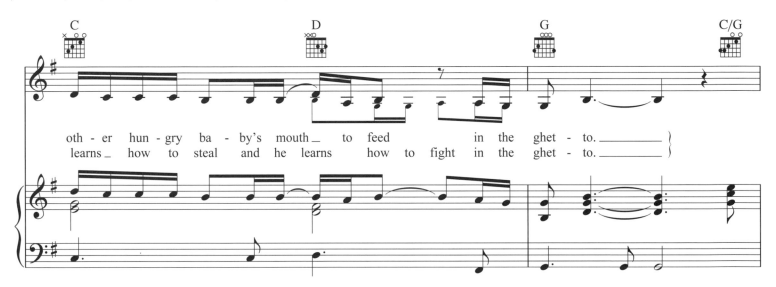

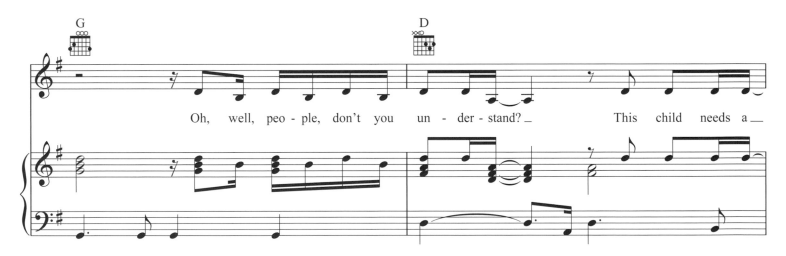

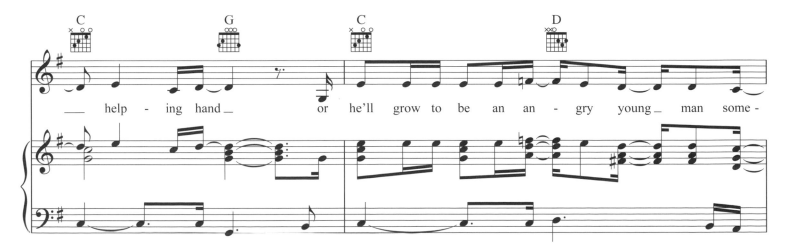

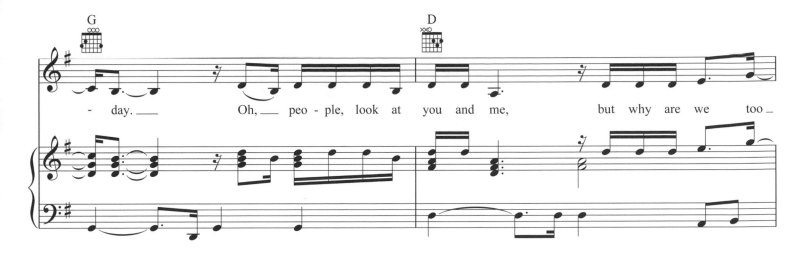

Oh, — peo-ple, look at you and me, but why are we too —

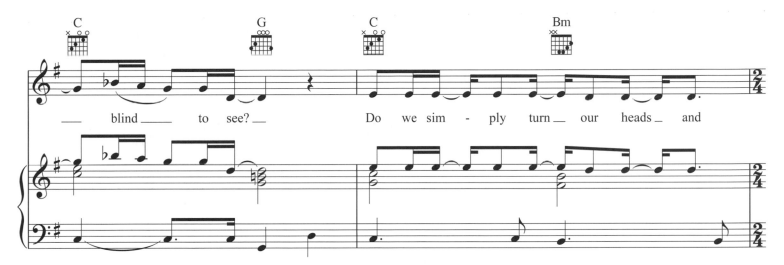

— blind — to see? — Do we sim-ply turn — our heads — and

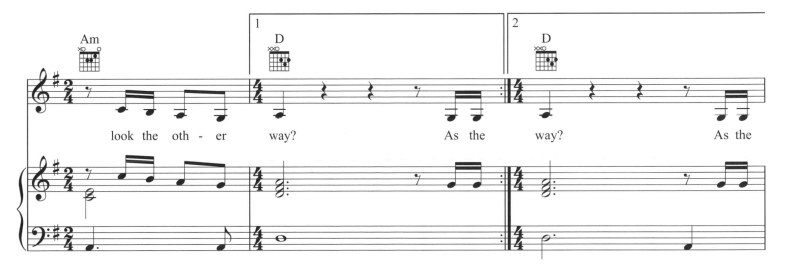

look the oth-er way? As the way? As the

world — turns. —

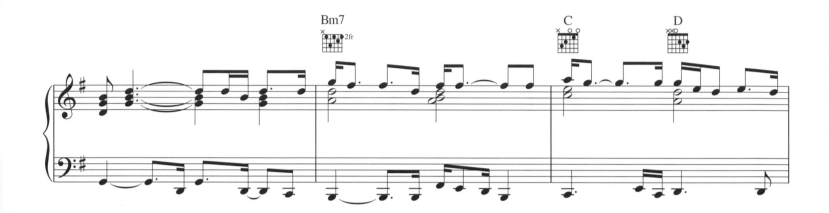

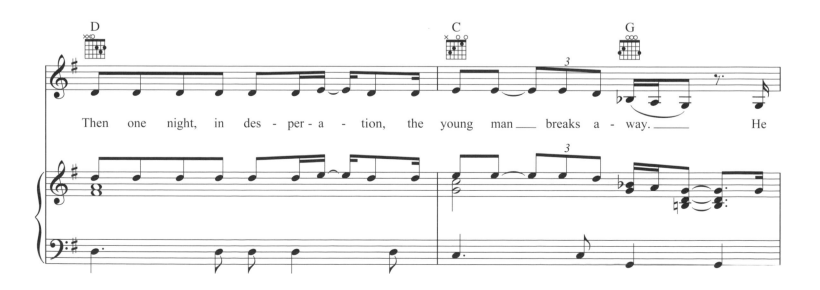

Then one night, in des - per - a - tion, the young man___ breaks a - way.___ He

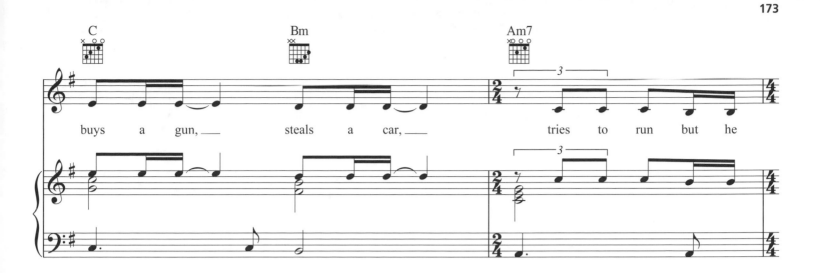

buys a gun, ____ steals a car, ____ tries to run but he

don't get far. And his oth-er hun-gry ba-by child ____ is born in the

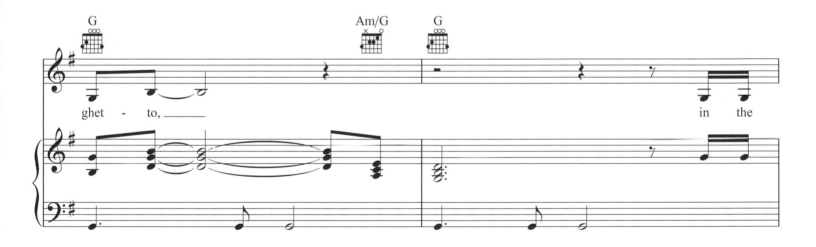

ghet - to, ____ in the

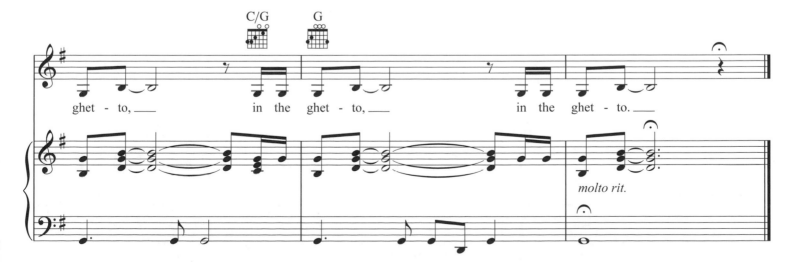

ghet - to, ____ in the ghet - to, ____ in the ghet - to. ____

molto rit.

JEREMY

Music by JEFF AMENT
Lyric by EDDIE VEDDER

Alternative Rock

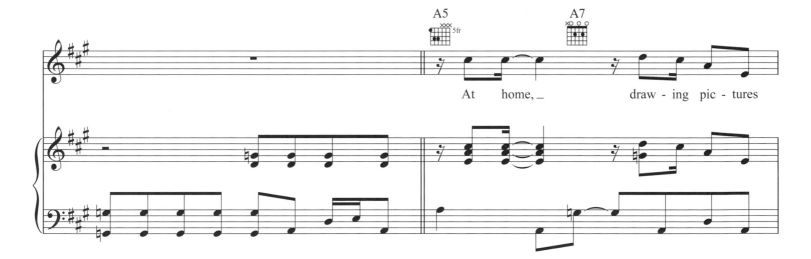

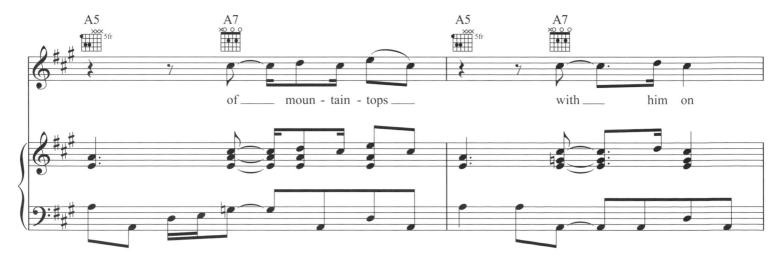

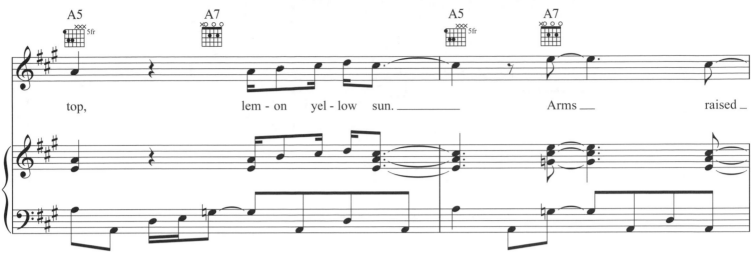

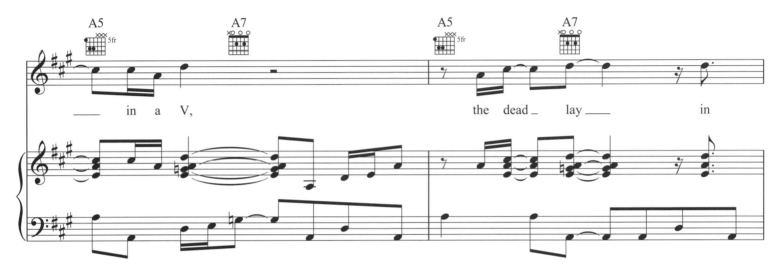

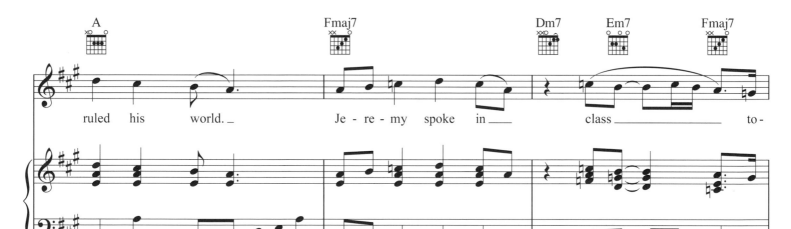

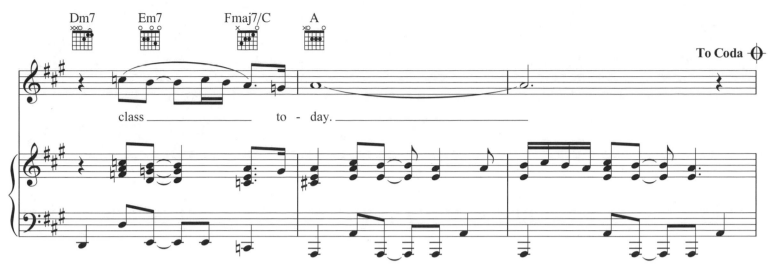

class _____ to - day. _____

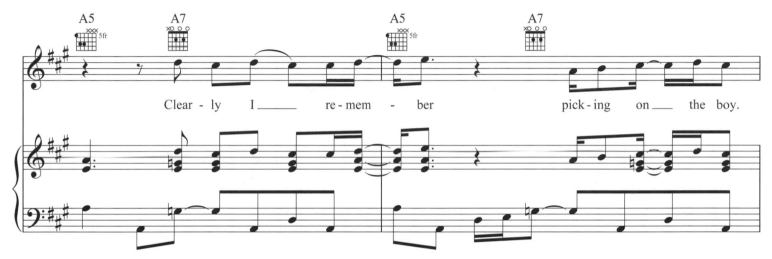

Clear - ly I _____ re - mem - ber   pick - ing on ____ the boy.

Seemed a harm - less _____ lit - tle fuck.

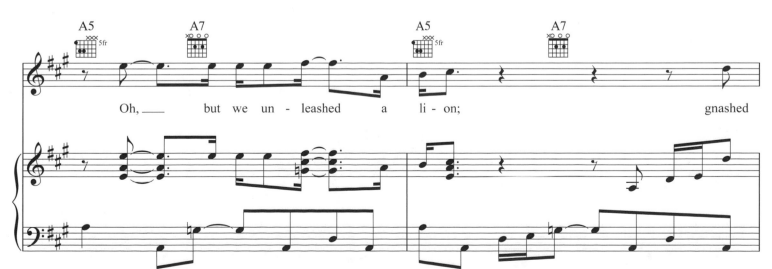

Oh, ____ but we un - leashed a li - on;   gnashed

178

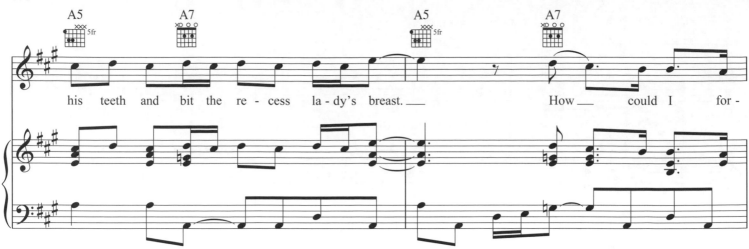

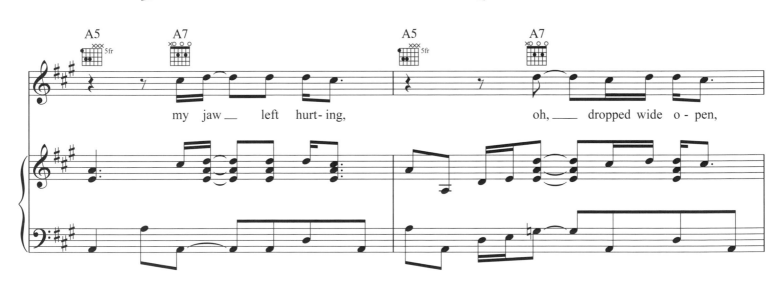

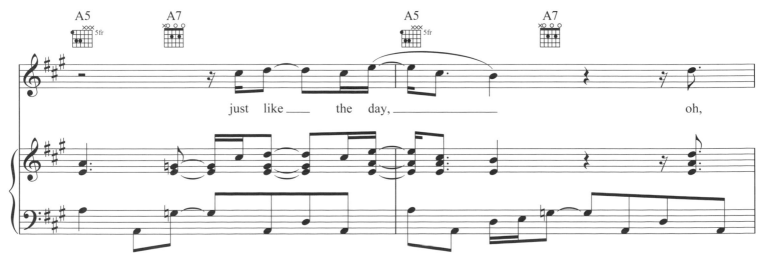

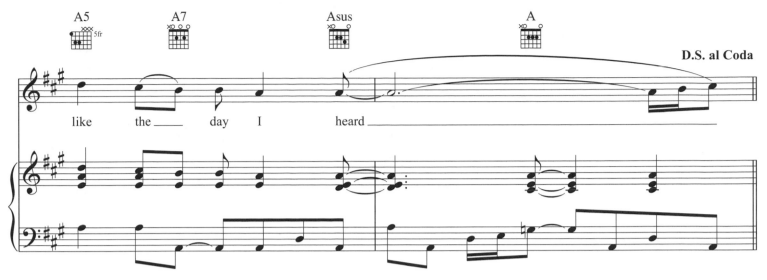

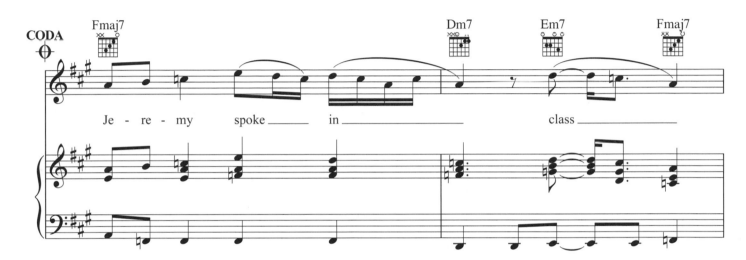

ooh   ooh.   Try ___ to for-get ___ this,   try ___   to for-get

this.   Try ___   to e-rase this,   try ___   to e-rase this   from _ the black -

Fmaj7   Dm7   Em7   Fmaj7   Am

board. _____

F/G   Dm7   Em7   Fmaj7

_____   Je - re - my spoke in ___   class _____ to-

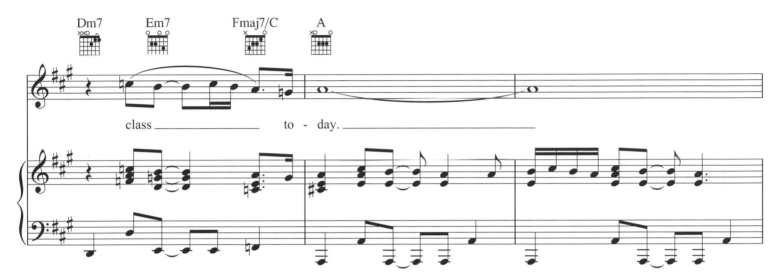

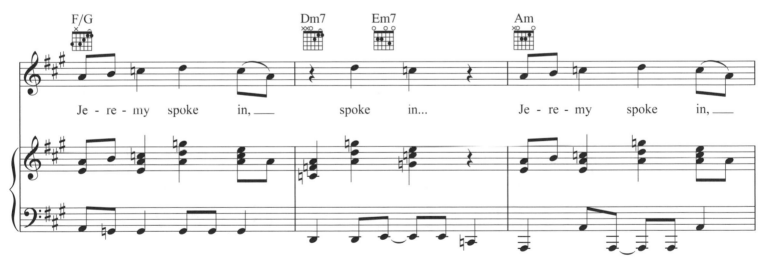

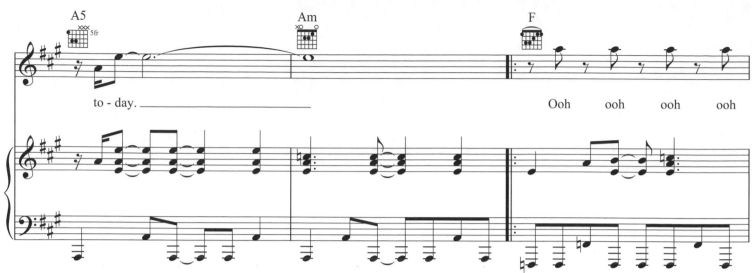

to - day. _____

Ooh   ooh   ooh   ooh

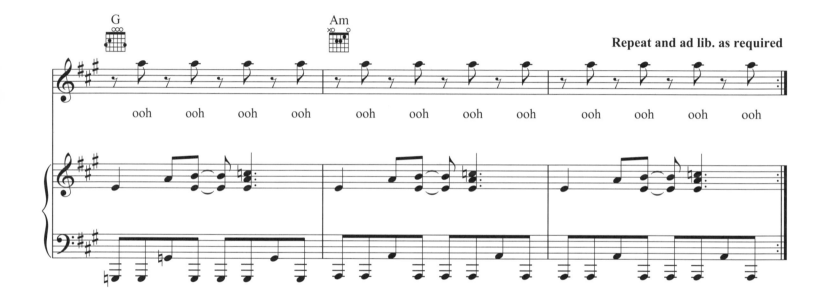

Repeat and ad lib. as required

ooh   ooh   ooh   ooh   ooh   ooh   ooh   ooh   ooh   ooh   ooh   ooh

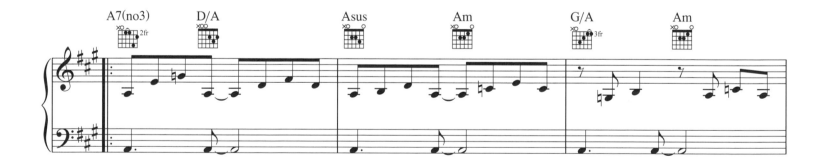

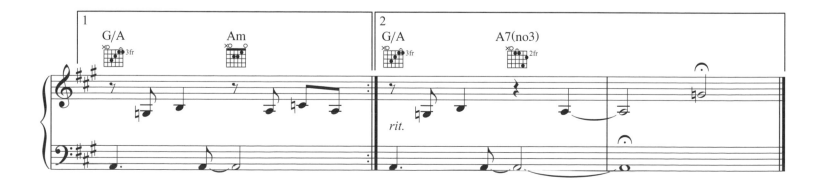

rit.

ODE TO BILLY JOE

Words and Music by
BOBBIE GENTRY

1. It was the third of June, _ an-oth-er
2.–5. *(See additional lyrics)*

sleep-y, dust-y del-ta day, _____ I was

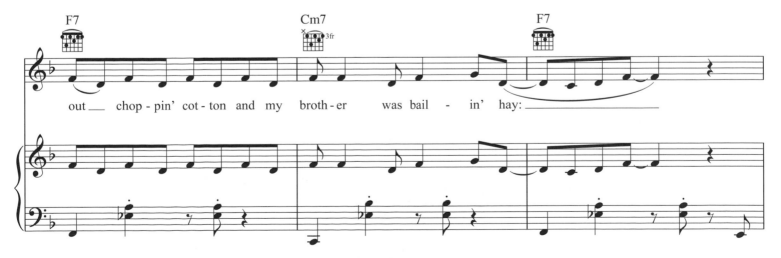

out _ chop-pin' cot-ton and my broth-er was bail-in' hay: _____

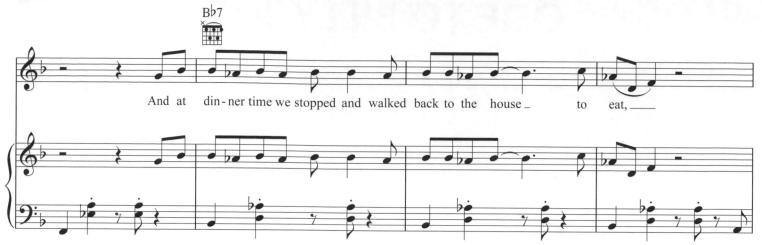

And at din-ner time we stopped and walked back to the house _ to eat, _

And Ma-ma hol-lered at the back door, "Y'all re-mem-ber to wipe your feet". _

Then she said, "I got some news this morn-

-in' from Choc-taw Ridge, _____ To-day _

Bil-ly Joe Mc-Al-lis-ter jumped off the Tal-la-hat-chee Bridge." —

Additional Lyrics

2. Papa said to Mama, as he passed around the black-eyed peas,
   "Well, Billy Joe never had a lick o' sense, pass the biscuits, please.
   There's five more acres in the lower forty I've got to plow,"
   And Mama said it was a shame about Billy Joe anyhow.
   Seems like nothin' ever comes to no good up on Choctaw Ridge,
   And now Billy Joe McAllister's jumped off the Tallahatchee Bridge.

3. Brother said he recollected when he and Tom and Billy Joe
   Put a frog down my back at the Carroll County picture show,
   And wasn't talkin' to him after church last Sunday night,
   I'll have another piece of apple pie, you know, it don't seem right.
   I saw him at the sawmill yesterday on Choctaw Ridge,
   And now you tell me Billy Joe's jumped off the Tallahatchee Bridge.

4. Mama said to me, "Child, what's happened to your appetite?
   I been cookin' all mornin' and you haven't touched a single bite.
   That nice young preacher Brother Taylor dropped by today,
   Said he'd be pleased to have dinner on Sunday. Oh, by the way,
   He said he saw a girl that looked a lot like you up on Choctaw Ridge
   And she an' Billy Joe was throwin' somethin' off the Tallahatchee Bridge."

5. A year has come and gone since we heard the news 'bout Billy Joe,
   Brother married Becky Thompson, they bought a store in Tupeolo.
   There was a virus goin' 'round, Papa caught it and he died last spring,
   And now Mama doesn't seem to want to do much of anything.
   And me I spend a lot of time pickin' flowers up on Choctaw Ridge,
   And drop them into the muddy water off the Tallahatchee Bridge.

JUST A DREAM

Words and Music by STEVE McEWAN,
GORDIE SAMPSON and HILLARY LINDSEY

Moderately, in 2

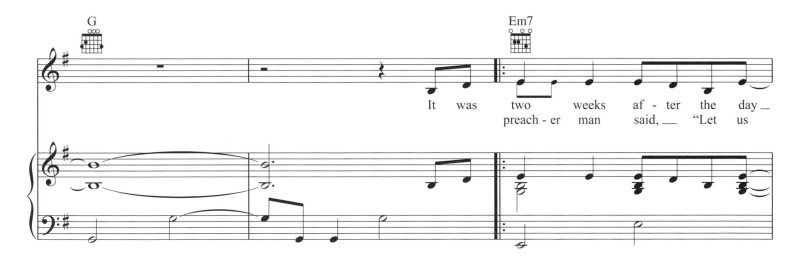

It was two weeks af-ter the day __
preach-er man said, __ "Let us

__ she turned __ eight - een, __
bow our heads __ and pray.

all dressed __ in white, __
Lord, please lift __ his soul __

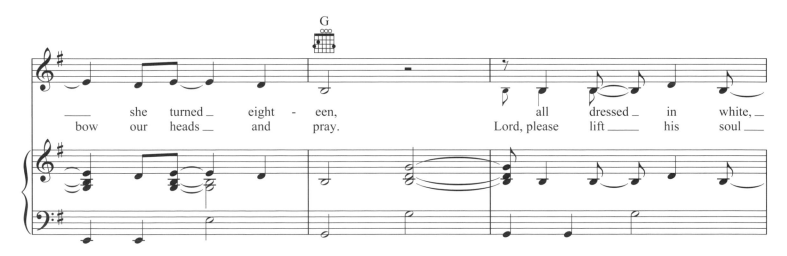

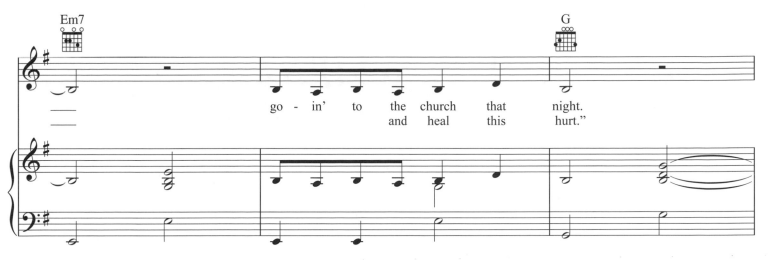

go - in' to the church that night.
and heal this hurt."

She had his box of let - ters in ____ the pas - sen - ger seat, ____
Then the con - gre - ga - tion all ____ stood up ____ and ____ sang ____

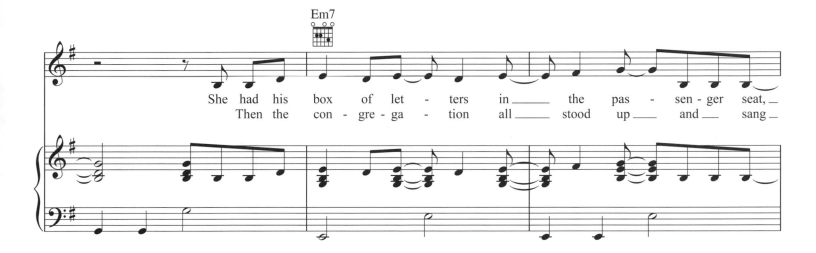

six - pence in a shoe, ____ some - thin'
the sad - dest song ____

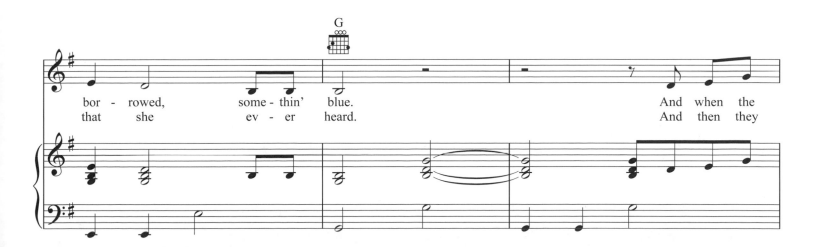

bor - rowed, some - thin' blue. And when the
that she ev - er heard. And then they

188

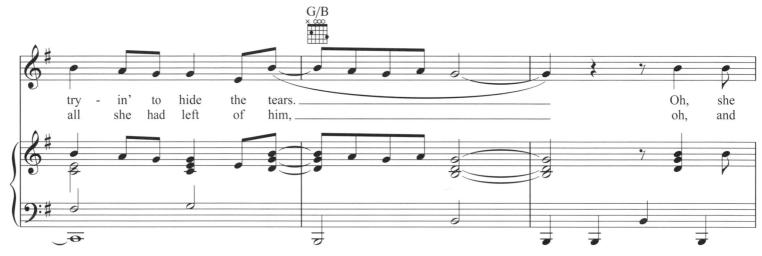

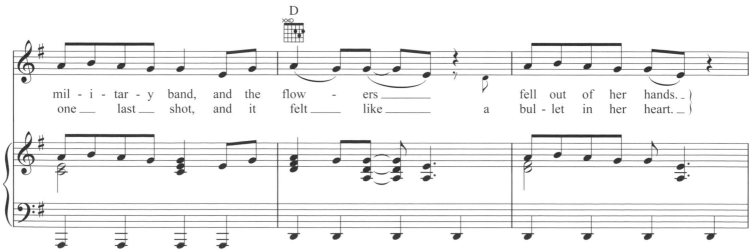

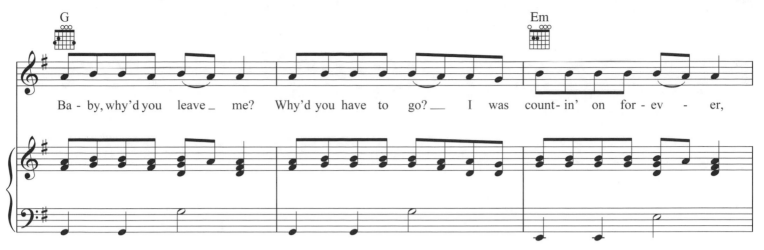

Ba - by, why'd you leave _ me? Why'd you have to go? _ I was count-in' on for - ev - er,

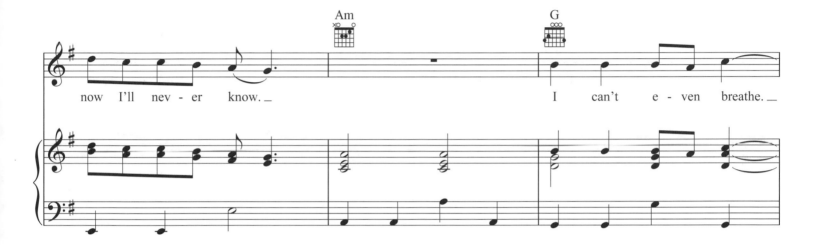

now I'll nev - er know. _ I can't e - ven breathe. _

It's like I'm _ look - in' from a dis - tance,

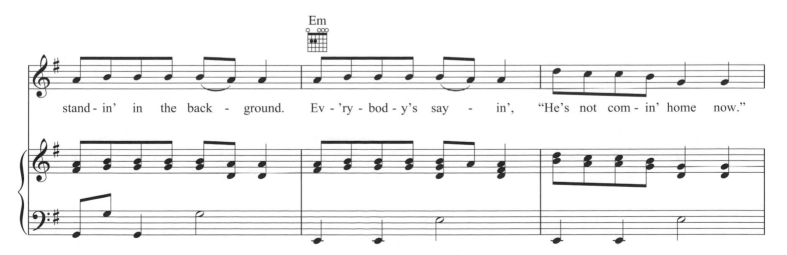

stand - in' in the back - ground. Ev - 'ry - bod - y's say - in', "He's not com - in' home now."

190

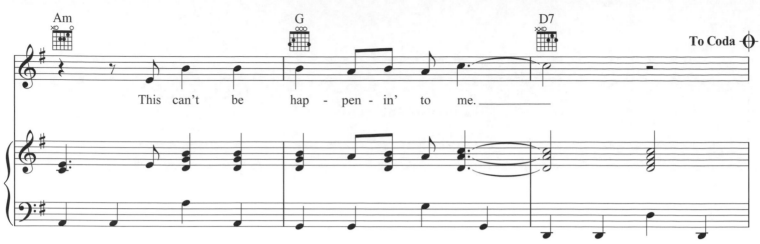

This can't be hap - pen - in' to me. ____

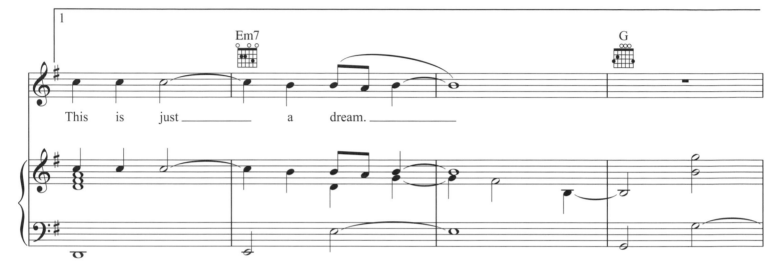

This is just ____ a dream. ____

The This is just ____ a

dream. ____

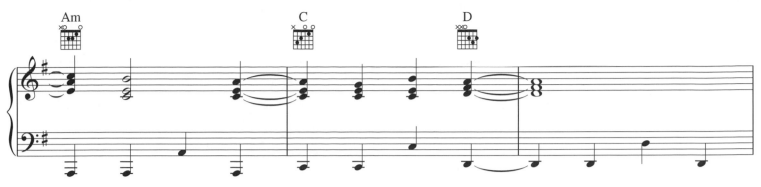

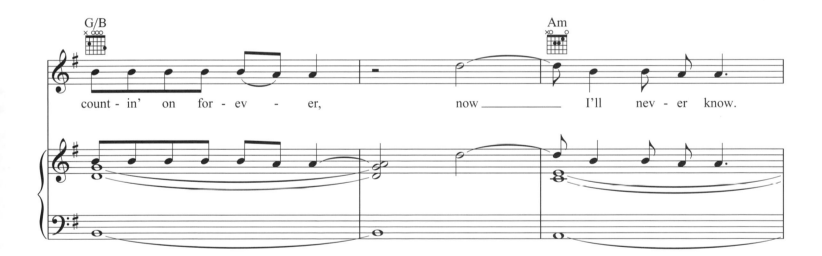

Oh, _____ ba - by, why'd you leave _ me? Why'd you have to go? ___ I was

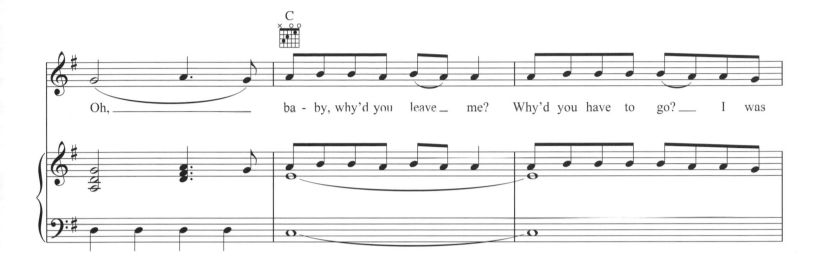

count - in' on for - ev - er, now _____ I'll nev - er know.

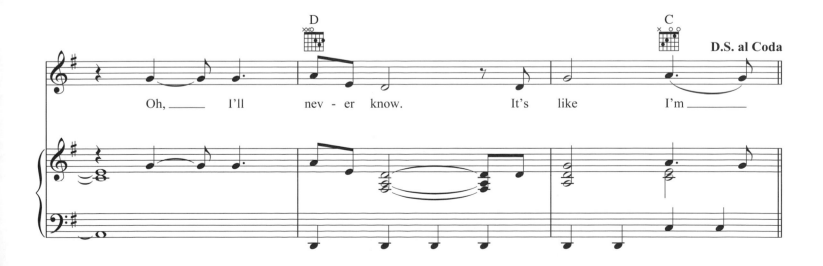

Oh, _____ I'll nev - er know. It's like I'm _____

D.S. al Coda

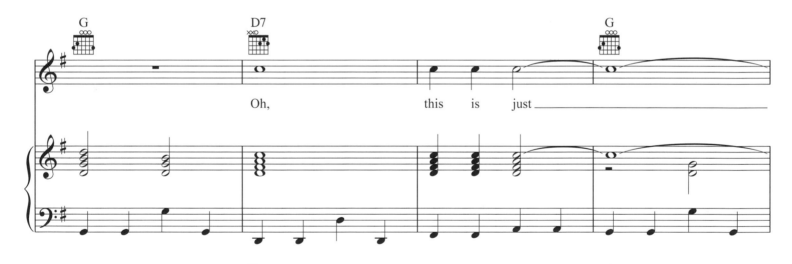

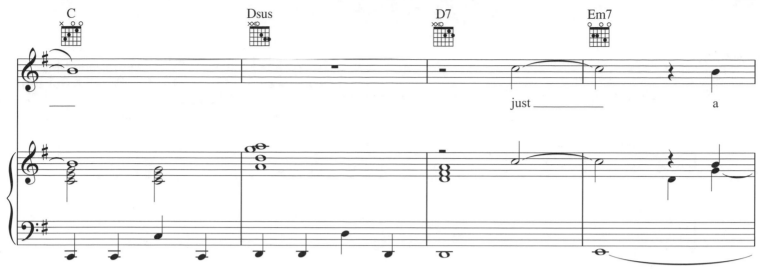

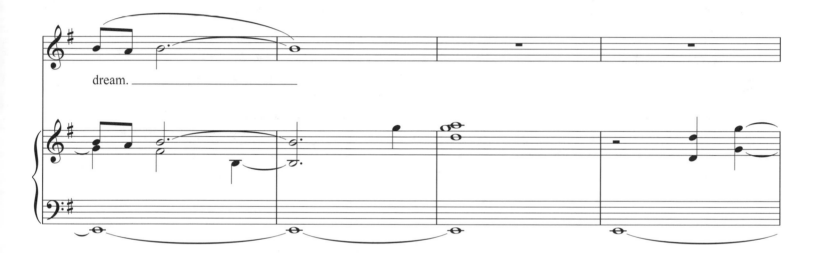

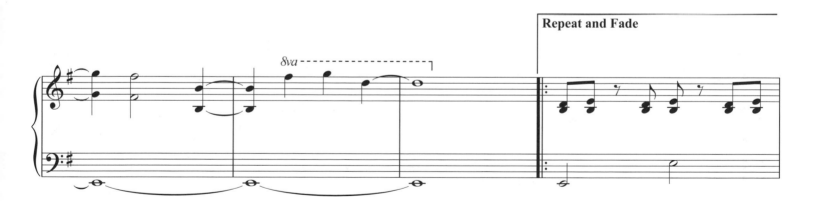

LAST KISS

Words and Music by
WAYNE COCHRAN

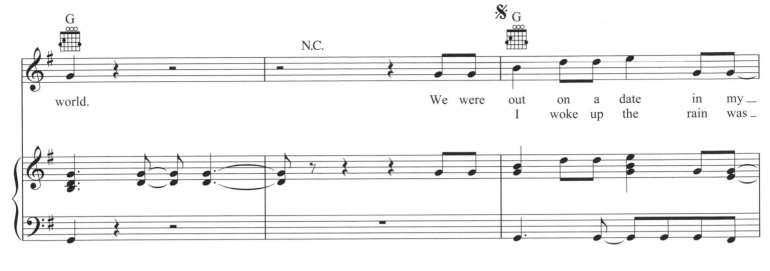

never forget ___ the sound that night, ___ the scream-in' tires, ____ the
"Hold me, dar-lin', just a lit-tle while." ___ I held her close. ___ I kissed her

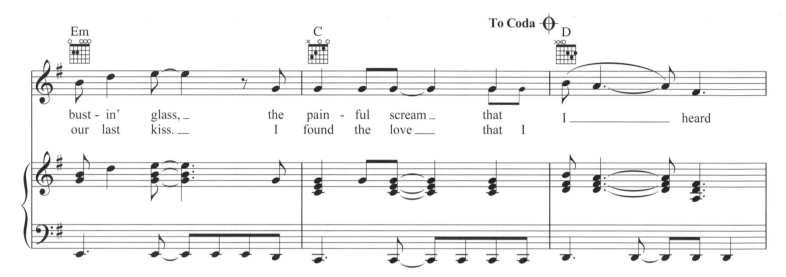

bust-in' glass, ___ the pain-ful scream ___ that I _____ heard
our last kiss. ___ I found the love ___ that I

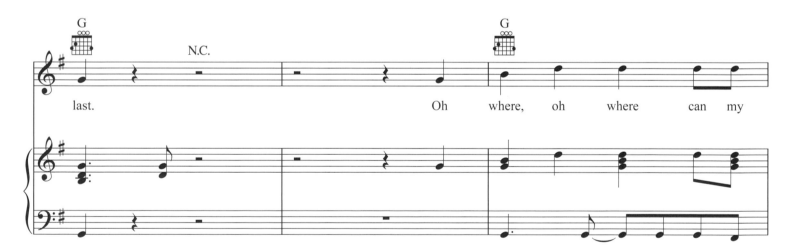

last. Oh where, oh where can my

ba - by be? The Lord took her a - way from me. ____

She's gone to heav-en, so I got to be good ____ so I can see my ba-by when I

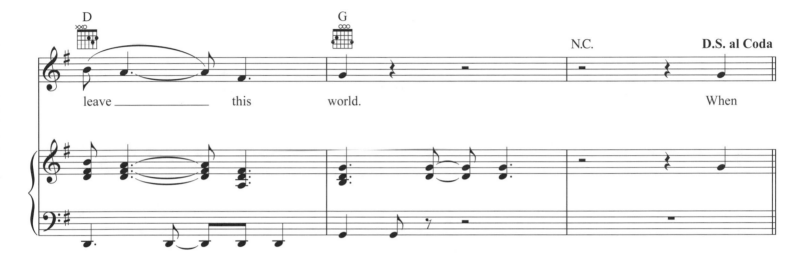

leave ____ this world. When

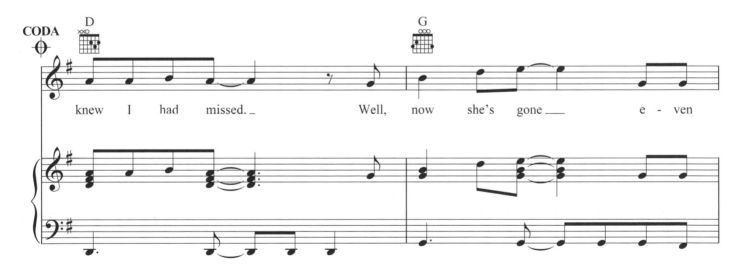

knew I had missed. _ Well, now she's gone ____ e - ven

though I hold her tight. I lost my love, _ my life ____ that

night. Oh where, oh where can my

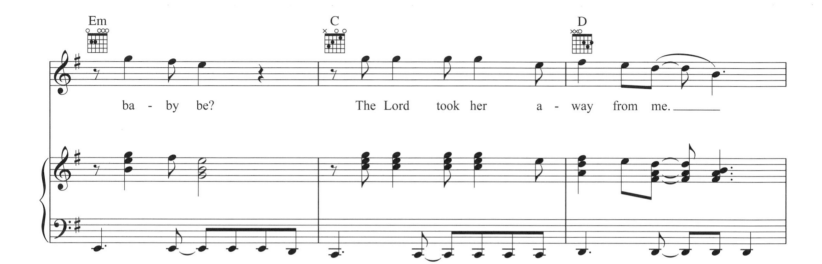

ba - by be? The Lord took her a - way from me.

She's gone to heav-en, so I got to be good so I can see my ba-by when I

leave this world.

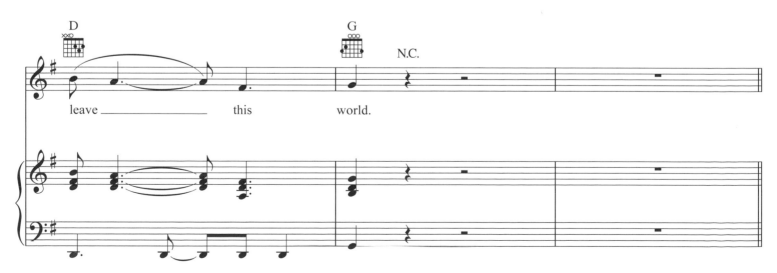

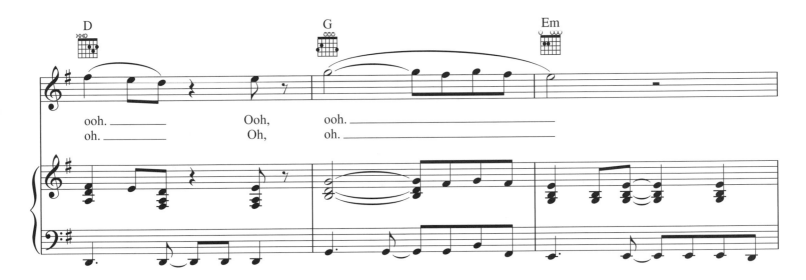

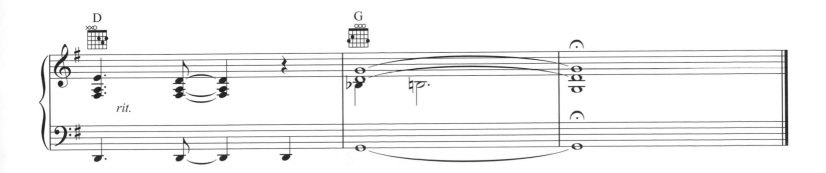

LIVIN' ON A PRAYER

Words and Music by JON BON JOVI,
DESMOND CHILD and RICHIE SAMBORA

(Spoken:) Once upon a time,

not so long ago...

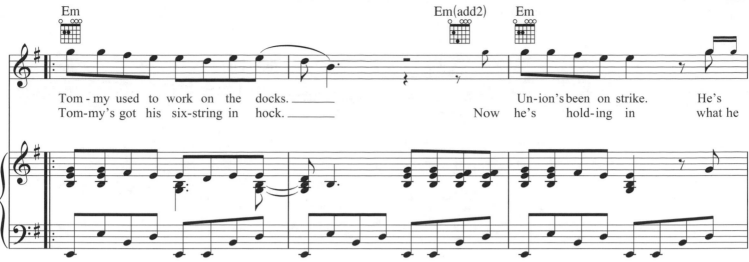

Tom - my used to work on the docks. _____ Un - ion's been on strike. He's
Tom-my's got his six-string in hock. _____ Now he's hold-ing in what he

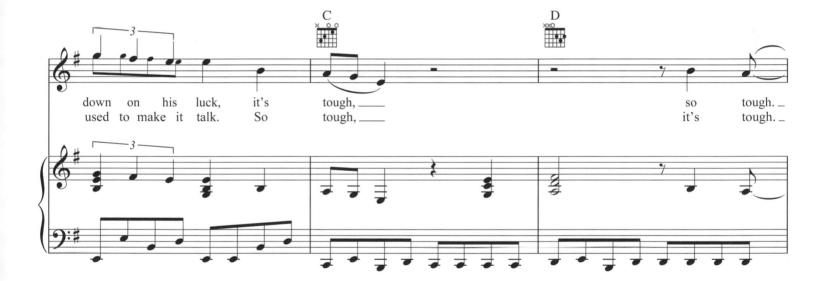

down on his luck, it's tough, _____ so tough. _
used to make it talk. So tough, _____ it's tough. _

_____ Gi - na works the din - er all day. _
_____ Gi - na dreams of run-ning a - way. _

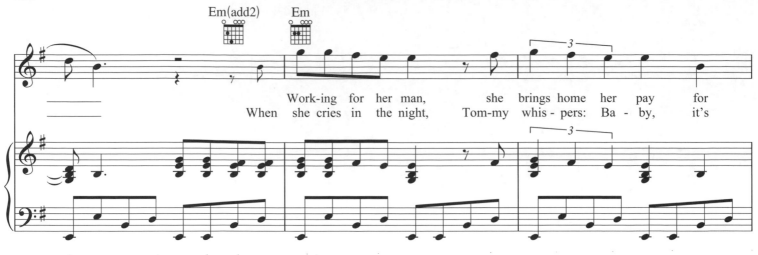

Working for her man, she brings home her pay for
When she cries in the night, Tom-my whis-pers: Ba - by, it's

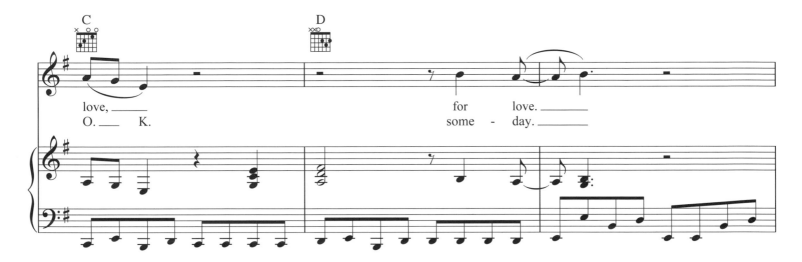

love, _____ for love. _____
O. ___ K. some - day. _____

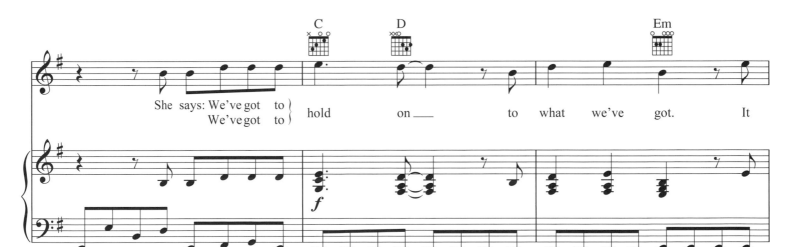

She says: We've got to } hold on ___ to what we've got. It
We've got to }

does-n't make a dif-f'rence if we make it or not. We've got each oth - er and

Em   C   D

that's a lot for ___ love. ___ We'll give it a shot.

Em   C   D   G   D7sus

Whoa, _____ we're half - way there. ___ Whoa, _____ liv -

Em   C   D

- in' on a prayer. ___ Take my ___ hand, ___ we'll make it, I swear. ___

G   C   D7sus   1. Em

Whoa, _____ liv - in' on a prayer. ___

Liv - in' on ___ a prayer. ___

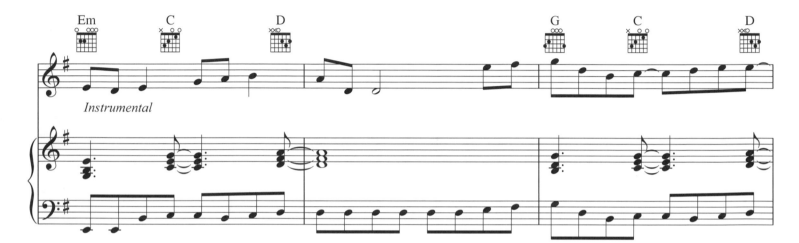

Instrumental

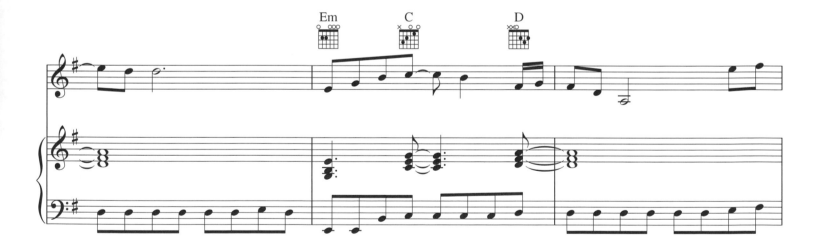

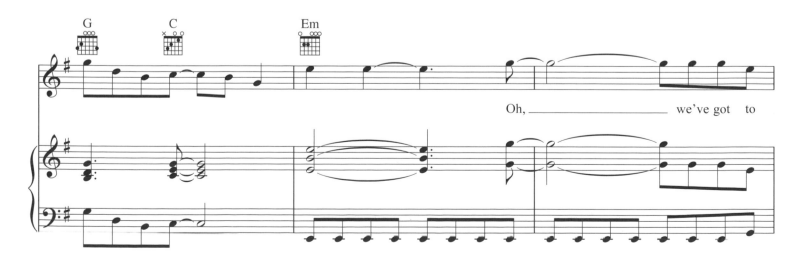

Oh, _____ we've got to

ME AND BOBBY McGEE

Words and Music by KRIS KRISTOFFERSON
and FRED FOSTER

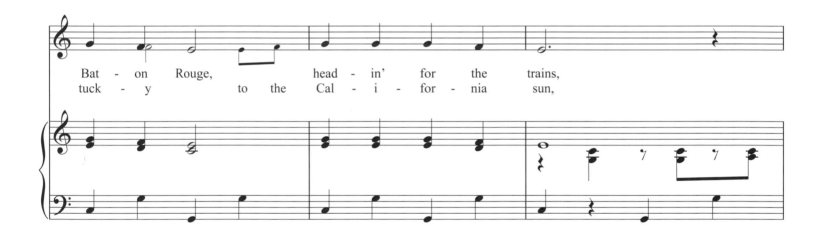

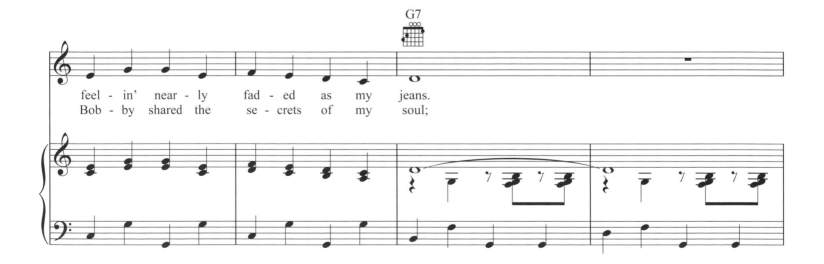

Bob - by thumbed a die - sel down just be - fore it rained;
stand - in' right be - side me, Lord, through ev - 'ry - thing I done,

took us all the way to New Or - leans.
ev - 'ry night she kept me from the cold. Then

I took my har - poon out of my dirt - y, red ban - dan - na and was
some - where near Sa - li - nas, Lord, I let her slip a - way,

blow - in' sad while Bob - by sang the blues. With them
look - in' for the home I hope she'll find. And I'd trade

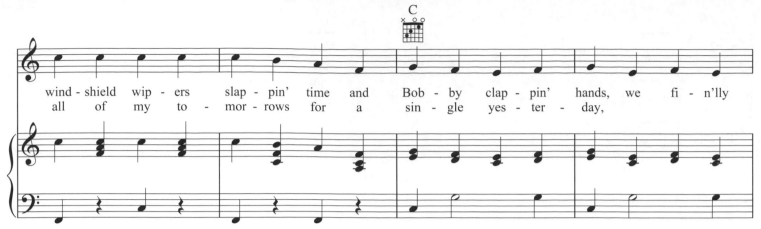

wind - shield wip - ers slap - pin' time and Bob - by clap - pin' hands, we fi - n'lly
all of my to - mor - rows for a sin - gle yes - ter - day,

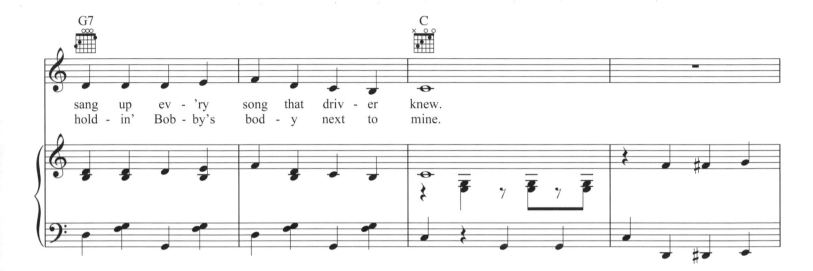

sang up ev - 'ry song that driv - er knew.
hold - in' Bob - by's bod - y next to mine.

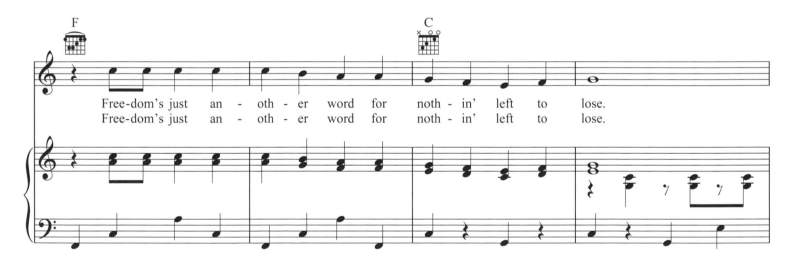

Free-dom's just an - oth - er word for noth - in' left to lose.
Free-dom's just an - oth - er word for noth - in' left to lose.

Noth - in' ain't worth noth - in', but it's free.
Noth - in' left is all she left for me.

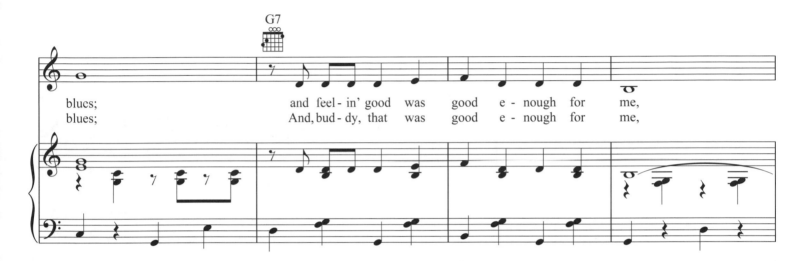

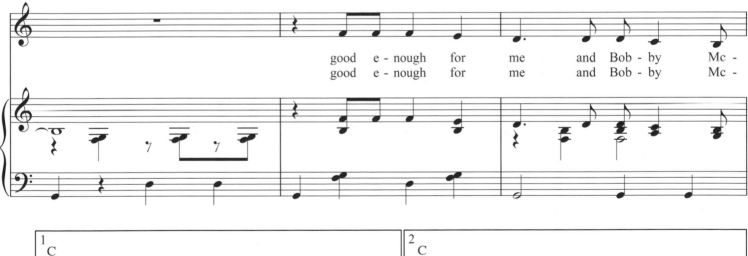

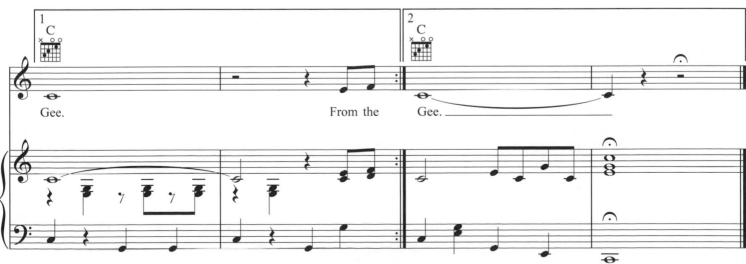

ME & MY UNCLE

Words and Music by
JOHN PHILLIPS

Brightly, in 2

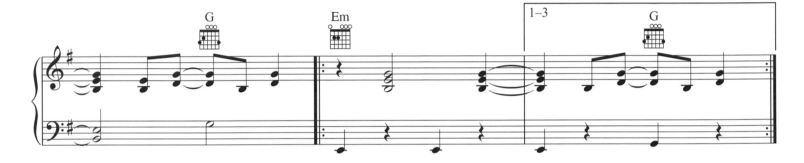

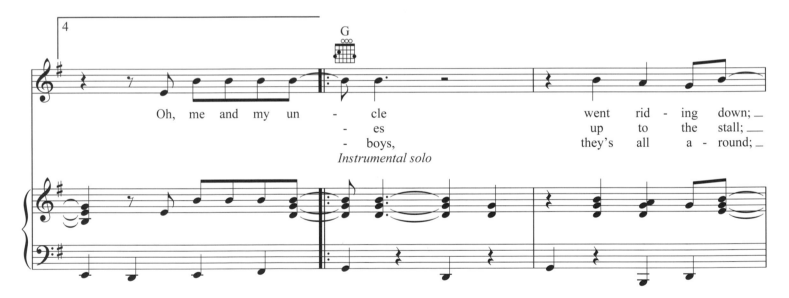

Oh, me and my un - cle went rid - ing down; ___
- es up to the stall; ___
- boys, they's all a - round; ___

Instrumental solo

South ___ Col - o - ra - do,
went ___ to the bar - room,
with liq - uor and mon - ey

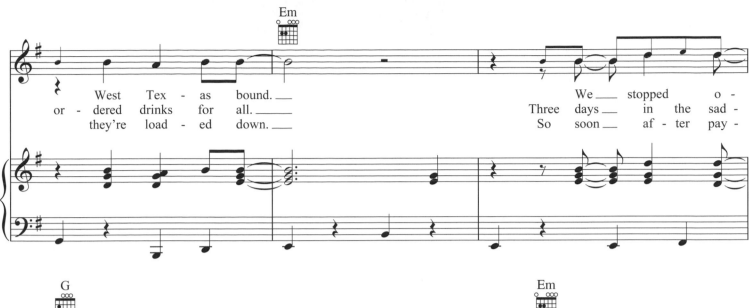

Em

West Tex - as bound. ___   We ___ stopped o -
or - dered drinks for all. ___   Three days ___ in the sad -
they're load - ed down. ___   So soon ___ af - ter pay -

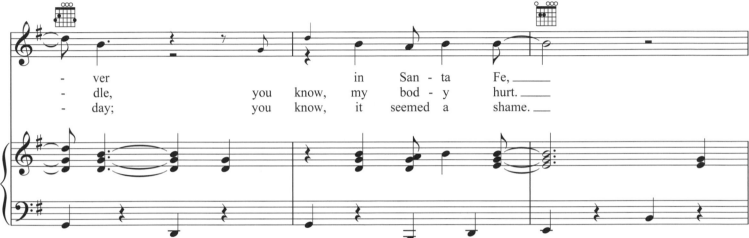

G   Em

- ver   in San - ta Fe, ___
- dle,   you know, my bod - y hurt. ___
- day;   you know, it seemed a shame. ___

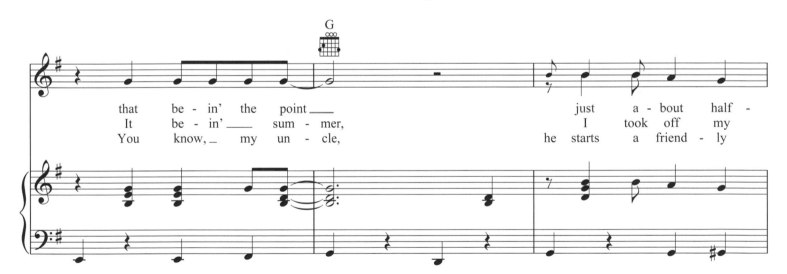

G

that be - in' the point ___   just a - bout half -
It be - in' ___ sum - mer,   I took off my
You know, ___ my un - cle,   he starts a friend - ly

A7   Em

way.   Hey, ___ and you know, it was the
shirt   and I ___ tried to wash off ___
game;   yeah, ___ High- Low Jack, and the

hot - test part ___ of the day. ___
some of that ___ dust - y dirt. ___
win - ner take ___ the hand. ___

And I took the hors -   *Solo ends*   My un - cle starts
West Tex - as cow -
Instrumental solo

win - ning;   cow - boys ___ got sore. ___
cow - boys,   he starts ___ to draw, ___

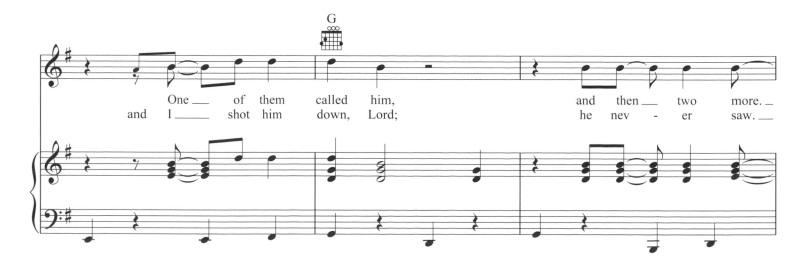

One ___ of them called him,   and then ___ two more. ___
and I ___ shot him down, Lord;   he nev - er saw. ___

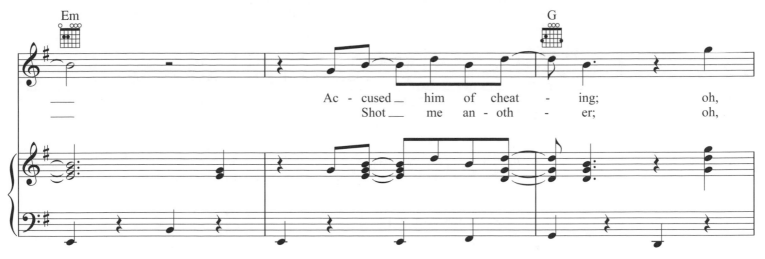

Ac - cused __ him of cheat - ing;   oh,
Shot __ me an - oth - er;   oh, oh,

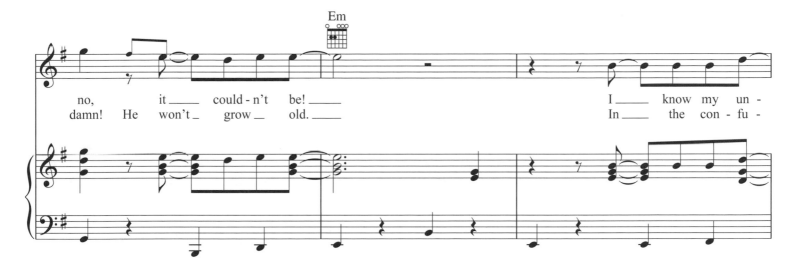

no,   it ____ could - n't be! _____   I ____ know my un -
damn! He won't _ grow _ old. _____   In ____ the con - fu -

- cle;   he's as hon - est as me, ____
- sion,   my un - cle grabbed ____ the gold, ____

and I'm as hon - est as a Den - ver man ____ can be. __
and we high - tailed ____ it ____ down to Mex - i - co. __

Oh, one of them

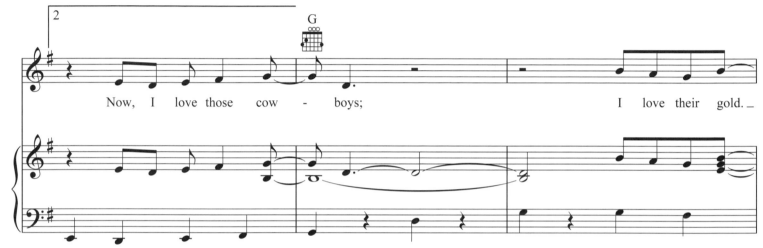

Now, I love those cow - boys; I love their gold. __

Love __ my __ un - cle, oh, God rest his soul. __

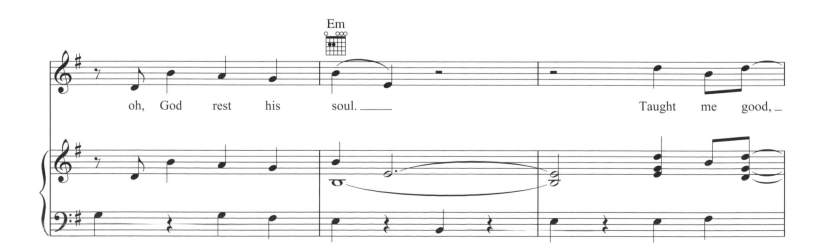

Taught me good, __

Lord, taught me all I know.

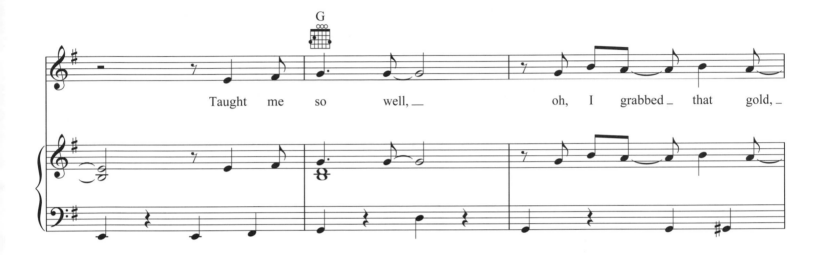

Taught me so well, __ oh, I grabbed __ that gold, __

and I left his dead ass

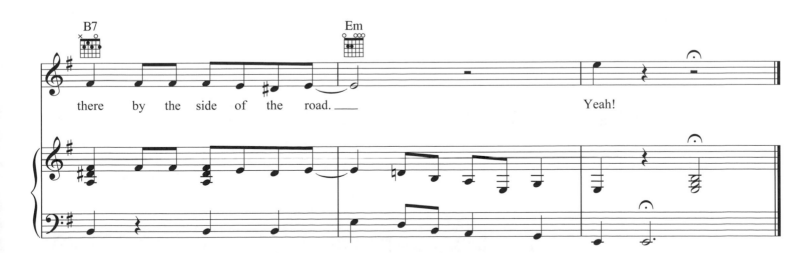

there by the side of the road. __ Yeah!

THE NIGHT THEY DROVE OLD DIXIE DOWN

Words and Music by
ROBBIE ROBERTSON

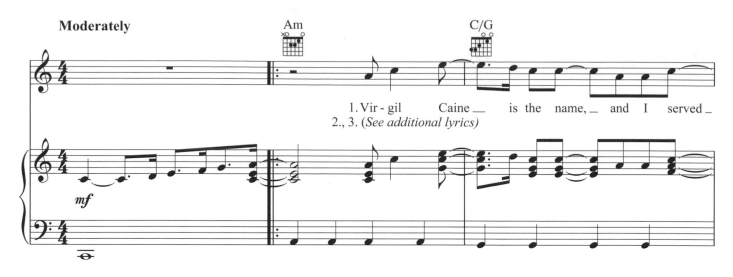

1. Vir - gil Caine is the name, and I served
2., 3. (See additional lyrics)

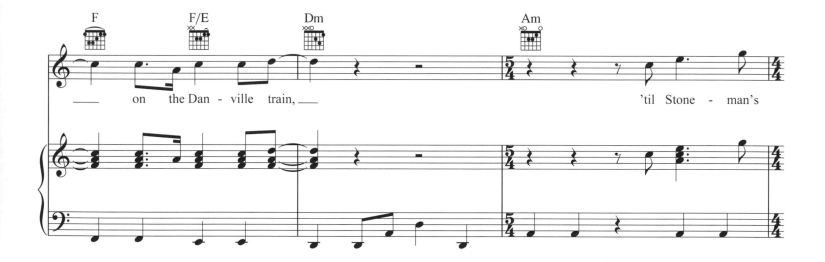

on the Dan - ville train, 'til Stone - man's

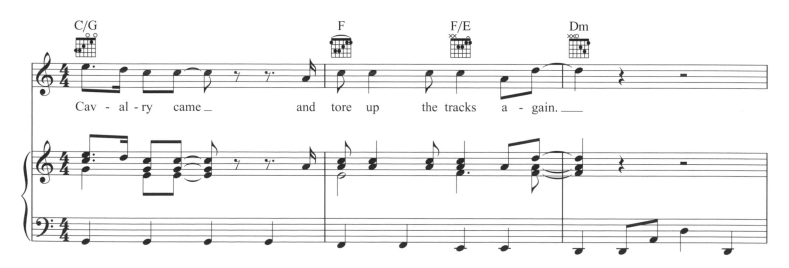

Cav - al - ry came and tore up the tracks a - gain.

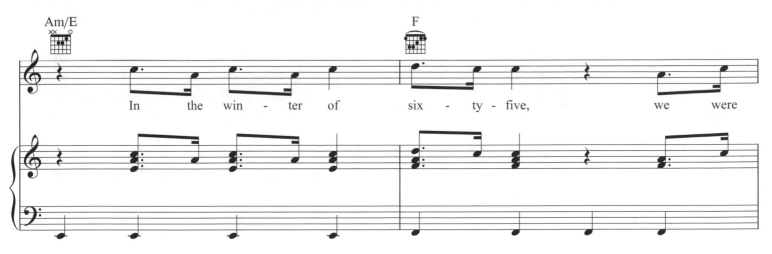

In the win - ter of six - ty - five, we were

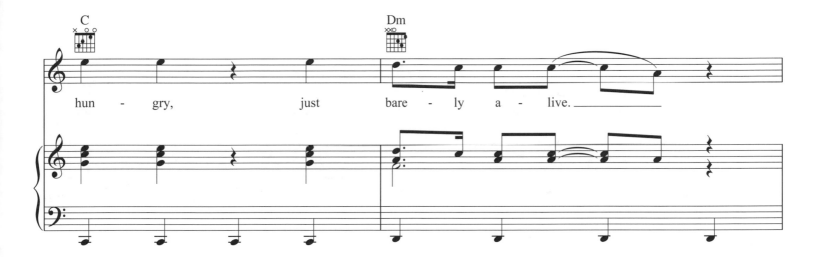

hun - gry, just bare - ly a - live.

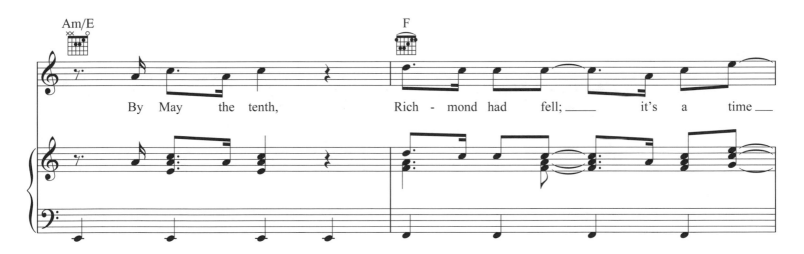

By May the tenth, Rich - mond had fell; it's a time

I re - mem - ber, oh, so well. The

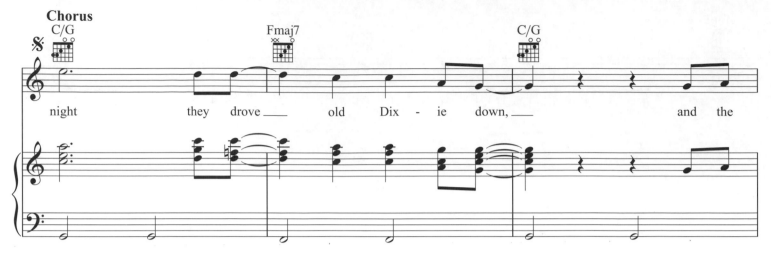

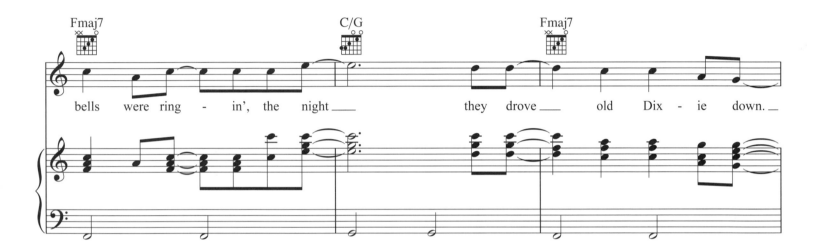

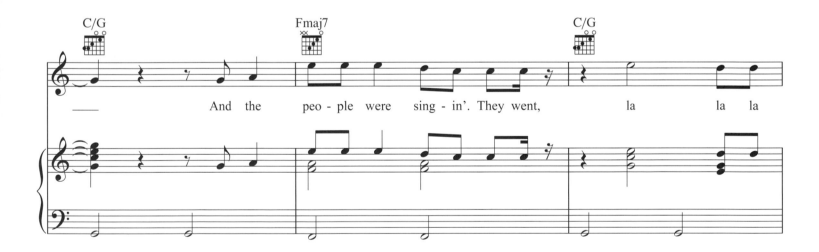

Additional Lyrics

2. Back with my wife in Tennessee
   When one day she called to me,
   "Virgil, quick, come see:
   There goes Robert E. Lee!"
   Now, I don't mind choppin' wood
   And I don't care if the money's no good,
   Ya take what ya need and ya leave the rest
   But they should never have taken
   The very best.
   (Repeat Chorus)

3. Like my father before me,
   I will work the land.
   And like my brother above me
   Who took a rebel stand.
   He was just eighteen, proud and brave,
   But a Yankee laid him in his grave.
   I swear by the mud below my feet,
   You can't raise a Caine back up
   When he's in defeat.
   (Repeat Chorus with final ending)

NORWEGIAN WOOD
(This Bird Has Flown)

Words and Music by JOHN LENNON
and PAUL McCARTNEY

I looked a-round and I no-ticed there was-n't a chair.
told her I did-n't and crawled off to sleep in the bath.

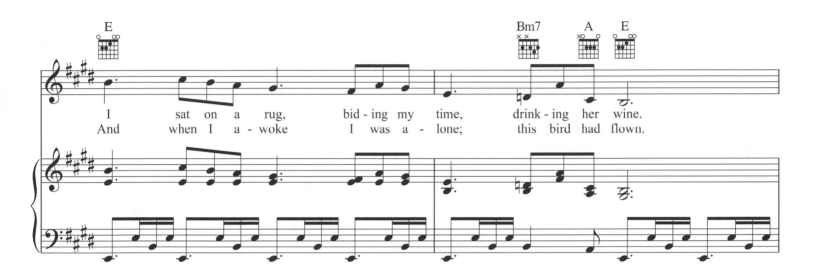

I sat on a rug, bid-ing my time, drink-ing her wine.
And when I a-woke I was a-lone; this bird had flown.

We talked un-til two and then she said, "It's time for bed."
So I lit a fire, is-n't it good Nor-we-gian wood.

rit.

ONE TIN SOLDIER

from BILLY JACK

Words and Music by DENNIS LAMBERT
and BRIAN POTTER

Moderately slow Rock tempo

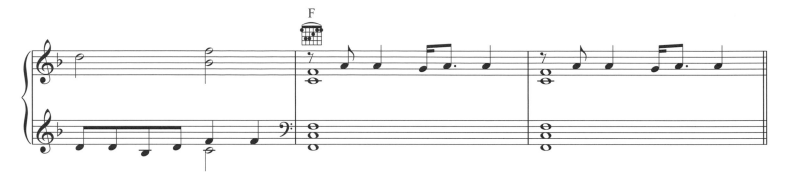

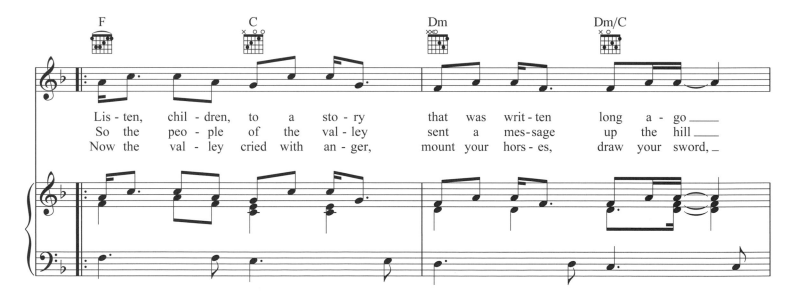

Lis - ten, chil - dren, to a sto - ry that was writ - ten long a - go
So the peo - ple of the val - ley sent a mes - sage up the hill
Now the val - ley cried with an - ger, mount your hors - es, draw your sword,

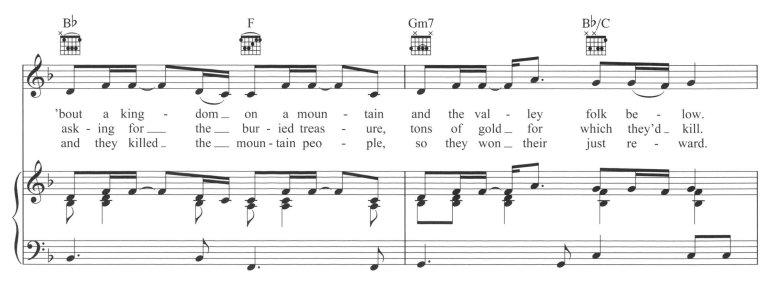

'bout a king - dom on a moun - tain and the val - ley folk be - low.
ask - ing for the bur - ied treas - ure, tons of gold for which they'd kill.
and they killed the moun - tain peo - ple, so they won their just re - ward.

223

Jus - ti - fy it in the end.___ There won't be an - y trum-pets blow - in'____

come the judg - ment day. On the blood - y morn - ing af - ter,_____

___ one tin sol - dier rides a - way.____

ONE PIECE AT A TIME

Words and Music by
WAYNE KEMP

Talking Blues tempo, in 2

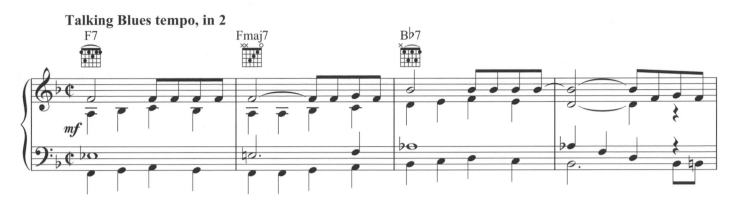

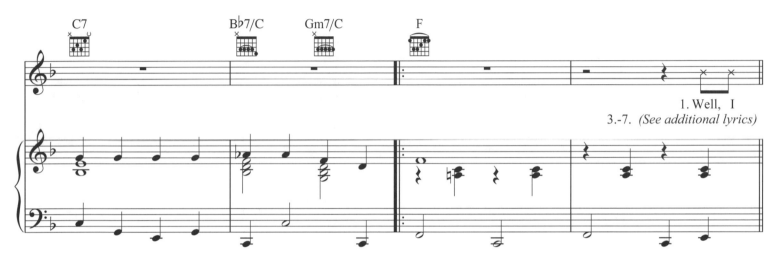

1. Well, I
3.-7. (See additional lyrics)

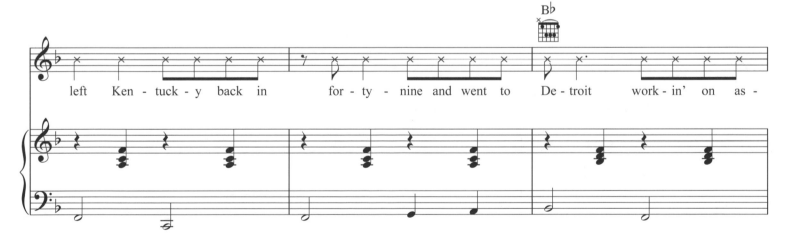

left Ken-tuck-y back in for-ty - nine and went to De-troit work-in' on as-

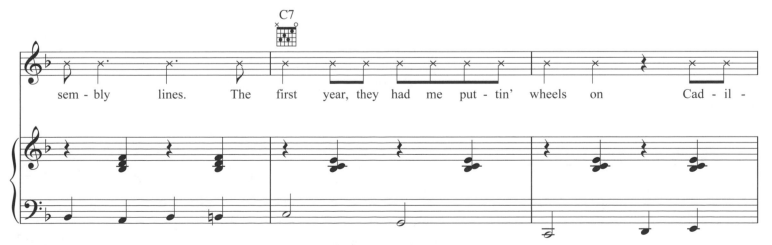

sem-bly lines. The first year, they had me put-tin' wheels on Cad-il-

lacs. Ev - 'ry day I'd watch them

beau - ties roll by, and some - times I'd hang my head and cry. 'Cause I

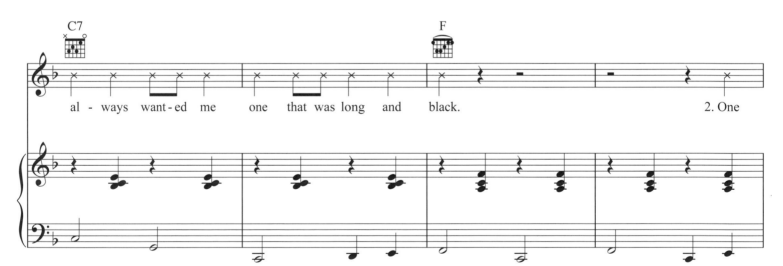

al - ways want-ed me one that was long and black. 2. One

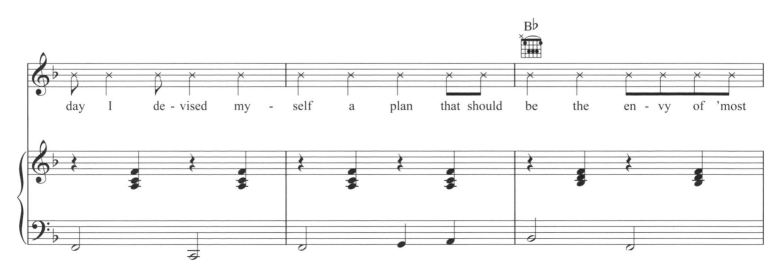

day I de - vised my - self a plan that should be the en - vy of 'most

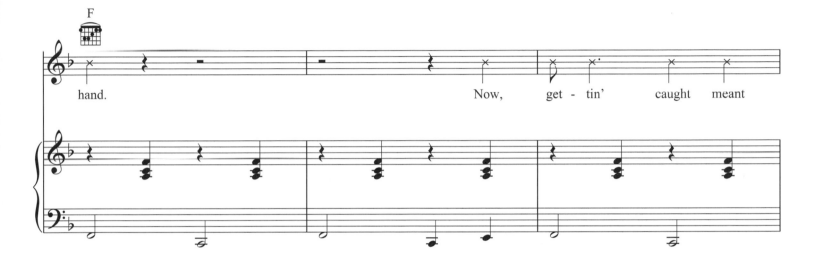

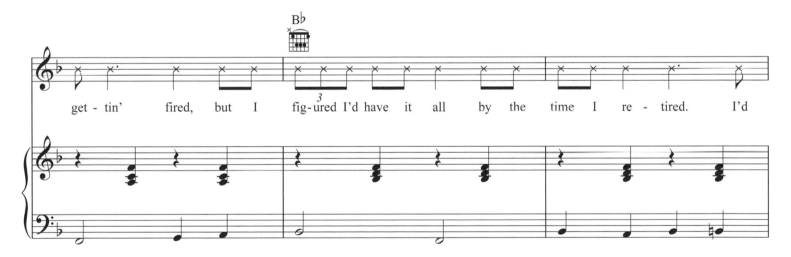

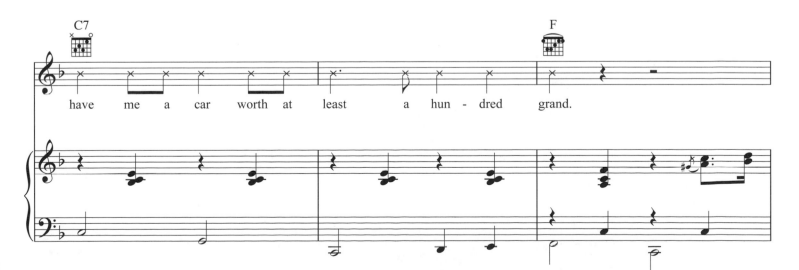

have the on - ly one there is a - round.

RECITATION

3. So, the very next day when I punched in with my big lunch box
   And with help from my friends, I left that day with a lunch box full of gears.
   I've never considered myself a thief, but GM wouldn't miss just one little piece
   Especially if I strung it out over several years.

4. The first day, I got me a fuel pump, and the next day I got me an engine and a trunk.
   Then I got me a transmission and all the chrome.
   The little things I could get in the big lunch box
   Like nuts and bolts and all four shocks.
   But the big stuff we snuck out in my buddy's mobile home.

5. Now, up to now, my plan went all right, 'til we tried to put it all together one night.
   And that's when we noticed that something was definitely wrong.
   The transmission was a '53, and the motor turned out to be a '73,
   And when we tried to put in the bolts, all the holes were gone.
   So, we drilled it out so that it would fit, and with a little bit of help from an adapter kit,
   We had the engine running just like a song.

6. Now the headlights, they was another sight,
   We had two on the left, and one on the right.
   But when we pulled out the switch, all three of 'em come on.
   The back end looked kinda funny, too.
   But we put it together, and when we got through, well, that's when we noticed that we only had one tail fin.
   About that time, my wife walked out, and I could see in her eyes that she had her doubts.
   But she opened the door and said, "Honey, take me for a spin."

7. So, we drove uptown just to get the tags, and I headed her right on down the main drag.
   I could hear everybody laughin' for blocks around.
   But, up there at the court house, they didn't laugh,
   'Cause to type it up, it took the whole staff.
   And when they got through, the title weighed sixty pounds.

2nd CHORUS: I got it one piece at a time, and it didn't cost me a dime.
   You'll know it's me when I come through your town.
   I'm gonna ride around in style; I'm gonna drive everybody wild,
   'Cause I'll have the only one there is around.

(Ad Lib): "Yeah, Red Rider, this is the Cottonmouth in the Psychobilly Cadillac, com'on? This
   is the Cotton-mouth, a negatory on the cost of this mo-chine, there, Red Rider, you might
   say I went right up to the factory and picked it up, it's cheaper that way. What model is
   it?.........Well, it's a 49, 50, 51, 52, 53, 54, 55, 56, 57, 58, 59 automobile....60, 61,
   62, 63, 64, 65, 66, 67, 68, 69 automobile....70, 71, 72, 73....."

PAPA WAS A ROLLIN' STONE

Words and Music by NORMAN WHITFIELD
and BARRETT STRONG

Moderately fast

It was the third of Sep-tem-ber.

nev-er got a chance to see ____

That day I'll al-ways re-mem-ber, yes, I will, ____ 'cause

____ him. Nev - er heard noth-in' but bad things a-bout him.

that was the day ___ that my dad - dy died. ___
Ma - ma, I'm de - pend - ing on you to tell me the truth. __

I ___ (Spoken:) *Mama just hung her head and said, "Son,*

Pa - pa was a roll - in' stone." __ Wher - ev - er he laid his hat

was his home. __ And when he died, __ all ___ he ___ left us was a -

and an - oth - er wife. _ And that ain't right.
pay his bills. _ Hey, Ma - ma,
truth.

(Spoken:)
Mama just hung her head and said,

Mama looked up with a tear in her eye and said, "Pa - pa was a roll - in' stone." _

Wher - ev - er he laid his hat was his home. _ And when he died, _ all _

Repeat and Fade

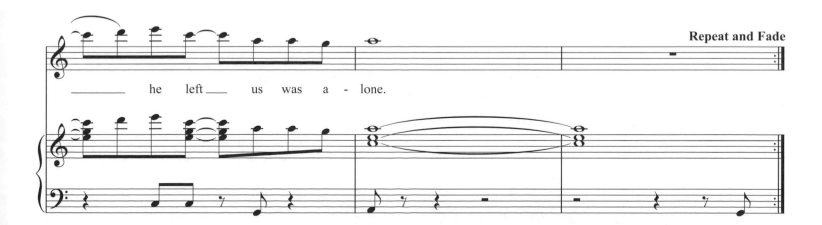

_____ he left _ us was a - lone.

PUFF THE MAGIC DRAGON

Words and Music by LENNY LIPTON
and PETER YARROW

Moderately, in 2

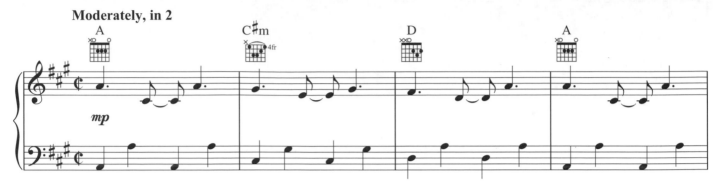

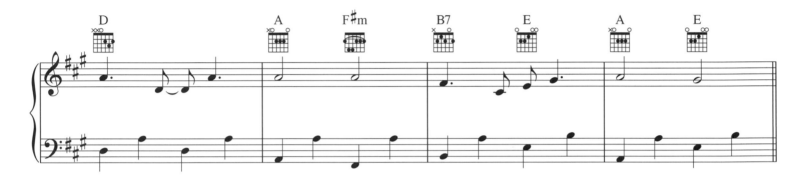

1. Puff the Mag - ic Drag - on lived by ____ the
2.–5. *(See additional lyrics)*

*3rd time, play verse twice
before proceeding to Chorus

sea ____ and frol - icked in ____ the au - tumn mist ____ in a

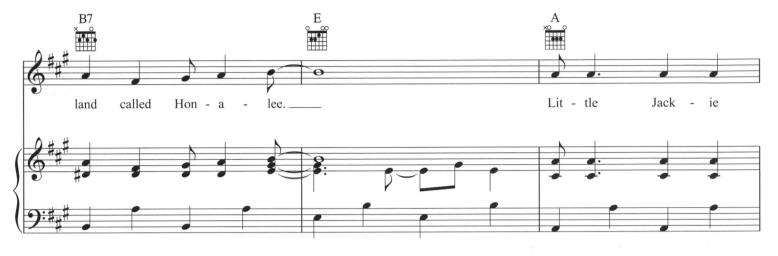

land called Hon - a - lee. _____ Lit - tle Jack - ie

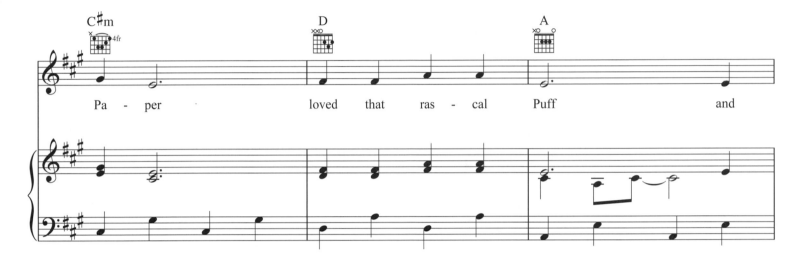

Pa - per loved that ras - cal Puff and

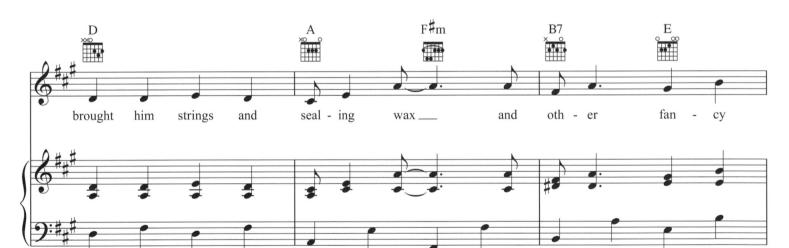

brought him strings and seal - ing wax _____ and oth - er fan - cy

Chorus

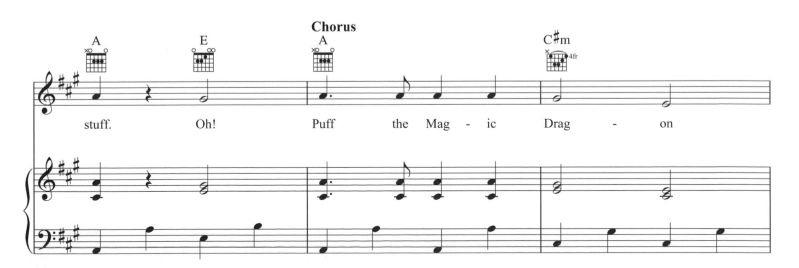

stuff. Oh! Puff the Mag - ic Drag - on

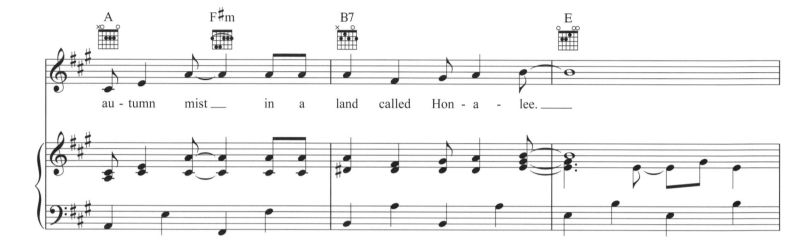

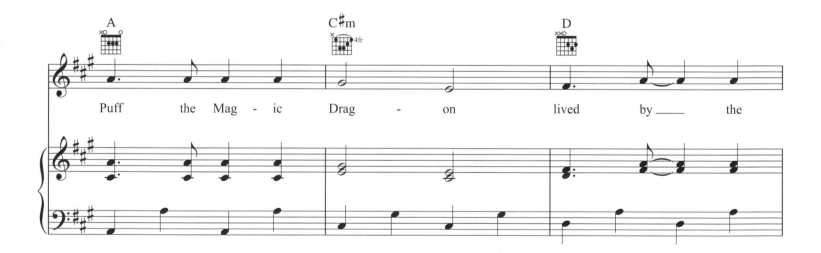

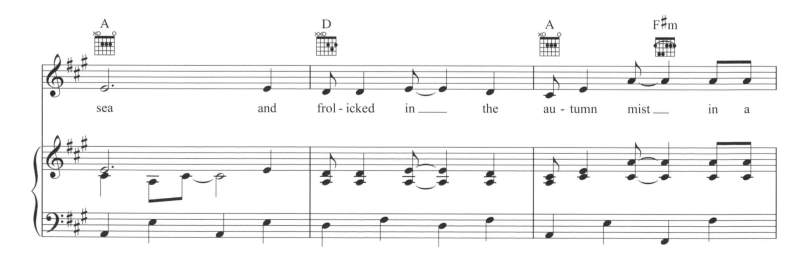

Additional Lyrics

2. Together they would travel on a boat with billowed sail.
Jackie kept a lookout perched on Puff's gigantic tail.
Noble kings and princes would bow whene'er they came.
Pirate ships would low'r their flags when Puff roared out his name. Oh!
Chorus

3. A dragon lives forever, but not so little boys.
Painted wings and giant rings make way for other toys.
One gray night it happened, Jackie Paper came no more,
And Puff that mighty dragon, he ceased his fearless roar.

4. His head was bent in sorrow, green tears fell like rain.
Puff no longer went to play along the Cherry Lane.
Without his lifelong friend, Puff could not be brave,
So Puff that mighty dragon sadly slipped into his cave. Oh!
Chorus

THE RETURN OF PUFF

5. Puff the magic dragon danced down the Cherry Lane.
He came upon a little girl, Julie Maple was her name.
She'd heard that Puff had gone away, but that can never be,
So together they went sailing to the land called Honalee.
Chorus

ROCKY RACCOON

Words and Music by JOHN LENNON
and PAUL McCARTNEY

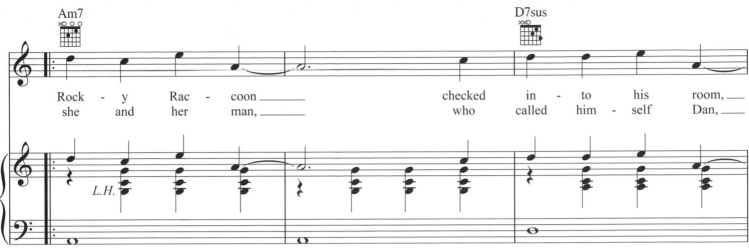

Am7 — D7sus

Rock - y Rac - coon _____ checked in - to his room, _____
she and her man, _____ who called him - self Dan, _____

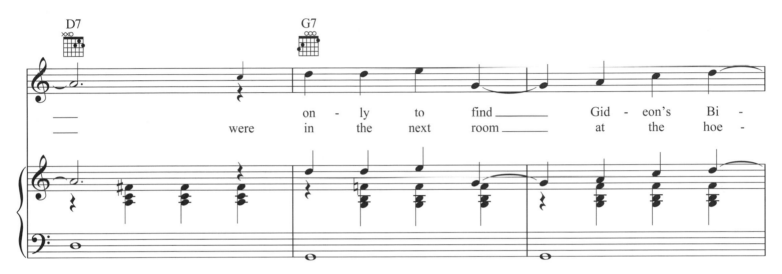

D7 — G7

_____ on - ly to find _____ Gid - eon's Bi -
_____ were in the next room _____ at the hoe -

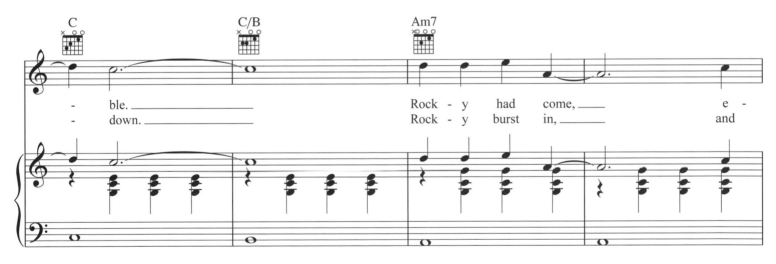

C — C/B — Am7

- ble. _____ Rock - y had come, _____ e -
- down. _____ Rock - y burst in, _____ and

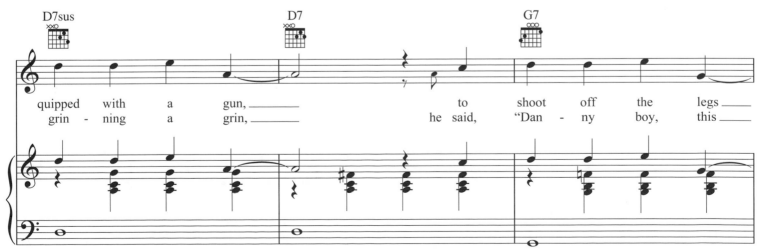

D7sus — D7 — G7

quipped with a gun, _____ to shoot off the legs _____
grin - ning a grin, _____ he said, "Dan - ny boy, this _____

of his ri - val. His
is a show - down." But

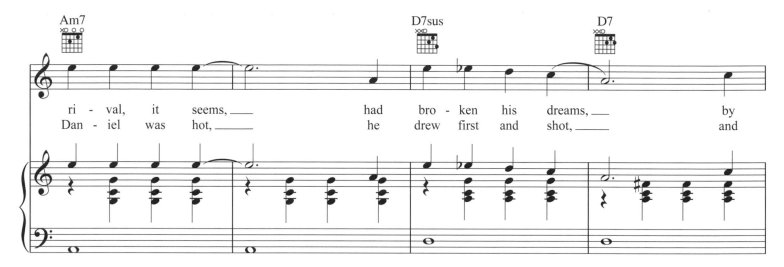

ri - val, it seems, had bro - ken his dreams, by
Dan - iel was hot, he drew first and shot, and

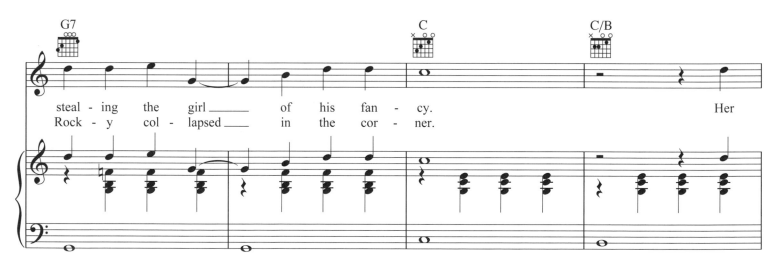

steal - ing the girl of his fan - cy. Her
Rock - y col - lapsed in the cor - ner.

name was Ma - gill, and she called her - self Lil, but

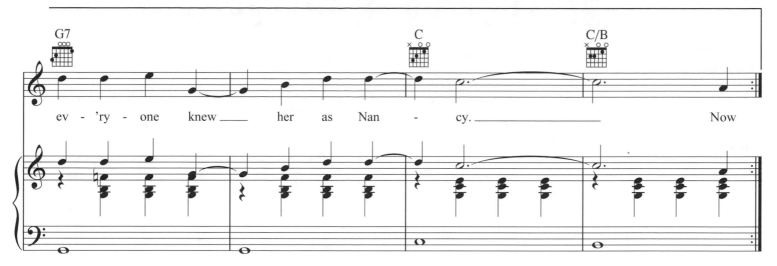

ev - 'ry - one knew ____ her as Nan - cy. ____ Now

2 **Barrelhouse style** (♫ = ♪♪)

Now, the doc - tor came in, ____

L.H.

stink - ing of gin, _____ and pro -

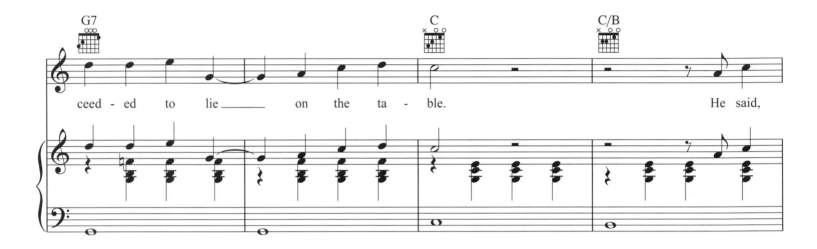

ceed - ed to lie _____ on the ta - ble. He said,

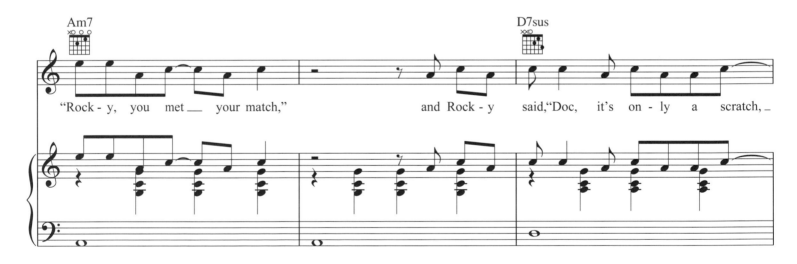

"Rock - y, you met __ your match," and Rock - y said, "Doc, it's on - ly a scratch, _

_ and I'll be bet - ter, I'll be bet - ter, Doc, as soon __ as I am

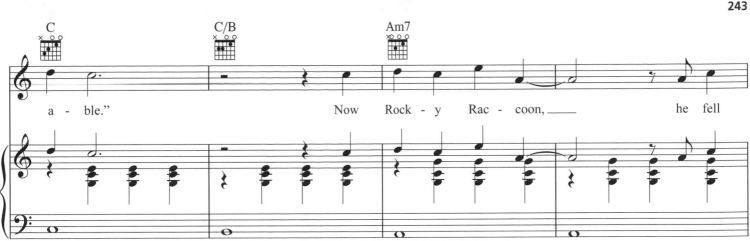

a - ble." Now Rock - y Rac - coon, _____ he fell

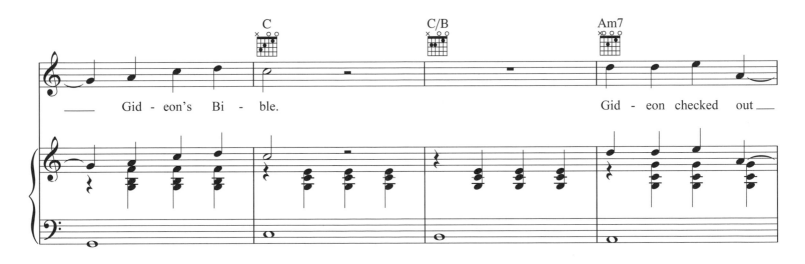

back in his room, _____ on - ly to find _____

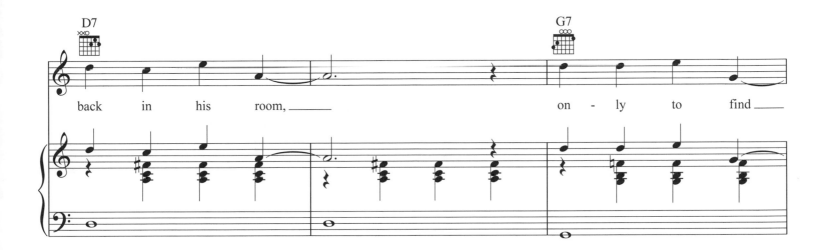

_____ Gid - eon's Bi - ble. Gid - eon checked out _____

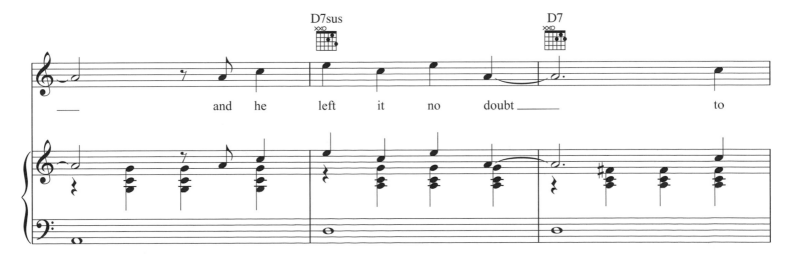

_____ and he left it no doubt _____ to

help with good Rock - y's re - viv - al. _____

Barrelhouse style

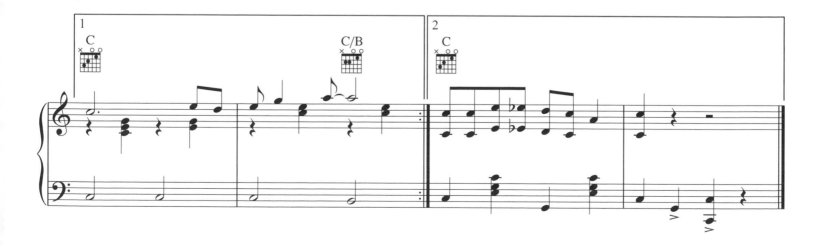

SCENES FROM AN ITALIAN RESTAURANT

Words and Music by
BILLY JOEL

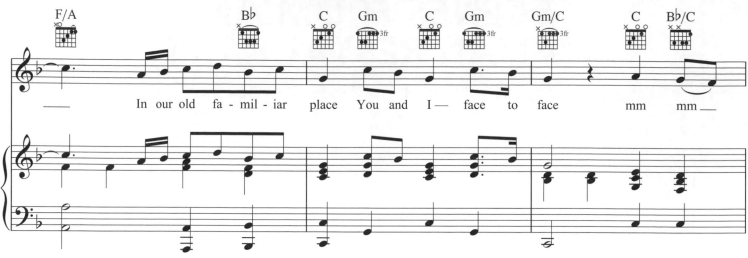

In our old fa - mil - iar place You and I — face to face mm mm __

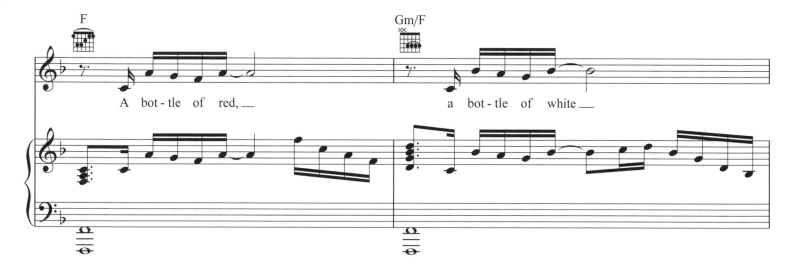

A bot - tle of red, __ a bot - tle of white __

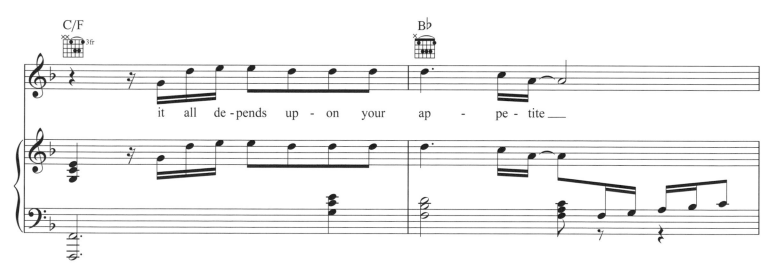

it all de - pends up - on your ap - pe - tite __

I'll meet you an - y time __ you want In our I - tal - ian ___ res -

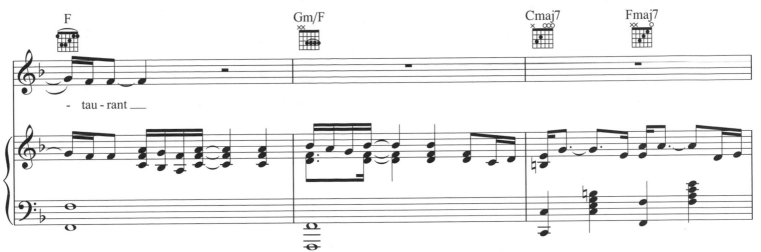

- tau - rant

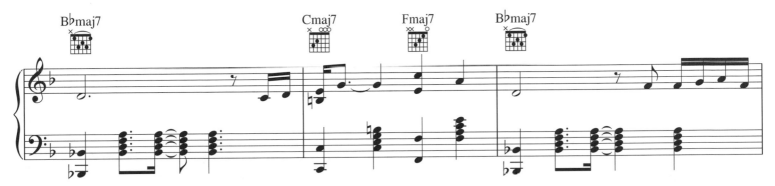

Fast Rock 'n' Roll

Things are o - kay _ with me these days _ Got a good job, _ got a good of - fice,

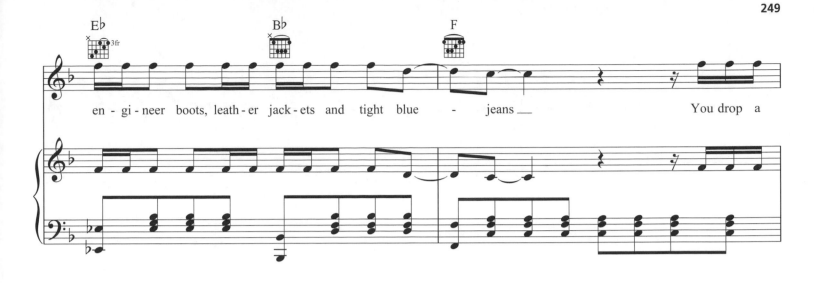

en-gi-neer boots, leath-er jack-ets and tight blue - jeans ___ You drop a

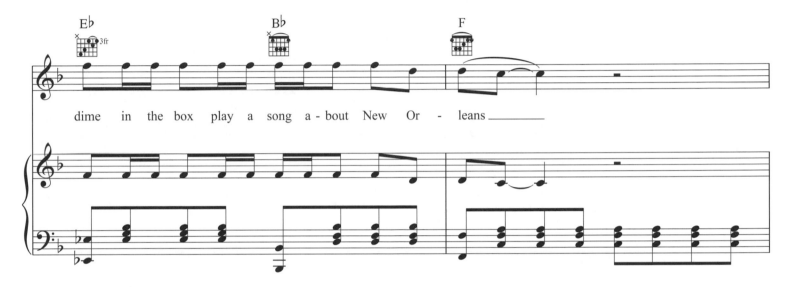

dime in the box play a song a-bout New Or - leans _____

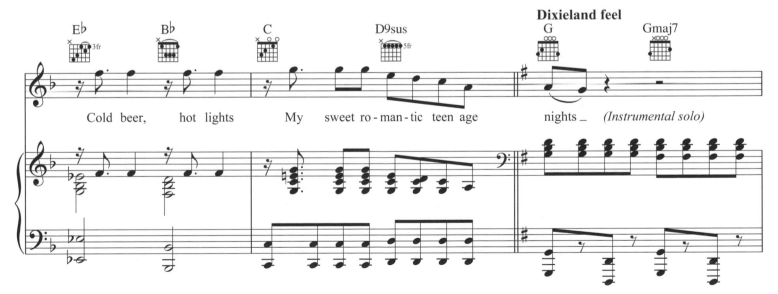

Cold beer, hot lights My sweet ro-man-tic teen age nights _ *(Instrumental solo)*

Dixieland feel

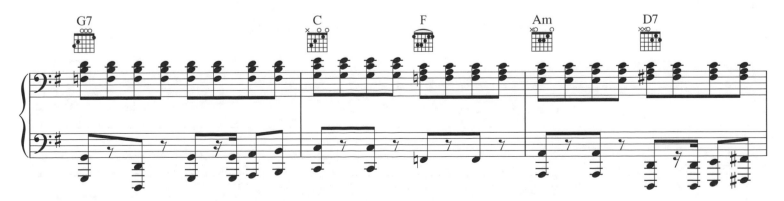

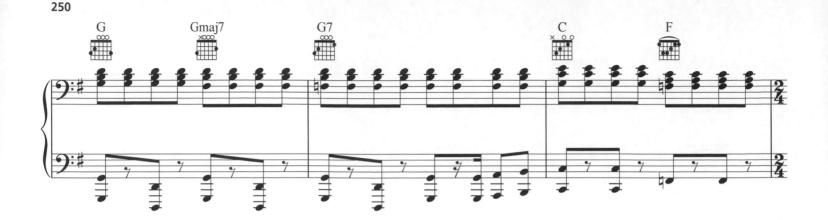

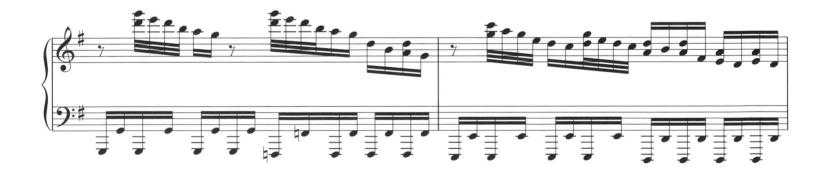

254

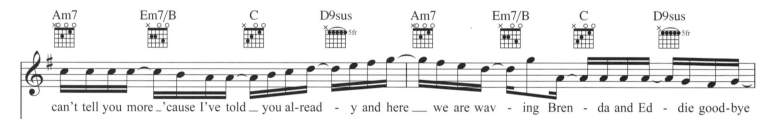

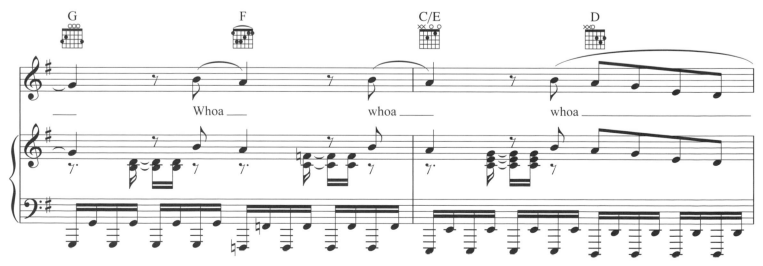

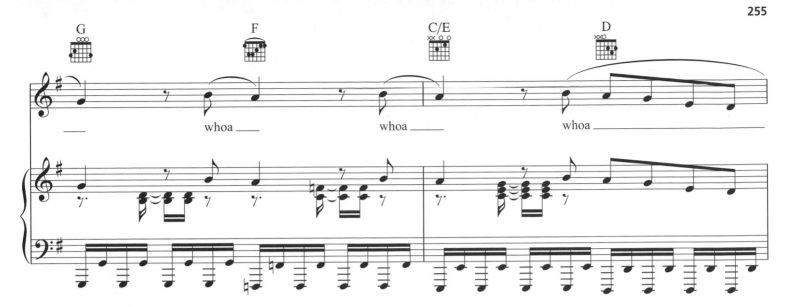

whoa ___ whoa ___ whoa ___

whoa ___ whoa ___ whoa ___

N.C.

rit.

Tempo I

With pedal

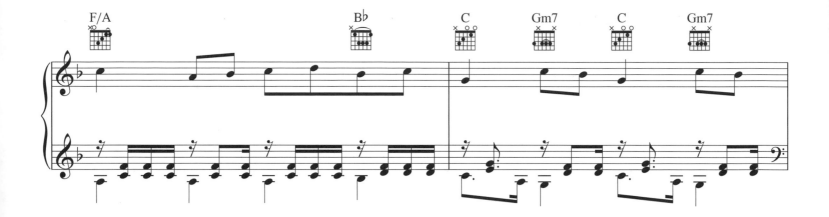

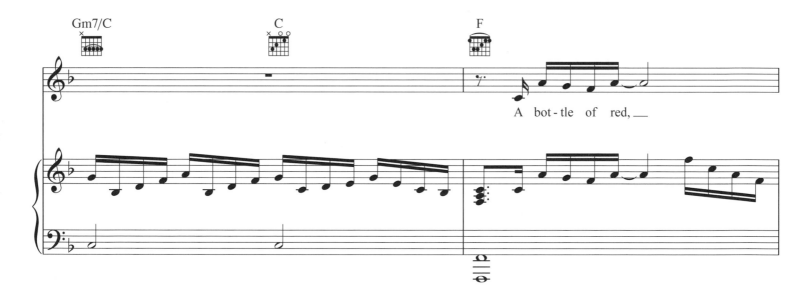

A bot-tle of red, ___

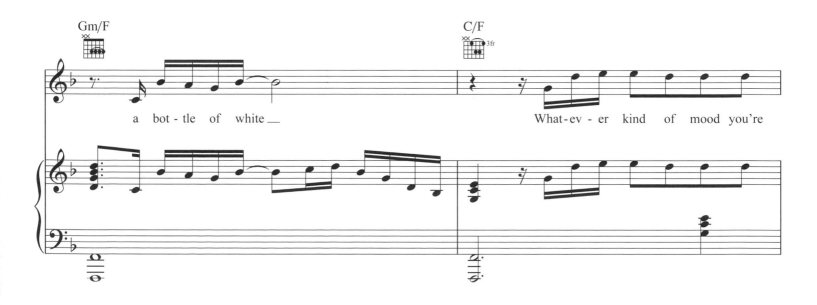

a bot-tle of white ___   What-ev-er kind of mood you're

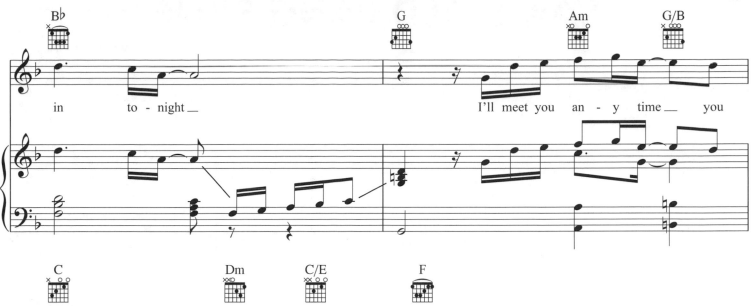

in to-night ___ I'll meet you an - y time ___ you

want in our I - tal - ian ___ res - tau - rant ___

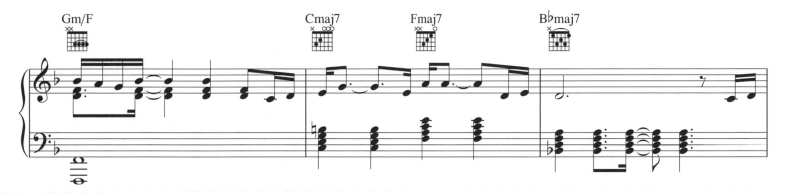

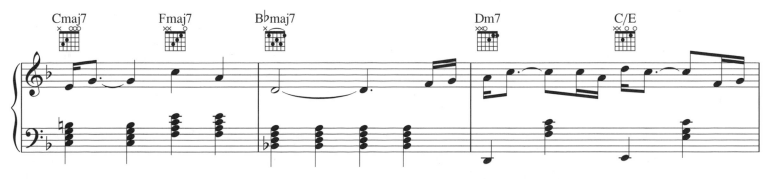

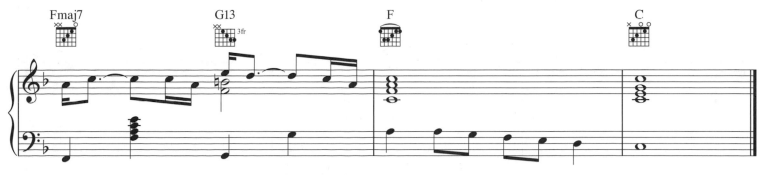

SAME OLD LANG SYNE

Words and Music by
DAN FOGELBERG

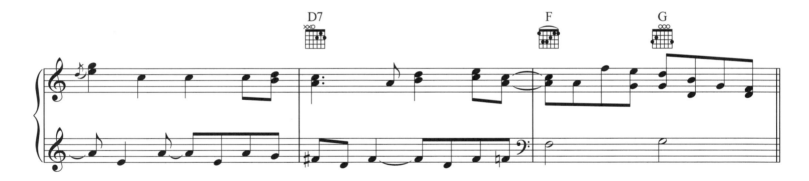

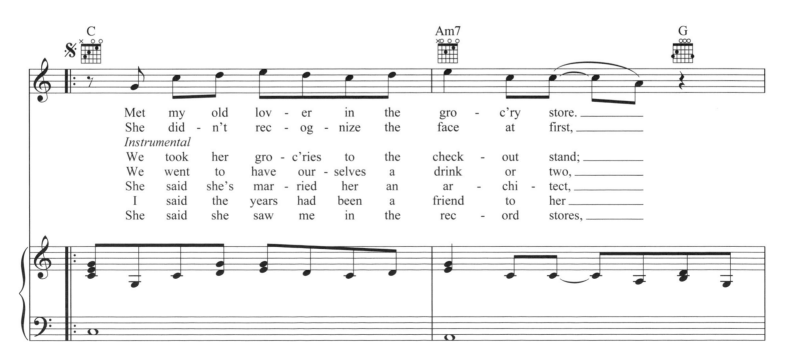

Met my old lov-er in the gro-c'ry store. _____
She did-n't rec-og-nize the face at first, _____
Instrumental
We took her gro-c'ries to the check-out stand; _____
We went to have our-selves a drink or two, _____
She said she's mar-ried her an ar-chi-tect, _____
I said the years had been a friend to her _____
She said she saw me in the rec-ord stores, _____

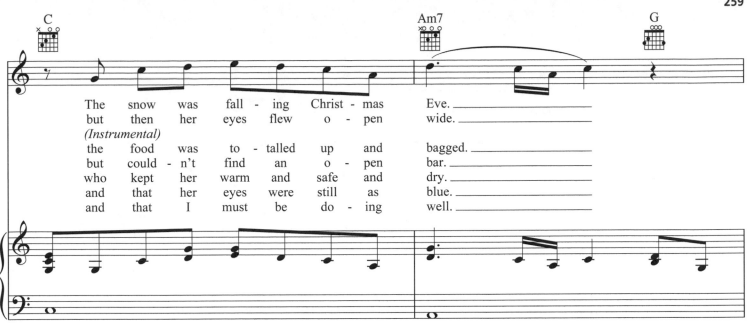

The snow was fall - ing Christ - mas Eve. _____
but then her eyes flew o - pen wide. _____
(Instrumental)
the food was to - talled up and bagged. _____
but could - n't find an o - pen bar. _____
who kept her warm and safe and dry. _____
and that her eyes were still as blue. _____
and that I must be do - ing well. _____

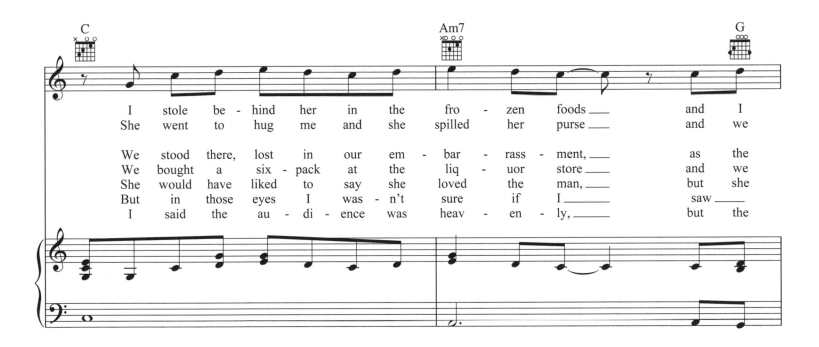

I stole be - hind her in the fro - zen foods ____ and I
She went to hug me and she spilled her purse ____ and we

We stood there, lost in our em - bar - rass - ment, ____ as the
We bought a six - pack at the liq - uor store ____ and we
She would have liked to say she loved the man, ____ but she
But in those eyes I was - n't sure if I _____ saw ____
I said the au - di - ence was heav - en - ly, ____ but the

touched her on ____ the sleeve. ____
laughed un - til ____ we cried. ____
Instrumental ends
con - ver - sa - tion lagged. ____
drank it in ____ her car. ____
did - n't like ____ to lie. ____
doubt or grat - i - tude. ____
trav - el - ing ____ was hell. ____

We drank a toast to in - no - cence; we

drank a toast ___ to now. ___ We tried to reach be - yond the

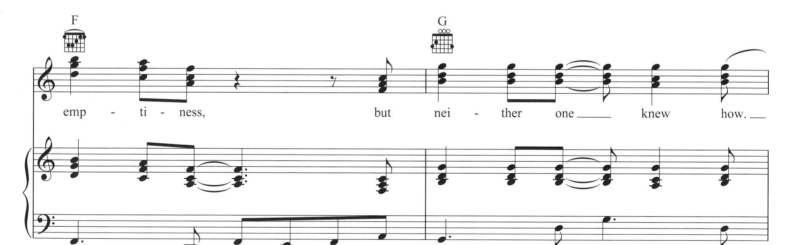

emp - ti - ness, but nei - ther one ___ knew how. ___

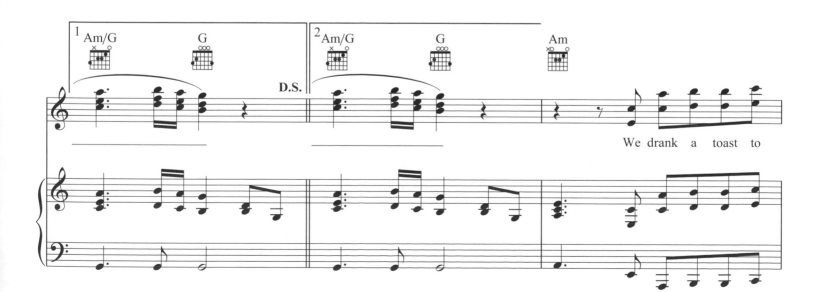

We drank a toast to

in - no - cence, we ___ drank a toast ___ to time; ___

re - liv - ing, in our

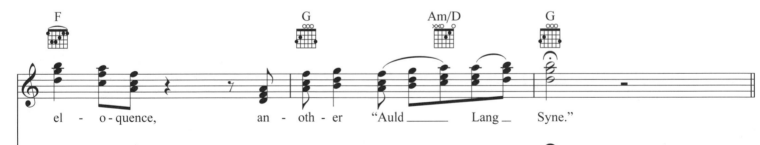

el - o - quence, an - oth - er "Auld ___ Lang ___ Syne."

rit. *a tempo*

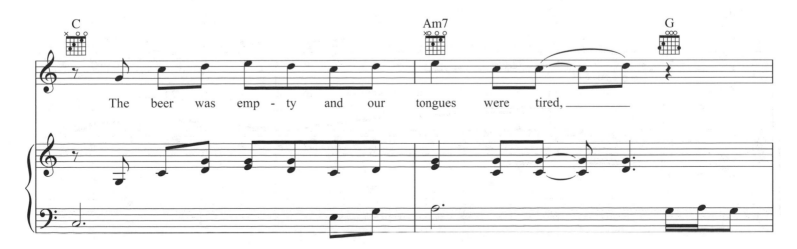

The beer was emp - ty and our tongues were tired, ___

and run-ning out _____ of things to say. _____

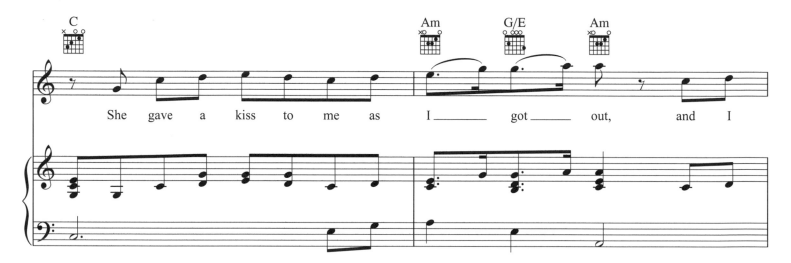

She gave a kiss to me as I _____ got _____ out, and I

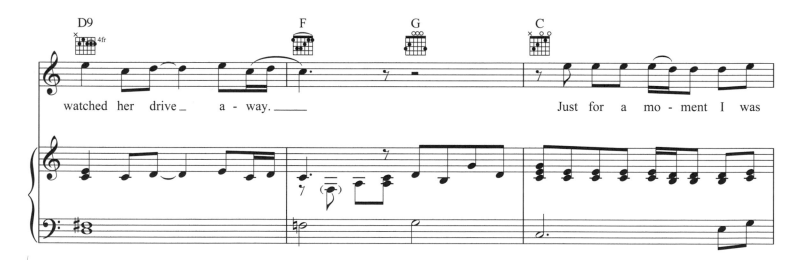

watched her drive _ a - way. _____ Just for a mo - ment I was

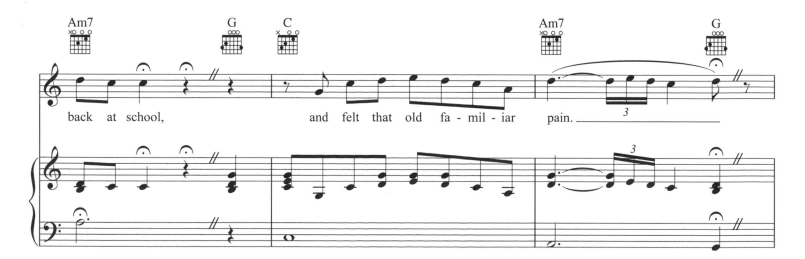

back at school, and felt that old fa - mil - iar pain. _____

And, as I turned to make my way ___ back ___ home, the snow turned in - to

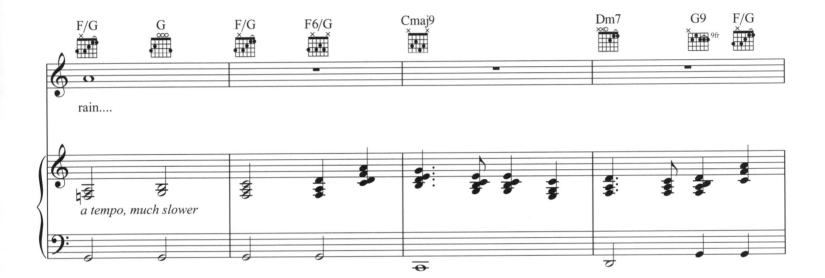

rain....

a tempo, much slower

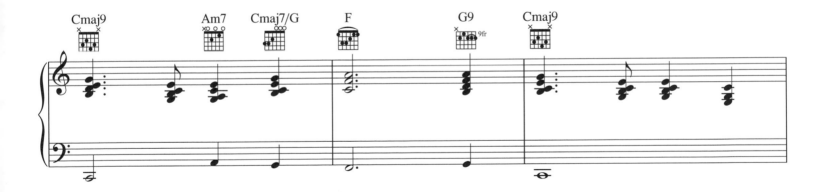

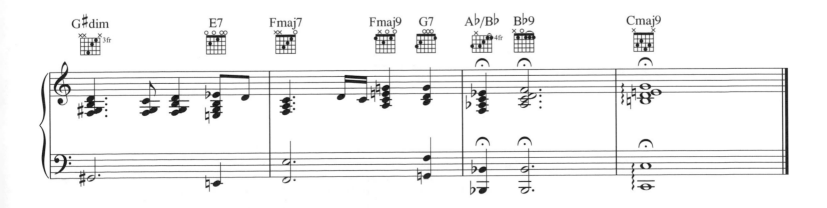

TANGLED UP IN BLUE

Words and Music by
BOB DYLAN

Moderately

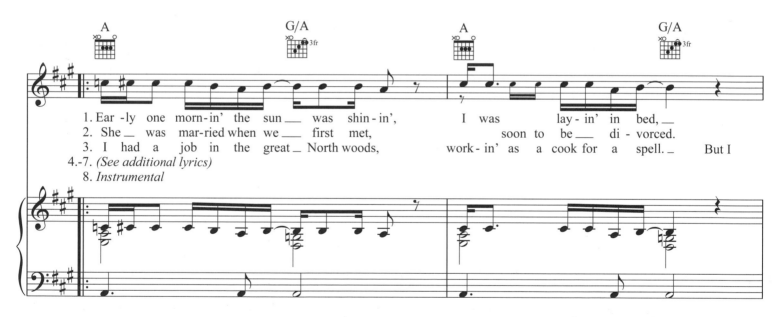

1. Ear-ly one morn-in' the sun __ was shin-in',   I was   lay-in' in bed, __
2. She __ was mar-ried when we __ first met,   soon to be __ di-vorced.
3. I had a job in the great __ North woods,   work-in' as a cook for a spell. __ But I
4.-7. *(See additional lyrics)*
8. *Instrumental*

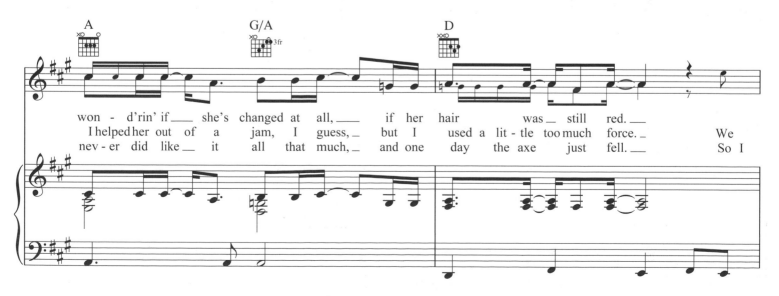

won - d'rin' if __ she's changed at all, __ if her hair was __ still red. __
I helped her out of a jam, I guess, __ but I used a lit - tle too much force. __ We
nev - er did like __ it all that much, __ and one day the axe just fell. __ So I

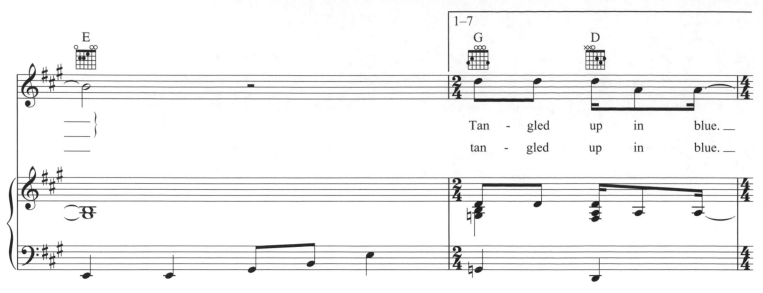

Tan - gled   up   in   blue. __
tan - gled   up   in   blue. __

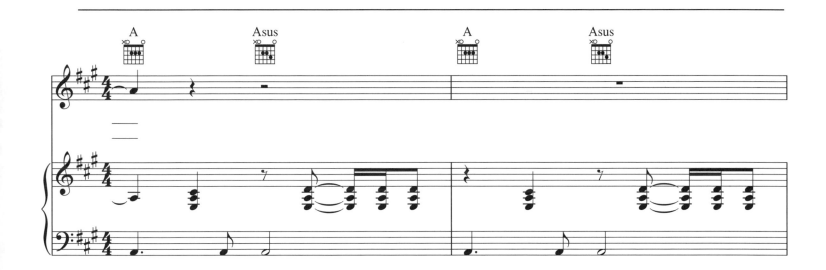

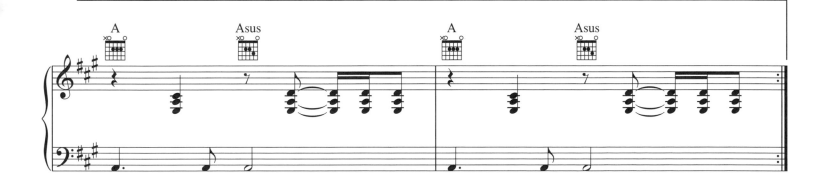

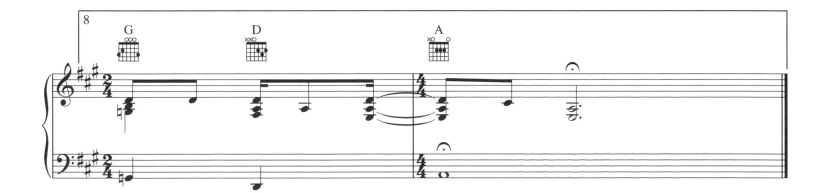

Additional Lyrics

4. She was working in a topless place
   And I stopped in for a beer.
   I just kept looking at the side of her face
   In the spotlight so clear.
   And later on when the crowd thinned out
   I was just about to do the same.
   She was standing there in back of my chair,
   Said to me, "Don't I know your name?"
   I muttered something underneath my breath.
   She studied the lines on my face.
   I must admit I felt a little uneasy
   When she bent down to tie the laces of my shoe,
   Tangled up in blue.

5. She lit a burner on the stove
   And offered me a pipe.
   "I thought you'd never say hello," she said.
   "You look like the silent type."
   Then she opened up a book of poems
   And handed it to me,
   Written by an Italian poet
   From the thirteenth century.
   And every one of them words rang true
   And glowed like burning coal,
   Pourin' off of every page
   Like it was written in my soul,
   From me to you,
   Tangled up in blue.

6. I lived with them on Montague Street
   In a basement down the stairs.
   There was music in the cafes at night
   And revolution in the air.
   Then he started in the dealing in slaves
   And something inside of him died.
   She had to sell everything she owned
   And froze up inside.
   And when finally the bottom finally fell out
   I became withdrawn.
   The only thing I knew how to do
   Was to keep on keeping on,
   Like a bird that flew
   Tangled up in blue.

7. So now I'm going back again.
   I got to get to her somehow.
   All the people we used to know,
   They're an illusion to me now.
   Some are mathematicians,
   Some are carpenter's wives.
   Don't know how it all got started,
   I don't know what they do with their lives.
   But me, I'm still on the road
   Headin' for another joint.
   We always did feel the same,
   We just saw it from a different point of view,
   Tangled up in blue.

TAXI

Words and Music by
HARRY CHAPIN

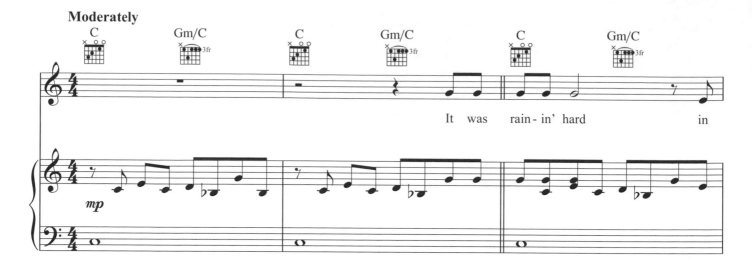

It was rain-in' hard in

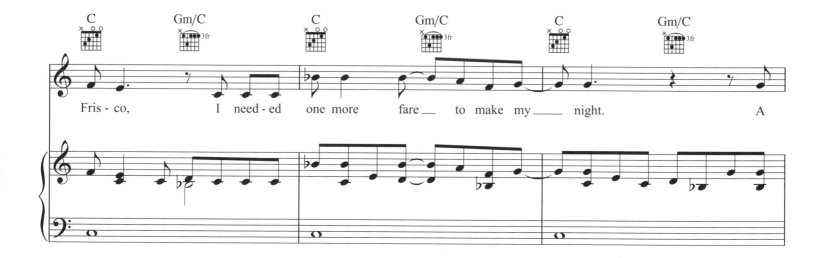

Fris-co, I need-ed one more fare __ to make my __ night. A

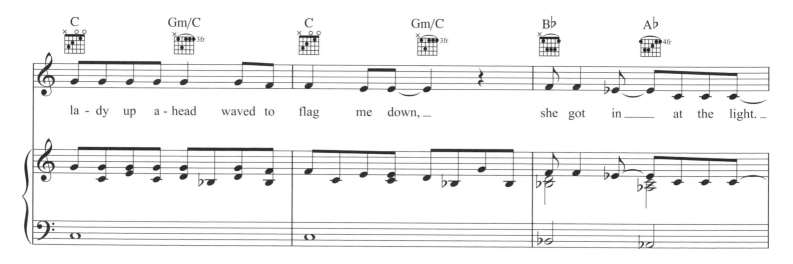

la-dy up a-head waved to flag me down, __ she got in __ at the light. __

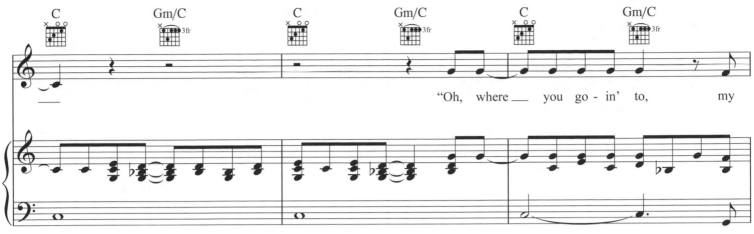

"Oh, where ___ you go - in' to, my

la - dy blue? It's a shame you ___ ru - ined your ___ gown _____ in the

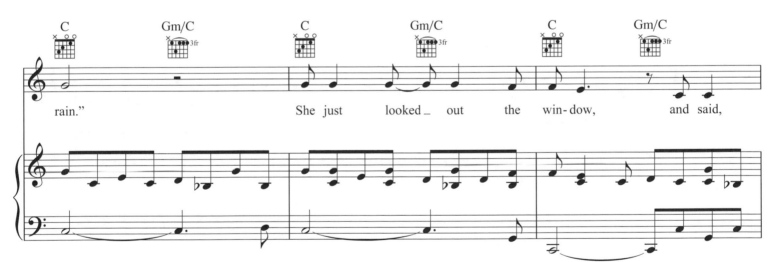

rain." She just looked ___ out the win - dow, and said,

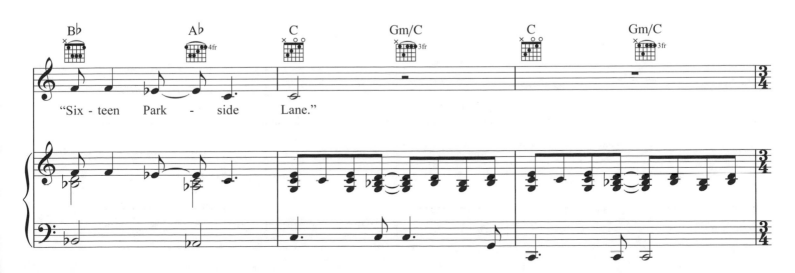

"Six - teen Park - side Lane."

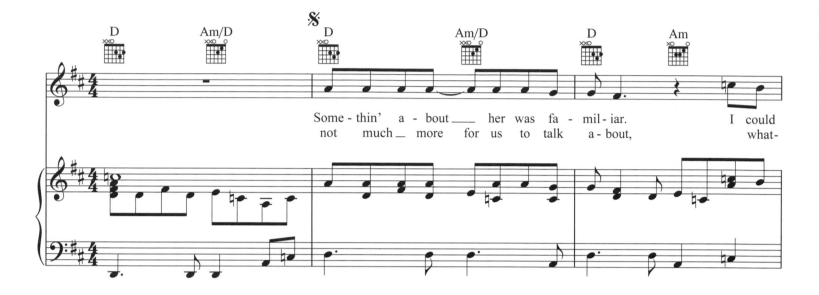

Some-thin' a-bout ___ her was fa-mil-iar. I could
not much __ more for us to talk a-bout, what-

swear I'd seen her face be-fore. ___ But she said, "I'm sure you're mis-
ev-er we had once was gone. ___ So I turned my cab in-to the

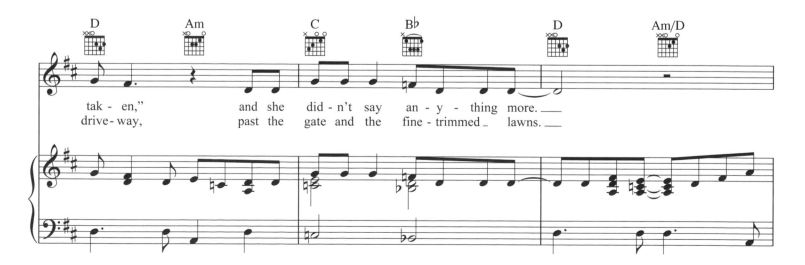

tak - en," and she did-n't say an-y-thing more. ___
drive-way, past the gate and the fine-trimmed _ lawns. ___

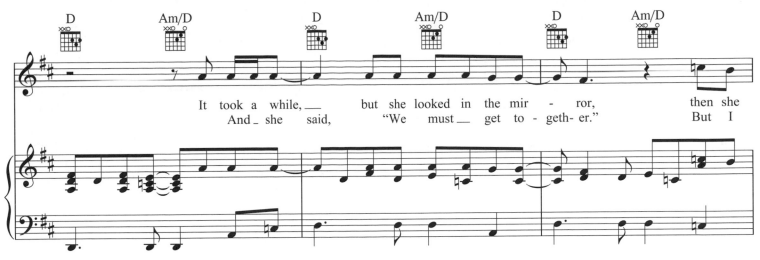

It took a while, ___ but she looked in the mir - ror, ___ then she
And _ she said, "We must ___ get to - geth- er." But I

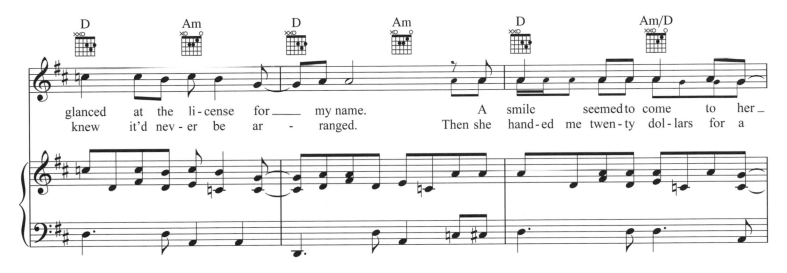

glanced at the li - cense for ____ my name. A smile seemed to come to her ___
knew it'd nev - er be ar - ranged. Then she hand - ed me twen - ty dol - lars for a

___ slow - ly. It was a sad smile, ___ just the same.
two - fif - ty fare, ___ she said, "Har - ry, ____ keep the change."

To Coda ⊕

And she said, "How _ are you, Har - ry?" I ___

said, "How are you, Sue?" Through the too man-y miles and the

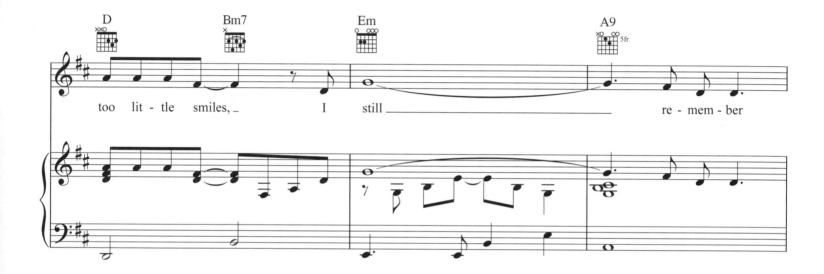

too lit-tle smiles, I still re-mem-ber

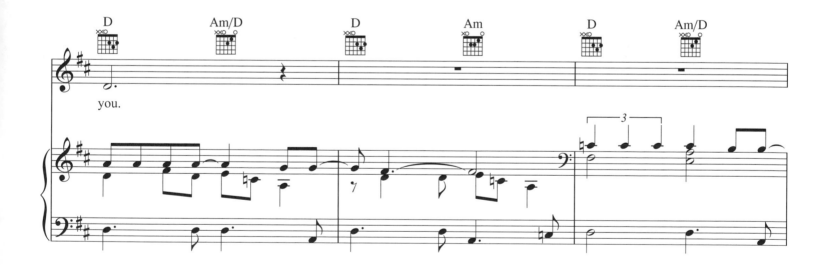

you.

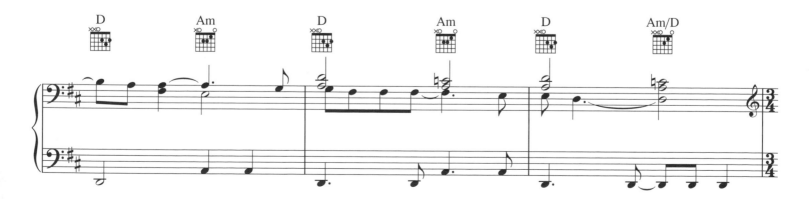

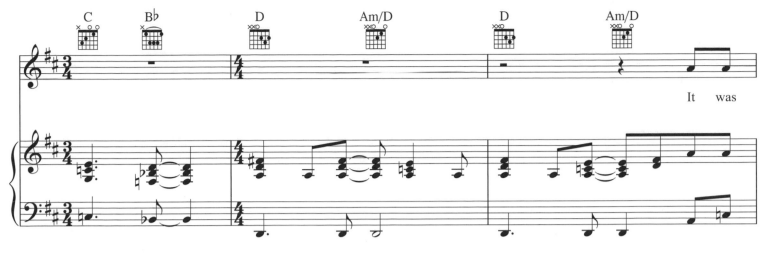

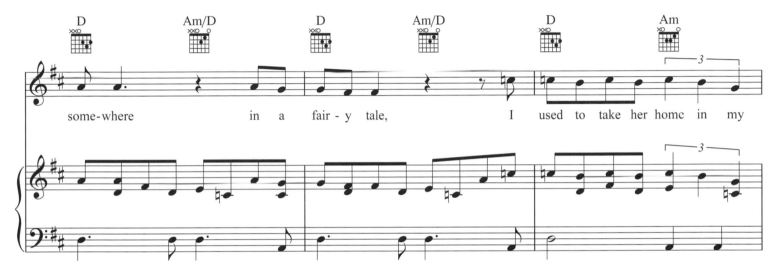

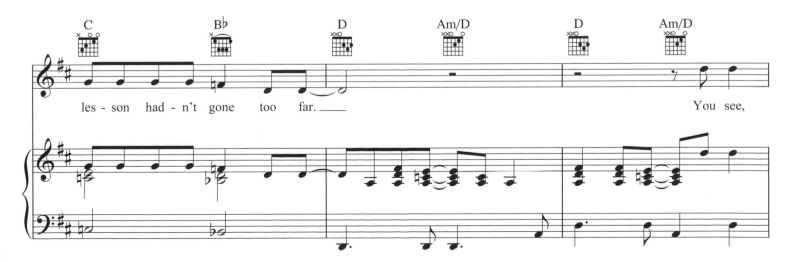

she was gon-na be an ac-tress, and I was gon-na learn to fly. _

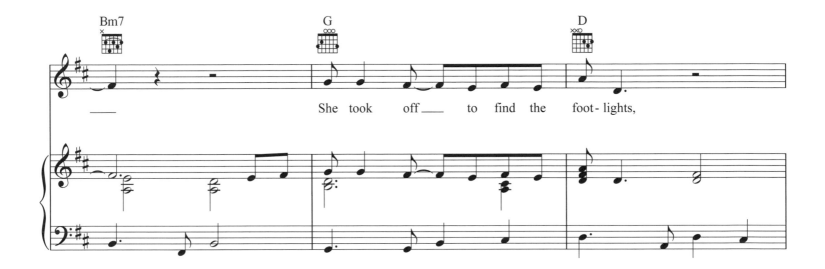

_ She took off ___ to find the foot-lights,

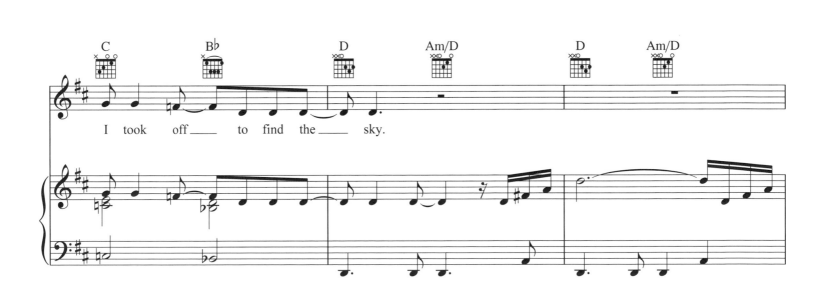

I took off ___ to find the ___ sky.

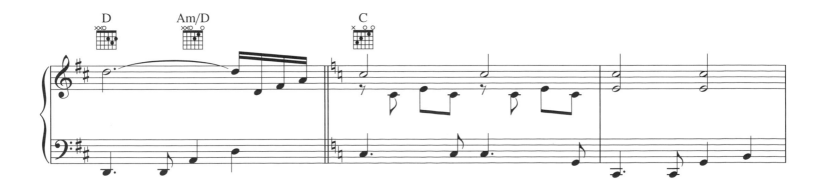

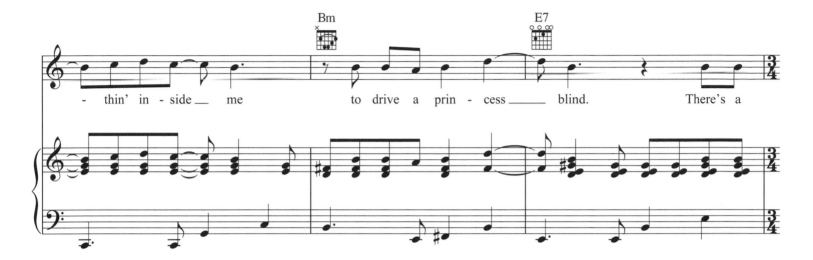

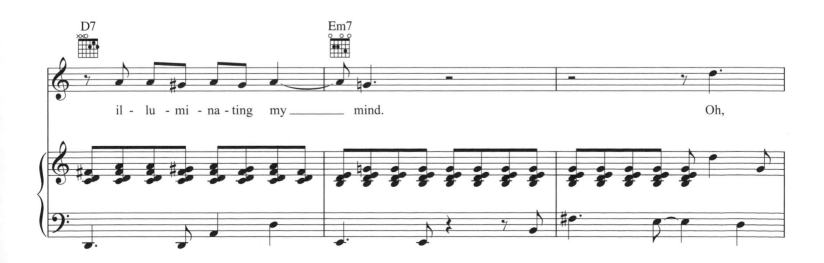

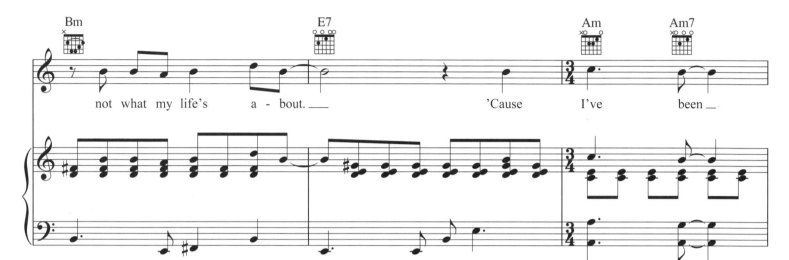

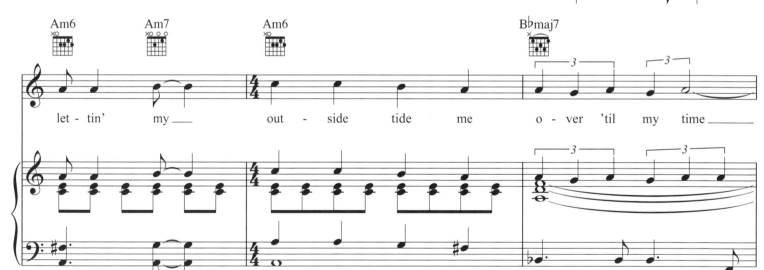

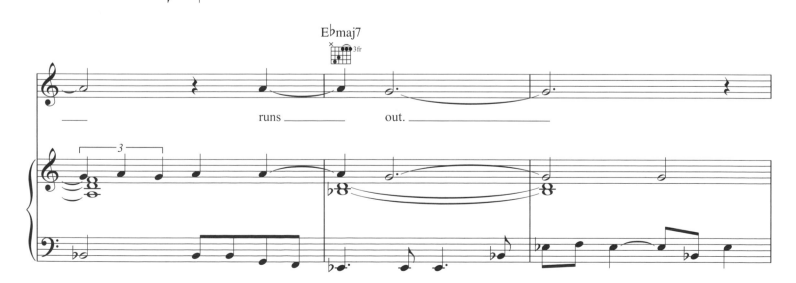

Ba - by's so high that she's sky - ing. ___

Yes, she's fly - ing, _____ a - fraid to

fall. _____ I'll tell you

why ba - by's cry - ing. _____ 'Cause she's

dy - ing, aren't we all? _____

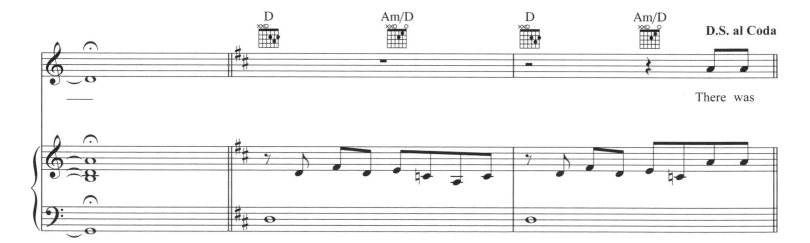

There was

si - lence. It's strange how you nev - er know. _____ But

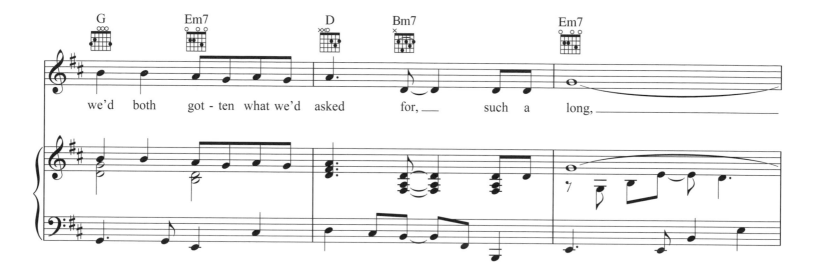

we'd both got - ten what we'd asked for, ___ such a long, _____

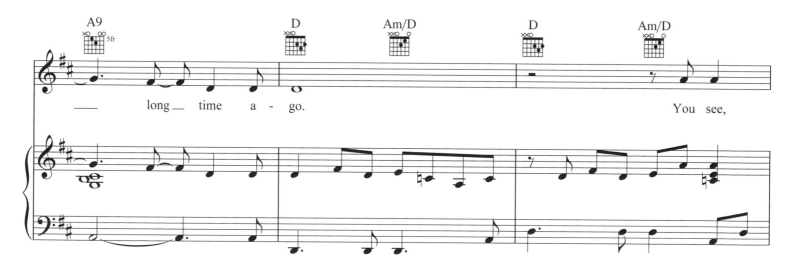

___ long ___ time a - go. You see,

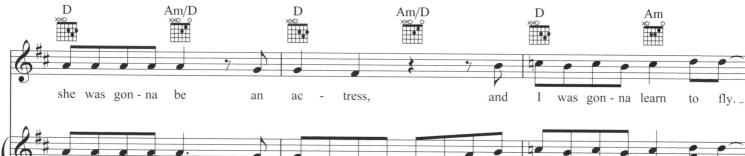

she was gon - na be an ac - tress, and I was gon - na learn to fly. _

She took off ___ to find the foot-lights,

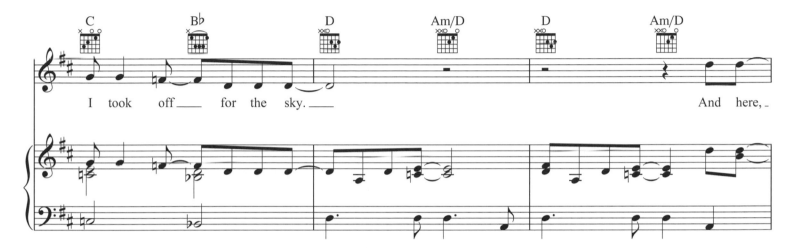

I took off ___ for the sky. ___ And here, ___

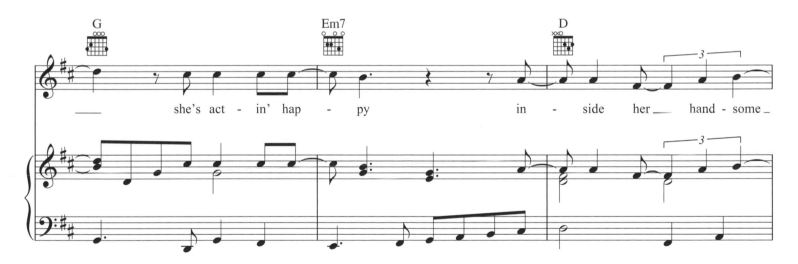

___ she's act - in' hap - py ___ in - side her ___ hand - some ___

___ home. And me, I'm fly - in' in my tax - i, tak - in'

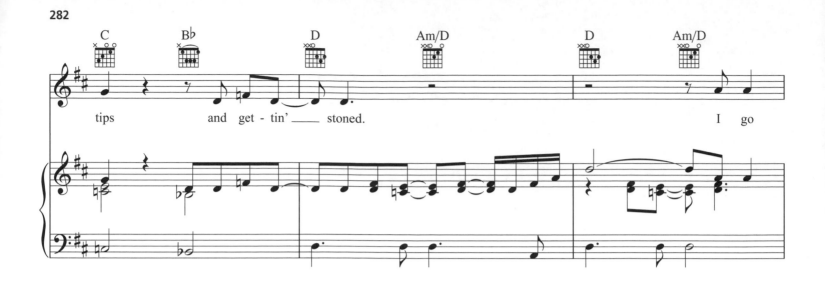

tips   and get - tin' _____ stoned.   I   go

fly   -   in'   so _____   high _____

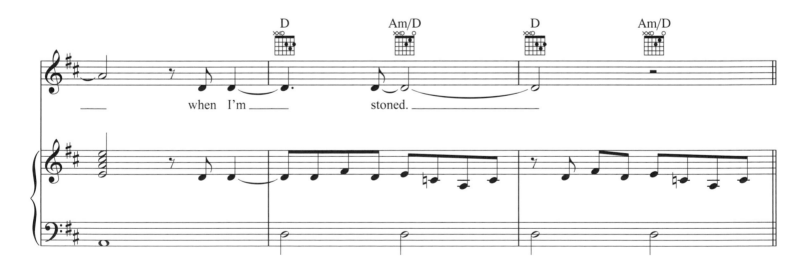

_____   when I'm _____   stoned. _____

Optional Ending

Repeat and Fade

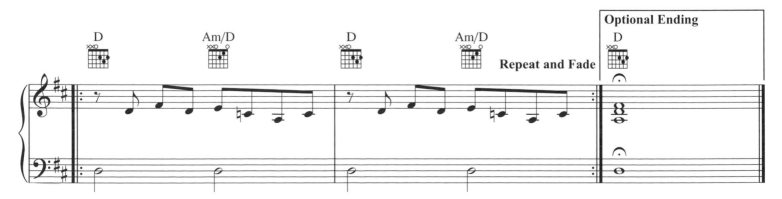

YOU DON'T MESS AROUND WITH JIM

Words and Music by
JIM CROCE

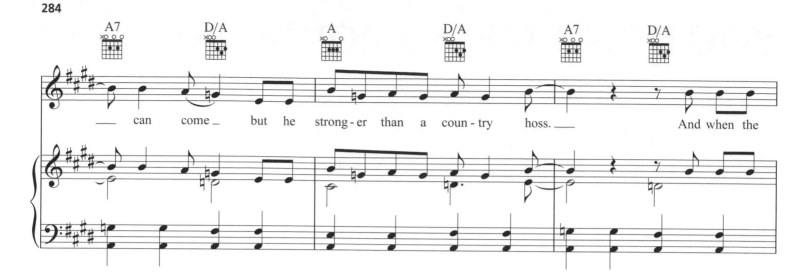

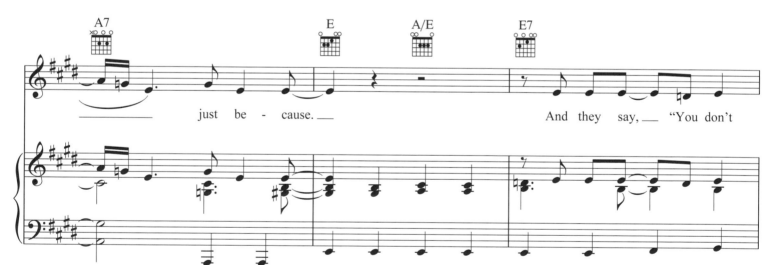

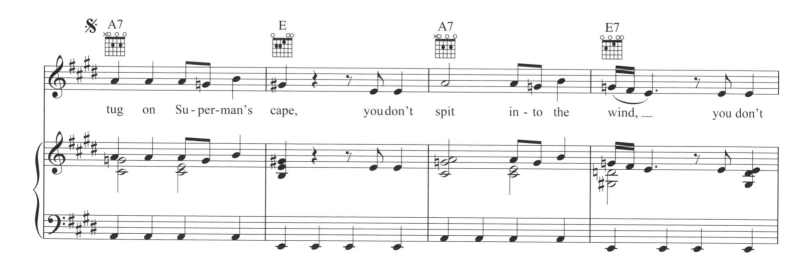

pull the mask off the old Lone Rang - er, and you don't mess a - round with Jim."

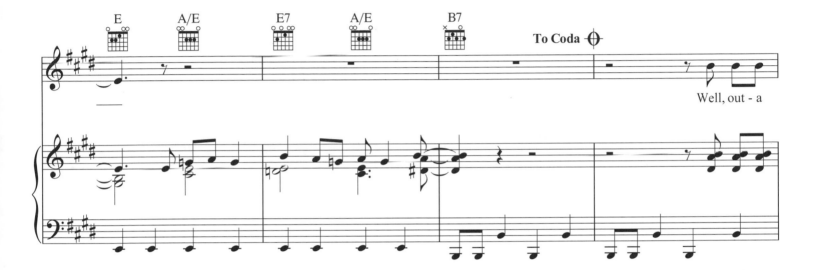

To Coda

Well, out - a

south Al - a - bam - a come a coun - try boy. He said, "I'm look - in' for a man named Jim. _

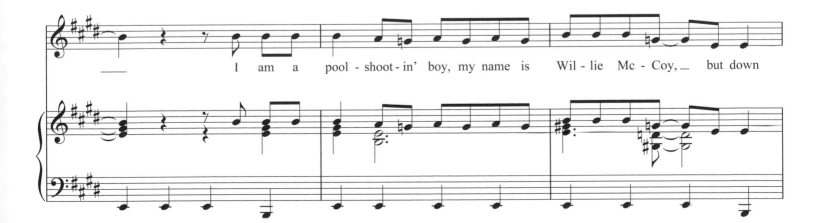

I am a pool - shoot - in' boy, my name is Wil - lie Mc - Coy, _ but down

home they call me "Slim." __ Yeah, I'm look - in' for the king of For - ty -

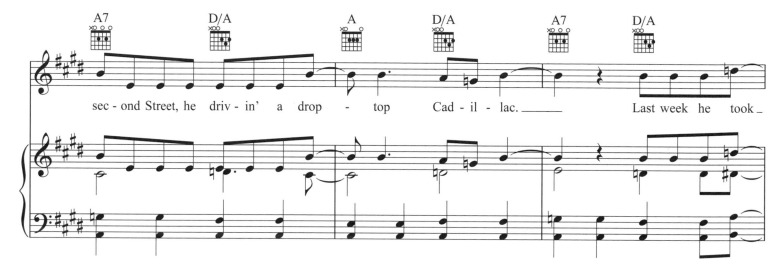

sec - ond Street, he driv - in' a drop - top Cad - il - lac. ___ Last week he took __

___ all my mon - ey and it may sound fun - ny but I come to get my mon - ey back." __

D.S. al Coda

___ And ev - 'ry - bod - y say, "Jack, don't you know that you don't

And you bet - ter be - lieve __ they sung a dif-f'rent kind of sto - ry when-a

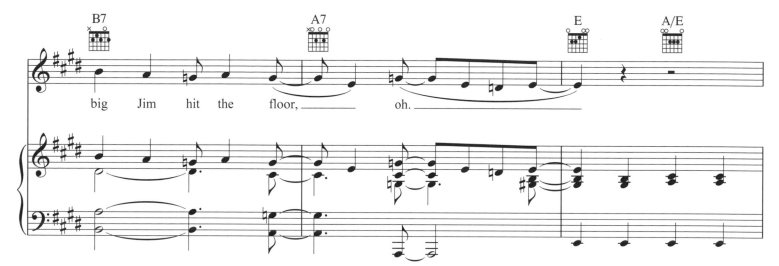

big Jim hit the floor, _____ oh. _____

𝄋 𝄋

Now they say you don't tug on Su - per - man's cape, you don't

spit in - to the wind, ___ you don't pull the mask off the

old Lone Rang - ger and you don't mess a - round with "Slim." __

(Spoken:) Yeah, big Jim got his hat,   *find out*
Even if you do got a two - piece custom - made pool cue.

D.S.S. and Fade

where it's at, and not hustling people strange to you.   Yeah, you don't

TOM'S DINER

Music and Lyrics by
SUZANNE VEGA

F#m9

da da da da da ___ da, da da da da da da da ___ da. Da da

F#m9

da da da da da ___ da, da da da da da da da ___ da. Da da

1
F#m

2
F#m

da da da da da ___ da. I am sit - ting in the morn - ing at the
al - ways nice to see ___ you," says the

din - er on the cor - ner. I am wait - ing at the coun - ter for the
man be - hind the coun - ter to the wom - an who has come ___ in. She is

man to pour the cof - fee. And he fills it on - ly half - way, and be -
shak - ing her um - brel - la. And I look the oth - er way __ as they are

fore I e - ven ar - gue, he is look - ing out the win - dow at some -
kiss - ing their hel - los, __ and I'm pre - tend - ing not to see __ them, and in -

F#m9

bod - y com - ing in. __ } Da da da da da da da __ da, da da
stead I pour the milk. __ }

F#m   F#m9

da da da da da __ da. Da da da da da da da __ da, da da

da da da da da da. "It is | da da da da da da. I

o - pen up the pa - per; there's a sto - ry of an act - or who had

died while he was drink - ing. It was no one I had heard of. And I'm

turn - ing to the hor - o - scope and look - ing for the fun - nies, but I'm

feel-ing some-one watch-ing me, and so I raise my head. Da da

F#m9   **F#m**

da da da da da ____ da, da da da da da da da ____ da. Da da

F#m9   **1**   **F#m**

da da da da da ____ da, da da da da da da da ____ da. Da da

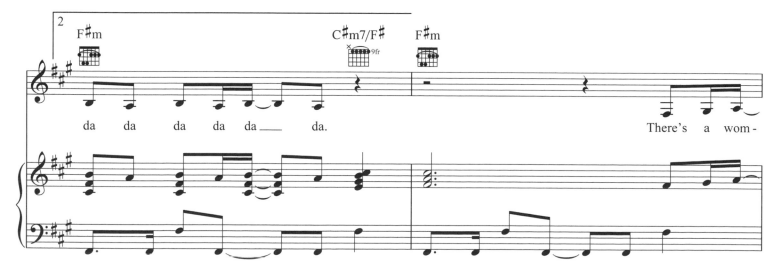

2   **F#m**   **C#m7/F#**   **F#m**

da da da da da ____ da.   There's a wom-

-an on the out-side look-ing in-side. Does she see __ me? No, she does __

__ not real-ly see me, 'cause she sees her own re-flec - tion. And I'm

try - ing not to no - tice that she's inch-ing up her skirt. And while she's

straight-en-ing __ her stock-ings, her hair has got - ten wet. __ Da da

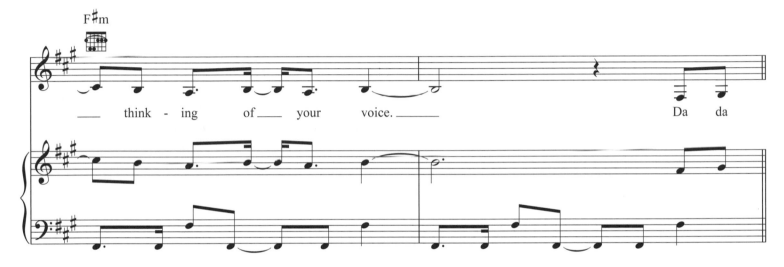

THE WRECK OF
THE EDMUND FITZGERALD

Words and Music by
GORDON LIGHTFOOT

Moderately slow, in 1

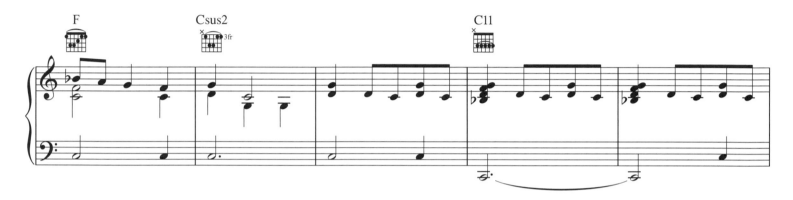

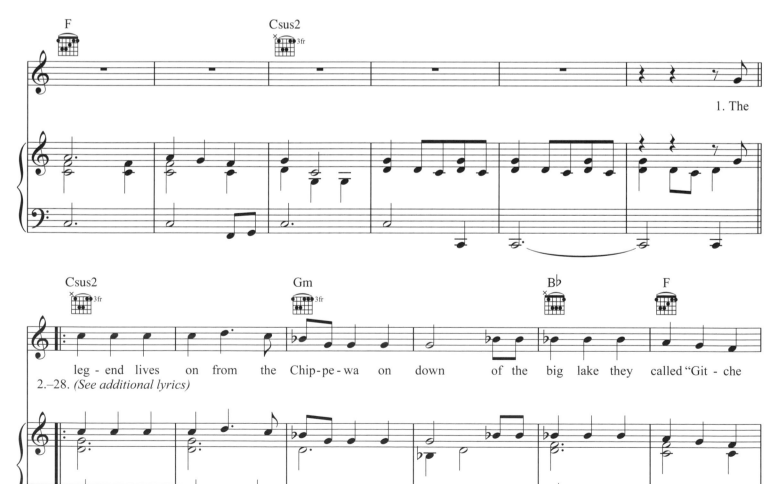

1. The
leg - end lives on from the Chip-pe - wa on down of the big lake they called "Git - che
2.–28. (*See additional lyrics*)

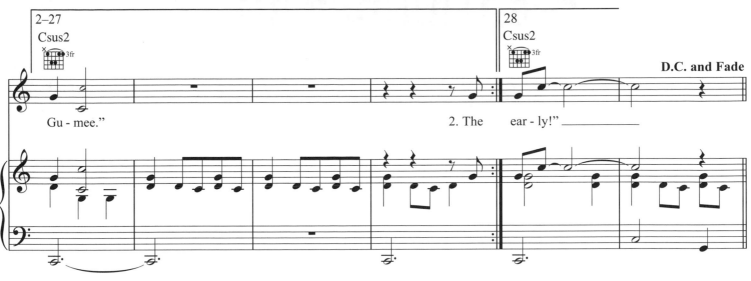

Additional Lyrics

2. The lake, it is said, never gives up her dead
   When the skies of November turn gloomy.

3. With a load of iron ore twenty-six thousand tons more
   Than the Edmund Fitzgerald weighed empty.

4. That good ship and true was a bone to be chewed
   When the gales of November came early.

5. The ship was the pride of the American side
   Coming back from some mill in Wisconsin.

6. As the big freighters go it was bigger than most
   With a crew and a captain well seasoned.

7. Concluding some terms with a couple of steel firms
   When they left fully loaded for Cleveland.

8. And later that night when the ship's bell rang,
   Could it be the north wind they'd been feelin'?

9. The wind in the wires made a tattletale sound
   And a wave broke over the railing.

10. And ev'ry man knew as the captain did too
    'Twas the witch of November come stealin'.

11. The dawn came late and the breakfast had to wait
    When the gales of November came slashin'.

12. When afternoon came it was freezin' rain
    In the face of a hurricane west wind.

13. When suppertime came the old cook came on deck
    Sayin', "Fellas, it's too rough t'feed ya."

14. At seven P.M. a main hatchway caved in;
    He said, "Fellas, it's been good t'know ya!"

15. The captain wired in he had water comin' in
    And the good ship and crew was in peril.

16. And later that night when 'is lights went outta sight
    Came the wreck of the Edmund Fitzgerald.

17. Does anyone know where the love of God goes
    When the waves turn the minutes to hours?

18. The searchers all say they'd have made Whitefish Bay
    If they'd put fifteen more miles behind 'er.

19. They might have split up or they might have capsized;
    They might have broke deep and took water.

20. And all that remains is the faces and the names
    Of the wives and the sons and the daughters.

21. Lake Huron rolls, Superior sings
    In the rooms of her ice-water mansion.

22. Old Michigan steams like a young man's dreams;
    The islands and bays are for sportsmen,

23. And farther below Lake Ontario
    Takes in what Lake Erie can send her.

24. And the iron boats go as the mariners all know
    With the Gales of November remembered.

25. In a musty old hall in Detroit they prayed,
    In the "Maritime Sailors' Cathedral."

26. The church bell chimed 'til it rang twenty-nine times
    For each man on the Edmund Fitzgerald,

27. The legend lives on from the Chippewa on down
    Of the big lake they called "Gitche Gumee."

28. "Superior," they said, "never gives up her dead
    When the gales of November come early!"

THE THUNDER ROLLS

Words and Music by PAT ALGER
and GARTH BROOKS

Rain-drops on the wind-shield; there's a storm ___ mov - in' in. ___

He's head-ing back from some - where ___ that he

nev - er should ___ have been. ___ And the thun-der rolls, ___

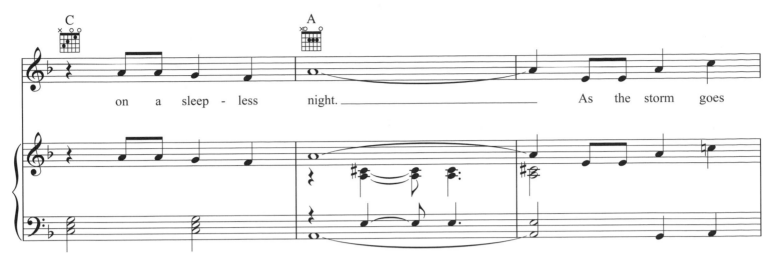

on a sleep - less night._____ As the storm goes

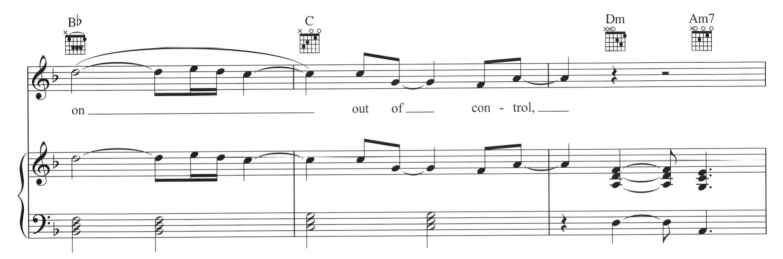

on _____ out of ____ con - trol, ____

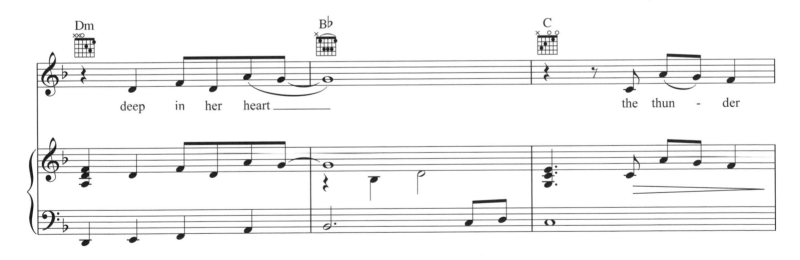

deep in her heart _____ the thun - der

rolls.

Additional Lyrics

2. Every light is burnin' in a house across town.
She's pacin' by the telephone in her faded flannel gown,
Askin' for a miracle, hopin' she's not right,
Prayin' it's the weather that has kept him out all night.
And the thunder rolls, and the thunder rolls.
Chorus

3. She's waitin' by the window when he pulls into the drive.
She rushes out to hold him, thankful he's alive.
But on the wind and rain, a strange new perfume blows,
And the lightnin' flashes in her eyes, and he knows that she knows.
And the thunder rolls, and the thunder rolls.
Chorus